VOLUME 570

JULY 2000

THE ANNALS

of The American Academy *of* Political
and Social Science

ALAN W. HESTON, *Editor*
NEIL A. WEINER, *Assistant Editor*

DIMENSIONS OF GLOBALIZATION

Special Editors of this Volume

LOUIS FERLEGER
Boston University
Massachusetts

JAY R. MANDLE
Colgate University
Hamilton
New York

Ⓢ Sage Publications, Inc. *THOUSAND OAKS   LONDON   NEW DELHI*

The American Academy of Political and Social Science

3937 Chestnut Street   Philadelphia, Pennsylvania 19104

Origin and Purpose. The Academy was organized December 14, 1889, to promote the progress of political and social science, especially through publications and meetings. The Academy does not take sides in controverted questions, but seeks to gather and present reliable information to assist the public in forming an intelligent and accurate judgment.

Meetings. The Academy occasionally holds a meeting in the spring extending over two days.

Publications. THE ANNALS of the American Academy of Political and Social Science is the bimonthly publication of The Academy. Each issue contains articles on some prominent social or political problem, written at the invitation of the editors. Also, monographs are published from time to time, numbers of which are distributed to pertinent professional organizations. These volumes constitute important reference works on the topics with which they deal, and they are extensively cited by authorities throughout the United States and abroad. The papers presented at the meetings of The Academy are included in THE ANNALS.

Membership. Each member of The Academy receives THE ANNALS and may attend the meetings of The Academy. Membership is open only to individuals. Annual dues: $61.00 for the regular paperbound edition (clothbound, $90.00). Add $12.00 per year for membership outside the U.S.A. Members may also purchase single issues of THE ANNALS for $14.00 each (clothbound, $19.00). Add $2.00 for shipping and handling on all prepaid orders.

Subscriptions. THE ANNALS of the American Academy of Political and Social Science (ISSN 0002-7162) is published six times annually—in January, March, May, July, September, and November. Institutions may subscribe to THE ANNALS at the annual rate: $327.00 (clothbound, $372.00). Add $12.00 per year for subscriptions outside the U.S.A. Institutional rates for single issues: $59.00 each (clothbound, $66.00).

Periodicals postage paid at Thousand Oaks, California, and at additional mailing offices.

Single issues of THE ANNALS may be obtained by individuals who are not members of The Academy for $20.00 each (clothbound, $31.00). Add $2.00 for shipping and handling on all prepaid orders. Single issues of THE ANNALS have proven to be excellent supplementary texts for classroom use. Direct inquiries regarding adoptions to THE ANNALS c/o Sage Publications (address below).

All correspondence concerning membership in The Academy, dues renewals, inquiries about membership status, and/or purchase of single issues of THE ANNALS should be sent to THE ANNALS c/o Sage Publications, Inc., 2455 Teller Road, Thousand Oaks, CA 91320. Telephone: (805) 499-0721; FAX/Order line: (805) 499-0871. *Please note that orders under $30 must be prepaid.* Sage affiliates in London and India will assist institutional subscribers abroad with regard to orders, claims, and inquiries for both subscriptions and single issues.

Printed on recycled, acid-free paper

THE ANNALS

Editorial Office: 3937 Chestnut Street, Philadelphia, PA 19104.

For information about membership (individuals only) and subscriptions (institutions), address:*

SAGE PUBLICATIONS, INC.
2455 Teller Road
Thousand Oaks, CA 91320

Sage Production Staff: MARIA NOTARANGELO, ALLISON TANGER, DORIS HUS, and ROSE TYLAK

From India and South Asia, write to:
SAGE PUBLICATIONS INDIA Pvt. Ltd
P.O. Box 4215
New Delhi 110 048
INDIA

From Europe, the Middle East, and Africa, write to:
SAGE PUBLICATIONS LTD
6 Bonhill Street
London EC2A 4PU
UNITED KINGDOM

Please note that members of The Academy receive THE ANNALS with their membership.
International Standard Serial Number I2SSN 0002-7162
International Standard Book Number ISBN 0-7619-2272-5 (Vol. 570, 2000 paper)
International Standard Book Number ISBN 0-7619-2271-7 (Vol. 570, 2000 cloth)
Manufactured in the United States of America. First printing, July 2000.

The articles appearing in the ANNALS are abstracted or indexed in *Academic Abstracts, Academic Search, America: History and Life, Asia Pacific Database, Book Review Index, CAB Abstracts Database, Central Asia: Abstracts & Index, Communication Abstracts, Corporate ResourceNET, Criminal Justice Abstracts, Current Citations Express, Current Contents: Social & Behavioral Sciences, e-JEL, EconLit, Expanded Academic Index, Guide to Social Science & Religion in Periodical Literature, Health Business FullTEXT, HealthSTAR FullTEXT, Historical Abstracts, International Bibliography of the Social Sciences, International Political Science Abstracts, ISI Basic Social Sciences Index, Journal of Economic Literature on CD, LEXIS-NEXIS, MasterFILE FullTEXT, Middle East: Abstracts & Index, North Africa: Abstracts & Index, PAIS International, Periodical Abstracts, Political Science Abstracts, Sage Public Administration Abstracts, Social Science Source, Social Sciences Citation Index, Social Sciences Index Full Text, Social Services Abstracts, Social Work Abstracts, Sociological Abstracts, Southeast Asia: Abstracts & Index, Standard Periodical Directory (SPD), TOPICsearch, Wilson OmniFile V,* and *Wilson Social Sciences Index/Abstracts,* and are available on microfilm from University Microfilms, Ann Arbor, Michigan.

Information about membership rates, institutional subscriptions, and back issue prices may be found on the facing page.

Advertising. Current rates and specifications may be obtained by writing to THE ANNALS Advertising and Promotion Manager at the Thousand Oaks office (address above).

Claims. Claims for undelivered copies must be made no later than six months following month of publication. The publisher will supply missing copies when losses have been sustained in transit and when the reserve stock will permit.

Change of Address. Six weeks advance notice must be given when notifying of change of address to ensure proper identification. Please specify name of journal. **POSTMASTER:** Send address changes to: THE ANNALS of the American Academy of Political and Social Science, c/o Sage Publications, Inc., 2455 Teller Road, Thousand Oaks, CA 91320.

THE ANNALS

of The American Academy of Political
and Social Science

ALAN W. HESTON, *Editor*
NEIL A. WEINER, *Assistant Editor*

─────────────── FORTHCOMING ───────────────

FEMINIST VIEWS OF THE SOCIAL SCIENCES
Special Editor: Christine L. Williams
Volume 571   September 2000

PRESIDENTIAL CAMPAIGNS: SINS OF OMISSION
Special Editors: Kathleen Hall Jamieson and Matthew Miller
Volume 572   November 2000

CULTURE AND DEVELOPMENT:
INTERNATIONAL PERSPECTIVES
Special Editors: Christopher K. Clague
and Shoshana Grossbard-Shechtman
Volume 573   January 2001

See page 2 for information on Academy membership and
purchase of single volumes of **The Annals.**

CONTENTS

PREFACE . . . . *Jay R. Mandle*
and Louis Ferleger   8

GLOBALIZATION: THE PRODUCT OF
A KNOWLEDGE-BASED ECONOMY . . . . *Lester C. Thurow*   19

THE GLOBALIZATION OF
HUMAN DEVELOPMENT . . . . *Richard A. Easterlin*   32

GLOBALIZATION IN SOUTHEAST
ASIA . . . . *Peter A. Coclanis*
and Tilak Doshi   49

REGULATING IMMIGRATION IN A
GLOBAL AGE: A NEW POLICY LANDSCAPE . . . . *Saskia Sassen*   65

LABOR VERSUS GLOBALIZATION . . . . *George Ross*   78

THE STUDENT ANTI-SWEATSHOP
MOVEMENT: LIMITS AND POTENTIAL . . . . *Jay R. Mandle*   92

THE BARK IS WORSE THAN THE
BITE: NEW WTO LAW AND
LATE INDUSTRIALIZATION . . . . *Alice H. Amsden*
and Takashi Hikino 104

COPING WITH GLOBALIZATION:
A SUGGESTED POLICY PACKAGE
FOR SMALL COUNTRIES . . . . *Frank B. Rampersad* 115

GLOBALIZATION AND JUSTICE . . . . *Jon Mandle* 126

GLOBALIZATION'S CULTURAL CONSEQUENCES . . . . *Robert Holton* 140

CORPORATE GOVERNANCE
AND GLOBALIZATION . . . . *Mary O'Sullivan* 153

SUSTAINABLE ECONOMIC
DEVELOPMENT IN RURAL AMERICA . . . . *Adam S. Weinberg* 173

BOOK DEPARTMENT 186

INDEX 222

BOOK DEPARTMENT CONTENTS

INTERNATIONAL RELATIONS AND POLITICS

BARNETT, MICHAEL N. *Dialogues in Arab Politics:*
Negotiations in Regional Order. Laurie A. Brand 186

BERGER, THOMAS U. *Cultures of Antimilitarism:*
National Security in Germany and Japan. Jeffrey J. Anderson 187

COOK, TIMOTHY E. *Governing with the News:*
The News Media as a Political Institution. William Haltom. 188

FRIMAN, H. RICHARD. *Narcodiplomacy: Exporting*
the United States War on Drugs. Donald J. Mabry 189

MUELLER, DENNIS C. *Constitutional Democracy.* Joseph F. Zimmerman 191

AFRICA, ASIA, AND LATIN AMERICA

EHRET, CHRISTOPHER. *An African Classical Age:*
Eastern and Southern Africa in World History,
1000 B.C. to A.D. 400. Ronald R. Atkinson 192

FABIAN, JOHANNES. *Moments of Freedom:*
Anthropology and Popular Culture. Arthur Asa Berger 193

EUROPE

PELINKA, ANTON. *Politics of the Lesser Evil: Leadership,*
Democracy and Jaruzelski's Poland. Bruce F. Pauley 194

REYNOLDS, ELAINE A. *Before the Bobbies:*
The Night Watch and Police Reform
in Metropolitan London, 1720-1830. Michael E. Buerger 195

UNITED STATES

BYBEE, KEITH J. *Mistaken Identity: The Supreme Court*
and the Politics of Minority Representation. Louis DeSipio 196

DERICKSON, ALAN. *Black Lung: Anatomy*
of a Public Health Disaster. Peter S. Barth 198

EISINGER, PETER K. *Towards an End*
to Hunger in America. Beth Osborne Daponte 199

ERENBERG, LEWIS A. *Swingin' the Dream:*
Big Band Jazz and the Rebirth
of American Culture. John Gennari 201

ETZIONI, AMITAI. *The Limits of Privacy.* Scott Sundby 202

GLAZIER, JACK. *Dispersing the Ghetto:*
The Relocation of Jewish Immigrants
Across America. Abraham D. Lavender 203

MAYERS, DAVID. *Wars and Peace: The Future
Americans Envisioned, 1861-1991*. Robert A. Divine 204

MELISH, JOANNE POPE. *Disowning Slavery:
Gradual Emancipation and "Race"
in New England, 1780-1860*. Jack P. Greene............................. 205

ROSSINOW, DOUG. *The Politics of Authenticity:
Liberalism, Christianity, and
the New Left in America*. Howard Brick................................. 206

SOCIOLOGY

DEUTSCH, FRANCINE M. *Halving It All: How
Equally Shared Parenting Works*. Janice M. Steil......................... 207

FLEISHER, MARK S. *Dead End Kids: Gang Girls
and the Boys They Know*. Arthur J. Lurigio.............................. 209

KILPATRICK, ALAN. *The Night Has a Naked
Soul: Witchcraft and Sorcery Among the
Western Cherokee*. Deward E. Walker, Jr................................ 210

MITCHELL, LAWRENCE E. *Stacked Deck:
A Story of Selfishness in America*. John R. Dalphin 211

SOWELL, THOMAS. *Conquests and Cultures:
An International History*. Jean W. Sedlar 212

STOCKER, MARGARETA. *Judith, Sexual Warrior:
Women and Power in Western Culture*. Constance Jordan 213

ECONOMICS

McNAMARA, PETER. *Political Economy and Statesmanship:
Smith, Hamilton and the Foundation
of the Commercial Republic*. Colin Wright.............................. 214

MINK, GWENDOLYN. *Welfare's End*. Sonya Michel......................... 215

PREFACE

The contributors to this collection explore their individual subjects within a common understanding of the term "globalization." There is agreement that "globalization" refers to the consequences of two phenomena that, in combination, have resulted in the global "compression of time and space" (Harvey 1989, quoted in Holton 1998, 8). The first is technological changes in the processing and dissemination of information related to finance and production. The second is the international spread of the technical competence necessary to use these advances efficiently.

What sets the current period of globalization off from other eras of international economic integration are the availability of new communicative tools and the fact that, worldwide, increasing numbers of potential users are sufficiently well educated to put these new tools to effective use. In this perspective, then, globalization represents the outcome both of the appearance and spread of the artifacts of the contemporary world—fax machines, personal computers, satellite broadcasting systems, and the Internet—and the worldwide growth in human capital. The combination of invention and user competence is the critical synergy. Because of it, there has been a dramatic increase in the ability of people rapidly to communicate, coordinate activities, and engage in long-distance, extremely rapid transactions. As a result, "the tyranny of distance has been obliterated" (Holton 1998, 8), and the geographic web of human interaction has been drawn together more tightly.

By conceptualizing globalization in this way, we affirm that this process represents something that is historically unique and of profound importance. We are not satisfied with Louis Uchitelle's quip in the *New York Times* that, "when it comes to globalization, the 20th century is ending on a note of deja vu: the world's economies are roughly as intertwined today as they were in 1913" (1998, 1). What is going on today is something that is only inadequately captured by the measures of globalization that Uchitelle employs: the growth rate of trade and foreign direct investment as a percentage of world output. Aside from the fact that the technology of communications is vastly more efficient than that used a century ago, the contemporary process of integration embraces a far higher proportion of the world's population than in that earlier period. Uchitelle's formulation misses what is distinctive in today's experience. It is only in recent decades that, as Robert Pollin has remarked, "we are moving in the direction of every country being able to produce everything" (quoted in Uchitelle 1998, 1).

We are eager to be sufficiently precise in our formulation to avoid being included among those who engage in "globe-talk," described by Holton (1998) as "the rhetoric, hype, and babble of voices . . . that may well testify to a certain modishness or fashion for global things" (1). We want our discussion of globalization not only to capture adequately the increased international integration of life, but as well to provide insight into the dynamic by which this process is occurring. It is for this reason that we identify the taproot of globalization in technological change and the spread of education internationally. We want to be able to identify the mechanisms by which change occurs and not simply report that many things seem to be occurring at once.

TECHNOLOGICAL CHANGE AND EDUCATION

In maintaining that technological change and education are the wellsprings of globalization, we do not mean to imply that these phenomena lack their own antecedents. The process of modern economic growth is at least two centuries old, and both technological change and advancing levels of educational attainment are positively and strongly linked to it. It is reasonable to argue that globalization represents the latest stage in that process. Globalization can be thought of as the geographic extension of processes that have long been under way. With that the case, globalization's ultimate origins are to be found in the same sources as those that have given rise to development generally.

This roughly is the position adopted by those who argue that Marx anticipated globalization when he predicted the international spread of capitalism. Marx did expect that "the country that is more developed industrially only shows to the less developed the image of its own future." Nevertheless, it is doubtful that even Marx had sufficient imagination to make his portrait, as Eric Hobsbawm puts it, "recognizably the world we live in 150 years later" (quoted in Lewis 1998, 1). As in the case of those who consider the four decades before World War I to be the same as today, this way of looking at the phenomena misses the distinctiveness of the global integration currently under way.

This distinctiveness is captured in a 1988 report prepared for the Council of Academies of Engineering and Technological Sciences that recognizes that "the world is in the throes of a technological revolution that differs from the periodic waves of technical change that have marked the progress of industrial society since its origins 200 years ago." It affirms that the key technologies are "the microelectronics-information technologies complex, the biotechnologies and the new materials science" (Colombo 1988, 23, 24). In this revolution, as Stever and Muroyama put it in the same collection, "sophisticated information technologies permit instantaneous communication among the far-flung operations of global enterprises." New materials, new production techniques, and improved air and sea transportation have "created and mandated greater interdependence among firms and nations" (Stever and Muroyama 1988, 1). With this mandate, globalization became possible.

But alone, the availability of new technology would not have resulted in globalization. Before that could occur, the level of education present in the Third World had substantially to advance. Only then could new means of communicating be effectively utilized. Universal literacy and substantial

TABLE 1

ILLITERACY RATES FOR MALES AND FEMALES AGED 15-24 IN UNDERDEVELOPED COUNTRIES WITH POPULATIONS OF FIFTY MILLION OR MORE, 1980-1997 (Percentage)

Country	Male		Female	
	1980	1997	1980	1997
Bangladesh	52	42	74	63
Brazil	15	10	13	7
China	4	1	16	4
Egypt	36	25	62	41
Ethiopia	59	47	78	51
India	32	23	61	44
Indonesia	7	2	15	4
Mexico	6	3	9	5
Nigeria	32	13	57	20
Pakistan	48	31	79	61
Philippines	5	2	5	2
Thailand	3	1	4	2
Turkey	6	2	25	8
Weighted average	19	12	36	22

SOURCE: World Bank 1999a, tab. 2.11.

levels of educational attainment have long been present in the developed world. As such, the populations of these countries have generally possessed the knowledge level necessary to use modern technology successfully. But the emergence of adequately educated people elsewhere—in the less developed countries of the world—is a recent phenomenon. By no means has this process been fully completed. Nevertheless, the data in Tables 1 and 2, concerned with the experience of the 13 largest poor countries in the world after 1980, suggest that in recent years real and important gains in education and literacy have been made.[1] Decreased illiteracy was experienced in each of these countries, in some cases by considerable amounts. For the entire grouping of countries, the weighted illiteracy rate for the male population decreased from 19 percent to 12 percent, while the female rate fell from 36 percent to 22 percent.

Corresponding to these declines in illiteracy, and almost certainly contributing to them, were advances in school enrollment. Overall, the proportion of the secondary-school-aged population who were enrolled in school in these 13 countries increased from 38 percent to 58 percent. As in the case of illiteracy, these data reveal that in a few countries the progress achieved has been dramatic. Thus in India the enrollment rate rose from 30 percent to 49 percent in this 16-year period and in Thailand the increase was from 29 percent to 56 percent. Sex differences remain, and the gains in enrollment do not mean that school attendance was as high in these poor countries as in the rich ones. But they do suggest that an increased fraction of the population in them now

TABLE 2

GROSS ENROLLMENT RATIOS FOR SECONDARY SCHOOLS IN UNDERDEVELOPED COUNTRIES WITH POPULATIONS OF FIFTY MILLION OR MORE, 1980-1996

Country	1998 Population (millions)	1980 Gross Enrollment Ratio	1996 Gross Enrollment Ratio
Bangladesh	126	18	—
Brazil	166	34	45
China	1,239	46	70
Egypt	61	51	75
Ethiopia	61	9	12
India	980	30	49
Indonesia	204	29	48
Mexico	96	49	61
Nigeria	121	18	33
Pakistan	132	14	—
Philippines	75	64	77
Thailand	61	29	56
Turkey	63	35	56
Total	3,385		
Weighted average		38	58

SOURCE: World Bank 1999a, tab. 2.10.

NOTE: Gross enrollment ratio is the ratio of total enrollment, regardless of age, to the population of the age group that corresponds to the level of education shown.

possesses the education necessary to gain access to the new technology of communications. Without literacy, such access clearly would be impossible.

POOR COUNTRIES AND INTERNATIONAL TRADE

The new technologies and the enhanced competence of the people of poor countries have resulted in a dramatic change in the role played in the international economy by the large poor countries. These countries are increasingly important participants in international trade, and there has been a dramatic change in what they export. No longer are countries such as Bangladesh, China, India, and Turkey largely self-contained, limiting their exports to raw materials and agricultural goods. As indicated in Table 3, among these countries, exports as a percentage of gross domestic product grew from 10 percent to 20 percent, proportionately doubling, while Table 4 shows that manufactured goods as a percentage of their total exports increased from 44 percent to 68 percent. The new technology of communications, transportation, and information transfer and the advancing educational achievements of the people of the poor large countries mean that, for the first time, the underdeveloped world is using the global market to industrialize.

But for this industrialization to have occurred, a legal framework to facilitate the process was required. Trade between nations best increases when

TABLE 3
EXPORTS AS A PERCENTAGE OF GROSS DOMESTIC PRODUCT,
SELECTED LARGE POOR COUNTRIES, 1980-1998

Country	1980	1998
Bangladesh	4	14
Brazil	9	7
China	6	22
Egypt	31	17
Ethiopia	11	16
India	6	12
Indonesia	34	28
Mexico	11	31
Nigeria	29	23
Pakistan	12	16
Philippines	24	56
Thailand	24	47
Turkey	5	25
Weighted mean	10	20
World weighted mean	20	25

SOURCE: World Bank 1999b, tab. 13.

tariff barriers are reduced and internationally agreed-upon rules concerning imports and exports are in place. Both were achieved in the institutional context provided by the General Agreement on Tariffs and Trade (GATT). Within that structure, numerous rounds of trade negotiations have occurred. The last round of negotiations, the Uruguay Round, was completed in 1994; it resulted in the establishment of the World Trade Organization (WTO) to supervise the system. The success of the process is widely acknowledged. According to Jagdish Bhagwati (1998), "The GATT trading system has achieved unprecedented trade expansion and world prosperity" (271).

The GATT negotiations were not over free trade, zero tariffs on imports. Instead, what was anticipated—and what did occur—was a series of negotiating rounds in which countries exchanged tariff concessions. In addition, the participants agreed to national treatment of imports. What this meant was that the imports of one country were to be treated identically to those of others and that countries could not subject imports to discriminatory tax or regulatory treatment compared to domestically produced goods. With both tariff reductions achieved and the principle of national treatment accepted, agreements between individual countries to reduce tariffs became universal. As Anne O. Krueger (1998) puts it, when "contracting parties negotiated with their key trading partners for reductions of tariffs on items they exported," those concessions had now to be extended to all nations participating in the GATT process. In this way, an "open multilateral [trading] system" was created (5, 4).

TABLE 4

**MANUFACTURES AS PERCENTAGE OF MERCHANDISE EXPORTS,
SELECTED LARGE POOR COUNTRIES, 1980-1997**

Country	1980	1997	Change
Bangladesh	68	87	+19
Brazil	37	54	+17
China	—	—	—
Egypt	11	40	+29
Ethiopia	—	66	—
India	59	72	+13
Indonesia	2	42	+40
Mexico	12	81	+69
Nigeria	0	—	—
Pakistan	48	86	+38
Philippines	21	45	+24
Thailand	25	71	+46
Turkey	27	75	+48
Population weighted mean	44	68	+24

SOURCE: World Bank 1999a, tab. 4.5.

It is likely that there was not any other basis than one that employed the principles of negotiated tariff reductions and import nondiscrimination that would have allowed the global trading system to expand as successfully as it did. Together, these principles permitted international trade to grow and to do so on a basis that allowed the benefits of such growth to be shared widely among trading countries. In their absence, it is almost certain that trade negotiations would have broken down because special interests and protectionist forces would have been able to insist upon tariff protection, discriminatory treatment, or both. Despite this progress, agreement on rules facilitating trade between nations is far from complete, a task put off indefinitely by the failure of the WTO Ministerial Meeting in Seattle in December 1999 to agree to a new negotiating agenda (World Trade Organization 1999).

Although it is clear that globalization has meant a greater degree of world economic integration than has ever before been the case, it nevertheless remains a process that is still in formation. As a result, the extent to which the new technology and enhanced educational attainment of the world's population will in fact result in enhanced human well-being remains uncertain. If the new technology represents a necessary condition for the acceleration of the international spread of development, it is policy formation and implementation that will determine the extent to which the promise of rising living standards, embodied in that technology, is fulfilled. Globalization was brought into being by technology and education, but its impact on people will be decisively influenced by politics.

THE NEED FOR SUPPORT

The reason this is so is that globalization is socially disruptive. With the spread of economic activity globally, some jobs are lost as well as gained; local cultural forms are changed by and sometimes superseded by imports; new forms of entrepreneurship, particularly in the financial service industries, become feasible. In each case, it is possible to argue that globalization represents a net advance. Structural change in the economy increases employment and overall productivity; the importing of music, information, sports, and new ways of thinking can be culturally enriching; the extension of financial markets can help to overcome capital shortfalls. But each, too, has its downside—downsides rooted precisely in the process of change that is the source of the advance.

Because of these disruptions, supportive and stabilizing policies are required. To date, however, not enough has been done in this regard. In the developed world, particularly the United States, globalization's restructuring frequently results in a serious income decline for workers. This occurs because often the new employment opportunities that become available to displaced workers do not pay as well as those that have been lost and the income supports that are in place are not sufficient to bridge the resulting shortfall. The same is the case in poor countries. Adequate support does not exist, for example, for the banana farmers in the West Indies whose protected market in Great Britain was lost because the marketing of their fruit violated WTO nondiscrimination principles.

A similar problem of support exists with regard to the arts and culture generally. It seems clear that commercial success should not be the only criterion employed in determining which cultural forms should survive. Too much of intrinsic value would be lost if, with globalization, profitability in markets became the sole criterion of viability. Yet to date, no consensus exists on the extent to which and how art forms, such as an indigenous film industry, should be protected from globalized sources of supply.

Finally, no one should need to be reminded that insufficient regulation of short-term capital flows has resulted in punishing dislocations emanating from financial markets. This is not the place to debate whether the reform process with regard to the latter should primarily reside in national legislation to strengthen regulatory regimes or whether the oversight of international finance should be at the supranational level. The point is that in this arena as in the others, insufficient attention has been paid to overcoming globalization's negative consequences.

One source of this neglect lies in the very process of technological change that produced globalization in the first place. Worries over economic disruption simply are not typically on the agenda of those whose work it is, for example, to build smaller and faster computer chips. Their triumph is in innovation. As was the case in the past when new products such as automobiles and home appliances were introduced, entrepreneurs do not focus on the wider social consequences of their actions. It is left for the rest of the society to cope with the ensuing need for adjustments.

A second source of the neglect of globalization's negative consequences resides in the nature of the political coalition that has fought for global economic liberalization. The negotiations that resulted in the increased freeing of trade occurred in a multilateral context. This context was chosen in the belief that the simultaneous lowering of trade barriers by large numbers of countries would encourage the construction of broad coalitions both nationally and internationally in support of liberalization. The wider the scope of the talks, the more industries and countries that would benefit from and champion the freeing of trade. Numerous rounds of arduous trade negotiations have occurred since the end of World War II, the last of which concluded in 1994 with the creation of the WTO. The latter organization, it was hoped, would further the process. According to the World Bank, the purpose of the WTO was to "facilitate trade reform." It would do so by sponsoring multilateral trade agreements that "[created] a set of concentrated 'winners' in member states—the exporting firms which benefit from lower tariffs in potential export markets" (World Bank 1999b, 53).

Critics of globalization therefore are not wrong when they claim, as Dani Rodrik (1998) has, that "in practice it turns out that the agenda of trade globalization, trade expansion and trade pacts has been captured largely by business interests" (94). Since it was by appealing to global business interests that the liberal agenda was advanced, there is very little to quarrel with in this formulation. But the conclusion Rodrik draws from his analysis too often is rejected by those who share his view of the trade negotiation process. Acknowledging that "trade is a source of gains for an economy precisely because it restructures economies," Rodrik argues that it is necessary to "think very seriously about what kinds of compensatory adjustment assistance measures we are going to put in place" (89). In his linking the benefits of a liberal global economy with the need for supportive safety nets, Rodrik is not breaking new ground. This has long been the mainstream position in the economics profession. As the authors of the recent book *Globaphobia* put it, "A standard remedy for the economic fallout from free trade is to require that the winners share some of their gains with the losers through some form of compensation. We take this seriously as a political requirement and a moral obligation" (Burtless et al. 1998, 131-32).

But instead of addressing the need to offset the costs of globalization with supportive and stabilizing policies, numerous critics of globalization attack the concept of a liberal trade order itself. David Morris (1993), for example, in a book entitled *The Case Against Free Trade*, argues, "We need to challenge the postulates of free trade head on, to preach a different philosophy, to embrace a different strategy" (157). In that same publication, Ralph Nader (1993) describes that alternative: "Societies need to focus their attention on fostering community-oriented production" (11). Jerry Mander (1996) as well does not shrink from the logic of this position, agreeing that what is involved in all of this is a rejection of the concept of economic development, favorably citing Wolfgang Sachs's remark that the only thing worse than the failure of economic development would be its success (6).

It is hard not to see in this counterattack a willful neglect of the interests of the poor people living in underdeveloped societies. Unanswered in this attack on globalization is the question of how else than through the sale of internationally marketed products can the standard of living in poor countries be raised. To tell small societies that they should orient their production to their limited local markets, as is done by many critics of globalization, is to condemn them to the permanent inefficiencies and resulting poverty associated with limited levels of output. At the same time, to tell Asian societies that they should eschew exports is to dismiss the very strategy that, though flawed, has succeeded in substantially raising human well-being there. It therefore is unlikely that the call to turn from liberal globalization will be warmly welcomed in the Third World. Defenders of the interests of displaced workers and industries in the developed world that suffer from growing international competition will simply have to turn their attention to putting in place domestic support policies, rather than trying to hold back the international sea change that the globalization of production represents.

Globalization is still a work in progress. The technology necessary for its attainment is in place, and the human capital essential for its success in the Third World is increasing. However, not yet created but needed are adequate control and compensating mechanisms to govern the emerging system. In both the developed and underdeveloped world, the creation of these mechanisms will require that supportive programs be put in place to protect the innocent victims of progress. Similarly, policies to achieve greater stability in financial markets are required in order to ensure that the potential of rising living standards is not dissipated. Both of these are needed to ensure that dissatisfaction with globalization does not result in victory for its critics, a victory that would have dire consequences for the poor people of the earth.

IN THIS VOLUME

The articles contained in this collection are presented to illuminate important dimensions of the globalization process. There is no thought that what is presented is definitive either in the range of subjects covered or in the treatment that is accorded them. Nevertheless, our hope is that these articles will provide perspective on the globalization phenomenon at a time when it is the subject of intense public scrutiny and debate.

The first three articles are the broadest in their scope. Lester C. Thurow traces the origins of globalization to new technologies that have created "brain-power industries." His argument is that, if countries are to succeed in the newly integrated world economy, they will have to promote and accommodate the needs of these new industries. Richard A. Easterlin provides a generally optimistic assessment of globalization's impact on human well-being, though he is at pains to note that its benefits remain unevenly distributed. The impact of the global economy on Southeast Asia is analyzed by Peter A. Coclanis and Tilak Doshi. That region is of particular importance in this context since it, arguably, is the part of the underdeveloped world that has been most profoundly transformed—both positively and negatively—by globalization.

The impact of globalization on migration and labor is the subject of the next three contributions. Saskia Sassen considers how the process has affected the determinants of international population movements and has complicated the ability of nation-states to control migration across borders. George Ross depicts the increased difficulties that nation-based unions face in an era of what he calls "transnationalization of markets." Jay R. Mandle also deals with labor issues, in this case analyzing the efforts of the student anti-sweatshop movement in the United States to improve the deplorable conditions endured by workers in the world apparel industry.

Important problems with regard to international trade are addressed in the contributions by Alice H. Amsden, Takashi Hikino, and the late Frank B. Rampersad. The article by Amsden and Hikino emphasizes the flexibility present in the rules of the WTO, a flexibility the authors believe permits the kinds of state subsidies that were important in stimulating the development of the leading latecomers to growth. Rampersad, however, argues that smallness of size acts to handicap countries like those in the Caribbean; he offers alternative strategies to help overcome these problems. Finally, the last group of articles considers cultural and other changes associated with globalization. Both Jon Mandle and Robert Holton argue that such cultural changes will not, in all likelihood, correspond to the nightmare projections of sterile uniformity that animate much of the objection to globalization. Similarly, Mary O'Sullivan doubts that the globalization of financial markets is the primary determinant of changes in corporate governance systems that have occurred in recent years. Adam S. Weinberg's case study illustrates the fact that education and political changes at the grass roots—even in the United States—are necessary if rural communities are to find successful niches for themselves in the newly integrated world economy.

JAY R. MANDLE

LOUIS FERLEGER

Note

1. Vietnam also would be included in this grouping of nations if adequate data for that country were available.

References

Bhagwati, Jagdish. 1998. *A Stream of Windows: Unsettling Reflections on Trade, Immigration and Democracy*. Cambridge: MIT Press.

Burtless, Gary, Robert Z. Lawrence, Robert E. Litan, and Robert J. Shapiro. 1998. *Globaphobia: Confronting Fears About Open Trade*. Washington, DC: Brookings Institution Press.

Colombo, Umberto. 1988. The Technology Revolution and the Restructuring of the Global Economy. In *Globalization of Technology: International Perspectives*, ed. Janet H. Muroyama and H. Guyford Stever. Washington, DC: National Academy Press.

Harvey, D. 1989. *The Condition of Postmodernity*. Oxford: Blackwell.

Holton, Robert J. 1998. *Globalization and the Nation-State*. New York: St. Martin's Press.

Krueger, Anne O. 1998. Introduction. In *The WTO as an International Organization*, ed. Anne O. Krueger. Chicago: University of Chicago Press.

Lewis, Paul. 1998. Marx's Stock Resurges on a 150-Year Tip. *New York Times on the Web*, 27 June.

Mander, Jerry. 1996. Facing the Rising Tide. In *The Case Against the Global Economy: And for a Turn Toward the Local*, ed. Jerry Mander and Edward Goldsmith. San Francisco: Sierra Club Books.

Morris, David. 1993. Free Trade: The Great Destroyer. In *The Case Against Free Trade: GATT, NAFTA and the Globalization of Corporate Power*, by Ralph Nader et al. San Francisco: Earth Island Press.

Nader, Ralph. 1993. Introduction: Free Trade and the Decline of Democracy. In *The Case Against Free Trade: GATT, NAFTA and the Globalization of Corporate Power*, by Ralph Nader et al. San Francisco: Earth Island Press.

Rodrik, Dani. 1998. Has Globalization Gone Too Far? Interview with Dani Rodrik. *Challenge* 41(2): 81-94.

Stever, H. Guyford and Janet H. Muroyama. 1988. Overview. In *Globalization of Technology: International Perspectives*, ed. Janet H. Muroyama and H. Guyford Stever. Washington, DC: National Academy Press.

Uchitelle, Louis. 1998. Some Economic Interplay Comes Nearly Full Circle. *New York Times on the Web*, 30 Apr.

World Bank. 1999a. *World Development Indicators 1999*. Washington, DC: World Bank.

———. 1999b. *World Development Report 1999/2000*. New York: Oxford University Press.

World Trade Organization. 1999. Background: The Seattle "Ministerial." Available at http://www.wto.org/wto/minist/backgr.htm. Accessed 8 Nov. 1999.

Globalization: The Product
of a Knowledge-Based Economy

By LESTER C. THUROW

ABSTRACT: The shift to an era of man-made brain-power industries is creating the technologies that are creating a global economy. Leaving behind the role of regulator or the function of controlling their national economies, governments are becoming platform builders that invest in infrastructure, education, and research and development to allow their citizens to have the opportunity to earn world-class standards of living. Countries themselves are being put into play, and inequality is rising. The rest of the world sees an invasion of the American system, but in reality, it is a brand-new global system. Intellectual property rights become a central and contentious unresolved issue.

Lester C. Thurow is a professor of management and economics and the former dean of MIT's Sloan School of Management. His most recent book is Building Wealth: New Rules for Individuals, Companies, and Nations in a Knowledge-Based Economy. *He is a member of America's national Trade Deficit Commission and is a regular columnist for newspapers in Asia, Europe, the Middle East, and America.*

GLOBALIZATION is just one of the impacts of the new technologies (microelectronics, computers, robotics, telecommunication, new materials, and biotechnology) that are reshaping the economies of the third millennium. Collectively, these technologies and their interactions are producing a knowledge-based economy that is systematically changing how all people conduct their economic and social lives. Often, globalization is seen as the cause of these changes, when it is in fact only one of many effects (Thurow 1999).

Bill Gates stands as the symbol of this new era. For all of human history until now, the richest person in the world has owned natural resources— land, gold, oil. But Bill Gates owns no land, no gold, and no oil. Owning no factories or equipment, he is not a capitalist in the old-fashioned sense. He has become the richest person in the world by controlling a knowledge process. As such, he marks a fundamental shift to a knowledge-based economy. This shift will come to be seen as the third industrial revolution—steam being the first, and electrification the second.

The third industrial revolution is spreading from the developed world to some, but not all, parts of the developing world. To participate in this new global economy, developing countries must be seen as attractive offshore production bases for multinational corporations. To be such bases, developing countries must provide relatively well-educated workforces, good infrastructure (electricity, telecommunications, transportation), political stability, and a willingness to play by market rules.

If these conditions are in place, multinational corporations will transfer via their offshore subsidiaries or to their offshore suppliers the specific production technologies and market linkages necessary to participate in the global economy. By themselves, developing countries, even if well educated, cannot produce at the quality levels demanded in high-value-added industries and cannot market what they produce even in low-value-added industries such as textiles or shoes. Put bluntly, multinational companies possess a variety of factors that developing countries must have if they are to participate in the global economy.

The geographical definition of any economy is given by the area across which business firms maximize profit—that is, across which they search to find the cheapest places to produce and the most profitable places to sell their goods and services. With today's communication and transportation technologies, business firms increasingly search the globe on both of these dimensions. In the process, a global economy is emerging that will in the end dissolve our existing national economies.

It is these search criteria and not any specific economic measure— profits earned abroad, exports relative to gross domestic product (GDP), and so on—that determine the existence of a global economy. No one economic statistic reflects the extent of globalization since globalization comes in many forms. When Proctor & Gamble produces and sells soap or shampoo inside China and keeps the profits within China to finance its expansion plans, it is part of globalization. A Toyota that exports cars and auto components to Europe and Japanese investors who buy securitized American home mortgages are part of globalization. A merger between Chrysler and Mercedes is part of globalization. A laptop computer built with "Intel Inside," a Microsoft operating system, a Japanese flat panel display, and Korean memory chips assembled in Taiwan to the specifications of a large variety of multinational sellers of computers is part of globalization. Keypunching American insurance forms in Jamaica, joint software design teams located in India and America, and teaching Third World foreign suppliers how to make components for First World products are all part of globalization. An American firm marketing Latin American bananas in Europe is part of globalization. So are the American movies, television programs, and music that dominate foreign programming. Internet commerce by its very technology is automatically global. While the forms of globalization differ, what is constant is the desire of business firms for profit maximization on a global basis.

THE NATION-STATE

The knowledge-based economy is fundamentally transforming the role of the nation-state. Instead of being a controller of economic events within its borders, the nation-state is increasingly having to become a platform builder to attract global economic activity to locate within its borders. In developing countries, platform building means creating the educated workforces, infrastructure, stability, and market frameworks necessary to play the economic game. In developed countries, governments must also finance the basic research and development that thrusts technology forward. But the nation-state cannot regulate the economic game or control its outcome as it has in the past in either developed or developing countries.

The decline in governmental powers is clearly seen in the 1997 Asian economic crisis. World capital markets, moving more than $1800 billion per day, dwarf and dominate all but the biggest governments. World capital markets can and do bring national economies down.

But global finance also undercuts the economic powers of even the biggest governments in the developed world. In September 1998, the chairman of the American Federal Reserve Board, Alan Greenspan, was forced to organize the rescue of a derivative hedge fund, Long Term Capital Management, that had borrowed more than $1000 billion dollars and whose imminent bankruptcy was threatening to bring down U.S. financial markets. He was criticized in the press for organizing a rescue rather than just closing the firm down. But what the press wanted him to do he could not do. Long Term Capital Management's physical headquarters was in the United States, but it was formally and legally a firm headquartered in the Grand Cayman Island. The chairman of the Federal Reserve Board had no legal regulatory powers to control the firm. All he could do was request that the American banks that were its equity investors (financial firms he did control) exercise their rights as owners and take control of the firm. Alan Greenspan, like central bankers in the developing world, was losing his powers to control.

Wishing to hold onto their present regulatory powers, governments, not surprisingly, talk about controlling the global flows of capital and regulating global financial institutions. But how is any one government, even one as big as that of the United States, to do so? Any government that tried to exert control would simply find its financial institutions legally and electronically moving offshore and outside of its jurisdiction of control.

A global government might regulate global financial institutions, but no one, least of all the United States, is about to give some global authority the power to directly regulate and control its financial institutions. But even if a global financial governance were to exist, there are reasons to doubt that it could control global capital flows to guarantee currency stability any more than national governments can now control the ups and downs of their domestic stock markets. When money can be moved across national boundaries electronically on personal computers, stopping global capital flows is technologically difficult and perhaps impossible—whatever its merits.

Because countries need corporations more than corporations need countries, the relative bargaining power of governments and multinational corporations is shifting in favor of corporations. High-profile multinational companies that bring technology, market linkages, and supplier networks with them no longer pay taxes to governments. Governments pay taxes to them. To get an Intel plant, the state of Israel paid Intel $600 million (in grants, the financing of plant infrastructure, tax rebates), and to get a Ford auto assembly plant, Brazil is promising to pay Ford $700 million. Countries can refuse to pay taxes to companies, but, if they do so, those companies simply locate elsewhere (Wilkinson 1999, 7).

Here again the reversal of traditional positions is not limited to developing countries. Huge sums were paid by the citizens of Alabama and South Carolina to get BMW and Mercedes Benz to locate auto assembly plants in their states. The United Kingdom, Norway, Germany, and the Netherlands all recently lowered taxes on shipping companies to keep them from legally reorganizing themselves in low-tax countries. The British bookmaker Ladbrokes is investigating ways to set up its betting offshore so that its customers do not have to pay British taxes. Electronic commerce is making it difficult to collect sales or value-added taxes on products and services (software, music, movies) that can be directly delivered electronically. In this new balance of power, governments (citizens) often pay taxes to multinational companies. Governments often cannot collect their traditional taxes.

Many other examples of the loss of governmental economic powers can be given. With modern transportation systems, countries find it impossible to stop illegal immigration. Millions see better standards of living elsewhere on their village television sets and decide to move to get those higher standards of living. In the process, what it means to be a country fades. A country that cannot control its own borders and its own workforce is in some fundamental sense not a real country. Similarly, pornography is produced electronically somewhere in the world (women with bare arms are regarded as pornographic in the Persian Gulf) where it is not illegal, put up on the Internet, and national governments lose their power to enforce their own standards of decency.

The economic interdependence that flows from globalization further undercuts the role of national governments. In the Latin American or East Asian meltdowns, the International Monetary Fund effectively replaced local governments when it came to economic decision making. The Japanese and East Asian meltdowns (purely locally generated in the case of Japan and locally triggered but globally intensified in the case of East Asia) threatened the world economy. What was feared did not happen because of the strength of the American economy, an economy bigger than those of Japan and East Asia combined. In the process, the continued prosperity of all parts of the world (Japan and Europe included) become dependent upon running export surpluses with the United States. For the continued prosperity of these economies, what happens to the American economy is more important than the activities of national economic policymakers at home.

Countries themselves are being put into play. Three factors are responsible.

1. With globalization, the scope, reach, and powers of national governments shrink, and the governments become less important. Attachments to existing governments grow weaker. If national governments cannot protect their citizens economically, why should their citizens support them politically?

2. The end of the Cold War means that superpowers have little interest in preventing other countries from disintegrating unless they are right next door and the chaos threatens to spread. Local civil wars in faraway places (Pakistan versus India, Israel versus Syria) are not going to bring the superpowers into military conflict with each other.

3. Small successful city-states, such as Singapore, demonstrate that one does not have to compromise with other ethnic groups so that one can live in larger countries that have the economies of scale necessary to produce high standards of living. National economies of scale are not all that important in a global economy. One can opt out and still succeed economically.

The empirical results of these three factors are clear. Many existing national states will not exist 50 years from now.

Fifteen countries have already emerged where the old USSR used to be. Czechoslovakia is divided in two. Yugoslavia has become at least five and will probably become seven different countries. The English have given quasi-independence to Scotland. The Basques and Catalans want independence from Spain. The Bretons and Corsicans agitate for autonomy in France. The northern Italians talk about kicking the southern Italians out of Italy. Quebec will at some point probably vote for independence from the rest of Canada.

In the non-Communist Third World, Indonesia is unlikely ever again to be one country. It was thousands of independent islands when it was conquered by the Dutch, forcibly made into their East Indies colony, and then ruled by two military dictators after World War II. An economic meltdown led to a political meltdown. There is no there there to glue it back together again.

Borders are going to be moving everywhere in Africa. Ten thousand different ethnic groups are not going to live forever in a handful of countries defined by the accidental meetings of British and French armies in the nineteenth century (Fisher and Onishi 1999).

The British unified India, the central planning of socialism held it together after the British left, but what is to hold it together now? Why should the prosperous parts be held back by the backward parts? Economic principalities will probably emerge looking much like the political principalities conquered by the British a few centuries earlier.

At the same time, in the developed world, countries are slowly disappearing. European countries without their own currencies are not fully independent countries. Eleven have become one. The remaining four members of the European Economic Community (EEC) will join—sooner rather than later. Others in Eastern Europe are knocking on the door. With the EEC imposing limits on national fiscal deficits, the determination of fiscal policies is now also outside of national control. Future steps, such as tax harmonization, will make members even less like real countries.

RISING INEQUALITY

The pressures fracturing the nation-state are also fracturing beliefs in, pressures for, and attainment of economic equality between individuals, companies, and countries. The economic gaps that have over the course of the last half-century shrunk are now widening.

In the first and second industrial revolutions, workers were leaving agriculture (a low-wage inegalitarian sector where patterns of land ownership dominate economic outcomes) and entering manufacturing and mining (intrinsically higher-waged and more egalitarian due to higher skill requirements). State-supported labor unions led to even more egalitarian distribution of wages. The social welfare state then used its tax and expenditure systems to further increase post-tax, post-transfer income equality.

But the knowledge-based economy essentially reverses all of these sources of equality. In the third industrial revolution, workers are leaving manufacturing and mining to enter services—a sector with a very wide dispersion of wages and average wages below those in mining and manufacturing (Thurow 1989). Services have also proven to be a difficult sector in which to organize unions. At the same time, globalization is driving unions out of existence in manufacturing. Why join a union if global competition means that unions cannot protect jobs or wages? Less than 10 percent of the private U.S. workforce is now unionized. Only in the public sector, where global competition plays no role, are unions still large and effective (U.S. Bureau of the Census 1998, 444).

Because of this shift in employment patterns, wage dispersions have increased sharply in America since 1973. Despite the booming prosperity of the 1990s in the United States, the trend toward sharply rising inequality has continued here. In the last three years of the decade, real wages ceased falling in absolute terms, but wage gaps between the top and bottom deciles continued to rise sharply (Mishel, Bernstein, and Schmitt 1998, 9, 23, 45, 85, 157, 51).

The egalitarian policies of the social welfare state are also in retreat. On both the tax and expenditure sides of the American federal government budget, redistributive activities have been sharply cut back (Council of Economic Advisors 1999, 357). International organizations such as the Organization for Economic Cooperation and Development repeatedly chastise Europe for not "deregulating its labor markets" and letting wages fall. The high payroll taxes necessary to finance a generous social welfare state are not globally viable since business firms will not expand in Europe as long as its

wages are out of line with those of the rest of the world. Firms will simply move to countries where they do not have to pay high payroll taxes. High social welfare benefits also mean that workers will not take the lower-wage service jobs that are their only alternative to unemployment. With European unemployment benefits higher than wages in America's expanding service sector, the result has to be high European unemployment rates. But Europeans do not want to dismantle their traditional social safety net and give up some of their hard-won benefits.

In GDP statistics, the economic returns to capital are up and the returns to labor are down (Bosworth 1995, 12, 14). This is not surprising, given that labor is more abundant relative to capital on a global basis than it is in the rich developed world. Similarly, among workers, the returns to skills are up and the wages of those without skills are down. This is not surprising, given that on a global basis the supply of unskilled workers far exceeds that of skilled workers and that new technologies are increasing the need for skilled workers.

Financial crises magnify these rising inequalities. Financial crises are not caused by globalization. They existed long before globalization occurred. But the austerity demanded by the International Monetary Fund to restore global macro-stability leaves countries with much greater levels of internal inequality. Years later, Mexico has still not restored the levels of equality that existed prior to its 1982 crisis. The same is going to be true in

East Asia. Levels of inequality are much higher then they were pre-crisis and are not going to return to pre-crisis levels any time soon.

Inequalities are rising between business firms as well as individuals. In a global economy, business firms find themselves confronting two strategic options: become a dominant global player or become a highly specialized, nimble niche player. The midsized national firm is doomed to extinction. In the auto industry, for example, it is widely believed that when the current consolidation is over, there will only be six firms left standing, and four of them (Volkswagen, Toyota, Ford, and General Motors) are already known. To have a chance at remaining viable, Mercedes bought Chrysler and Renault bought Nissan. The Volvos, Saabs, Jaguars, Rolls Royces, and Rovers are all gone as independent auto companies. How can the Fiats, Hyundais, and Peugeots survive?

In financial services, firms become global players such as Goldman Sachs or highly specialized niche players such as Long Term Capital Management (only 16 partners with more than $1000 billion focused on a very narrow range of derivative investments). Among those who would be corporate survivors, slice and dice (merge to get larger and sell divisions where it is not possible to be a global player) is the name of the game.

Among countries, the convergence in per capita GDPs that was occurring in the 1960s and 1970s is being replaced by divergence. Those countries that do not play in the global knowledge economy fall behind (Africa); those countries that can play the game leap ahead (China). Within Asia or South America, the gaps between the most successful and the least successful countries are larger than they were in the past. In the 1990s, the wealthiest big country, America, widened the income gap between itself and the rest of the world. Even the income gap between America and its closest and most similar neighbor, Canada, is up by a third.

The inequalities flowing from globalization and a knowledge-based economy are not important economically. Capitalistic economies can easily adjust to more unequal distributions of purchasing power. Middle-class stores find themselves with smaller markets (Sears) or go out of business (Gimbels). Upscale stores (Bloomingdale's) and downscale stores (Wal-Mart) boom.

The problems are political. Democracy (one person, one vote) implicitly assumes some degree of economic equality. A majority of the voters have to feel that they are benefiting from the economic system. As a result, all democracies have a heavy redistributive social welfare emphasis in their spending patterns. Governments have to deliver something to the majority of voters. As market forces produce ever more unequal distributions of economic wealth and as democratic governments lose their power to alter the market's distribution of earnings and wealth, political deliverables become harder to find. Over the past 25 years, America has illustrated that inequalities, if they grow slowly, can become very much larger than they were in the past, without evident political kickback. Yet it is difficult to believe that economic inequality can just keep on growing without limits in democracies.

EXPORTING THE AMERICAN SYSTEM

In the rest of the world, globalization is often seen as being forced to adopt American practices. (Europeans often call it "cowboy capitalism"). But the traditional American system is not being exported to the rest of the world (Calabrese 1998). A new global knowledge-based economy is being built, much of it in America, but what is emerging is not a global copy of traditional American practices.

Like those in the rest of the world, Americans see the new costs of globalization that they have to bear more clearly than they see the costs that others have to bear. Everyone, Americans included, is painfully adjusting to a new knowledge-based global economy. The American steel industry is a good example. Selling prices are down 25 percent because Asian steel production cannot be sold in Asia in the aftermath of Asia's meltdown. In 1998, steel imports surged into the United States from Asia (Korea, up 56 percent; Australia, up 98 percent; Japan, up 219 percent; and China, up 245 percent), American production fell 25 percent, and one third of America's steelworkers were laid off. These American steelworkers are essentially being asked to pay for Asia's mistakes. Not surprisingly, they object to this interdependence (Dunne 1999, 4).

Large labor force downsizings among profitable firms are new to America. Moving jobs to offshore production bases is new to Americans. An economy essentially without unions is not the economy of mid-twentieth-century America. Among men, wage inequalities are larger than they ever have been. Real inflation-adjusted median family incomes are slightly below where they were in 1973 (Council of Economic Advisors 1999, 366). Economic uncertainty is very high, and a majority of Americans expect their children to have real incomes below what they have.

Traditionally, culture is older people telling younger people what they should believe and how they should act. What is frightening about the new electronic culture is that it is a "for-sale" culture that jumps right across the generations directly to the young. In contrast to older forms of culture, this culture does not have any specific values that it wants to inculcate. Those who produce this culture provide whatever sells— whatever the young will buy. It is a culture of economics (profits) rather than a culture of values (morals). In that sense, it is profoundly different—and disturbing to many.

The television network MTV is a good example of the new global culture. From country to country, the songs and the languages in which the songs are sung are different, but the style in which the songs are presented is the same. That MTV style first appeared in America—but not all that long ago. The style is the same everywhere because the style seems to sell everywhere.

The electronic culture that frightens many in the rest of the world also frightens many Americans and has brought forth a religious-fundamentalist backlash in the United States that rivals that found anywhere else. In what other countries are there religious militia (Christian, in this case) who engage in shoot-outs with the police and their neighbors? One has to go to Algeria to find something more extreme. The fight going on within the Republican Party between the religious Right and the party's traditional business base vividly illustrates the power of those Americans who do not like the new electronic culture.

Economically, the interesting question is why Americans seem to create more than their fair share of this new for-sale culture. Games, movies, music, and television programs have become a major part of America's exports. Part of the answer may be found in an immigrant society that does not have a tight conception of what the American culture is. Others are welcome to add to that culture. As new immigrant groups have come to America, they have changed the American culture. Such changes have come to be expected. Foreign words become English words without anyone worrying about their origin. Asking what the potential clients (the young, in this case) want rather than trying to make them into a preconceived conception of what a young American ought to be is something a diverse country learns to do.

Because of this history, American companies are very good at bringing talented foreign performers into their operations and making them feel like first-class participants. Anyone good at creating cultural products that will sell is quickly invited to visit America, feels at home, and may decide to stay. These individuals quickly come to be seen by everyone inside and outside of the United States as an element of American culture despite their place of birth or the national heritage they bring with them.

With the new communication technologies, many of the new groups that are being invited to become Americans come electronically, not physically. In the process, they will change American culture just as those who came physically changed it. But the new amalgam will still probably be seen as American culture.

INTELLECTUAL PROPERTY RIGHTS

Not surprisingly in this new economy, the rules of engagement are uncertain and major unresolved problems will arise. The ownership of intellectual property rights—the ultimate source of wealth in a knowledge-based economy—is one of the most important and most contentious unresolved issues (Thurow 1997, 95).

The private ownership of productive assets and the ability to appropriate the output that flows from those assets lie at the heart of capitalism. Capitalism does not work unless who owns what is clear. But ownership rights are anything but clear in the area of intellectual property. Historically, efforts to establish and enforce ownership rights to intellectual property have revolved around patents, copyrights, trademarks, and trade secrets, but there are two problems. First, the current system was not built to deal with today's technologies. Second, there is no global system of enforceable intellectual property rights.

New technologies have created new potential forms of intellectual property rights: for example, can genetic pieces of a human being be patented, what ownership rights exist when humans build new genes that can replace defective natural human genes, what ownership rights exist when someone discovers what a gene does? New technologies have also made old rights unenforceable. When books and music can be downloaded from an electronic library, what does a copyright mean? If a software's look and feel cannot be patented, software can be legally copied as long as one does not use exactly the same programming. What does a software patent mean in this case? Put bluntly, a patent system created for a mechanical age simply does not fit an electronic age or a biological age.

What different countries want, need, and should have in a system of intellectual property rights is very different depending on their level of economic development. Developing countries need to copy in order to catch up, yet developed countries need to prevent copying to ensure adequate rates of return on investments in research and development. National systems that have been developed for advanced countries such as the United States are not going to evolve into de facto world standards. A global system will have to allow for a diversity of economic positions and beliefs, but how is that system to come into existence?

Meanwhile, everyone can feel aggrieved. From the perspective of the developed world, intellectual pirates are stealing property that belongs to others; from the perspective of the developing world, those seeking to enforce intellectual property rights are depriving them of the knowledge they need in order to develop. As they argue, they are doing nothing that today's wealthy countries were not doing when they were developing. The Americans blatantly copied the British textile mills in the nineteenth century. The Japanese blatantly copied the American auto and consumer electronics industries in the twentieth century.

CONCLUSION

Globalization has come in two waves. The illusion that national governments can choose to participate or not participate in globalization flows from the fact that choice was an important element in the first wave of globalization.

Seeing rampant economic nationalism as one of the causes of the Great Depression and World War II and facing a confrontation between capitalism and communism, both sides of the Cold War conflict set out in the 1950s to create more integrated transnational economies. The EEC in Western Europe and Comicon in Eastern Europe were both expressions of the same mind-set. Each of the two superpowers felt it had to more tightly tie its military partners together economically. Although America was not in Europe and is not a member of the EEC, it was the EEC's biggest supporter. The "United States of Europe" was a phrase commonly used on both sides of the Atlantic in the 1950s.

For the non-Communist world, the trading rounds of the General Agreement on Tariffs and Trade, starting with the Kennedy round in the 1960s, set out to achieve a capitalistic open trading regime globally. Governments dismantled tariffs and quotas deliberately in the 1950s, 1960s, and 1970s to create a more integrated capitalistic global economy. Companies reacted to these new economic opportunities created by governments by expanding across national borders. Then China, by choice in the late 1970s, and the Soviet Union, by default in the early 1990s, decided to abandon the idea of a competing Communist global economy and participate in a single capitalistic global market economy.

The second wave of globalization that started in the 1980s and accelerated in the 1990s is, however, very different. It was not created as a matter of public choice. It is a tsunami wave created by a seismic shift in technology. Responding to the new global profit-making opportunities created by technology, corporations started surfing the new technologies in this second wave. Governments lagged behind. Governments did not decide to start global sourcing and marketing. Governments did not encourage cross-border corporate mergers. Governments did not start

electronic commerce. All can be traced to shifts in technology.

The second wave of globalization is not a process that governments can start or stop, or speed up or slow down; nor can they pick and choose where they want to participate. Underdeveloped countries can opt out—the can refuse to provide the educated workforces and infrastructure necessary to participate—but that means opting out on the process of economic development itself. There is no other process for getting wealthy.

Developed countries cannot even opt out. They are already past the point of no return. Their corporations have committed themselves to the global economy, they have restructured themselves to fit that global economy, and they could not return to serving solely national economies even if they wished to do so. In the developed world, too many citizen-voters depend upon the global economy for their livelihoods for their governments even to think about opting out.

References

Bosworth, Barry. 1995. *Prospect for Savings and Investment in Industrial Countries.* Brookings Institution Discussion Paper no. 113. Washington, DC: Brookings Institution, May.

Calabrese, Michael. 1998. Should Europe Adopt the American Economic Model? *Policywire* (Center for National Policy), 6 Aug.

Council of Economic Advisors. 1999. *Economic Report of the President 1999.*

Washington, DC: Government Printing Office.

Dunne, Nancy. 1999. US Steel Demand Quota Protection. *Financial Times*, 11 Jan.

Fisher, Ian and Norimitsu Onishi. 1999. Congo's Struggle May Unleash Broad Strife to Redraw Africa. *New York Times*, 12 Jan.

Mishel, Lawrence, Jared Bernstein, and John Schmitt. 1998. *The State of Working America*. Ithaca, NY: Cornell University Press.

Thurow, Lester C. 1989. *Towards a High-Wage High-Productivity Service Sector*. Washington, DC: Economic Policy Institute.

———. 1997. Needed: A New System of Intellectual Property Rights. *Harvard Business Review* Sept.-Oct.: 95-103.

———. 1999. *Building Wealth: New Rules for Individuals, Companies and Nations in a Knowledge-Based Economy*. New York: HarperCollins.

U.S. Bureau of the Census. 1998. *Statistical Abstract of the United States 1998*. Washington, DC: Government Printing Office.

Wilkinson Max. 1999. They Can Run and They Can Hide. *Financial Times*, 14-15 Aug.

ANNALS, *AAPSS*, **570**, July 2000

The Globalization of
Human Development

By RICHARD A. EASTERLIN

ABSTRACT: By many measures, a revolution in living conditions is sweeping the world. Most people today are better fed, clothed, and housed than their predecessors two centuries ago. They are healthier, live longer, and can read and write. Women's lives are less centered on bearing and raising children, and political democracy has gained a foothold. Western Europe and its offshoots have been the leaders of this advance in the human condition. Most of the less developed world joined in the twentieth century, with the newly emerging nations of sub-Saharan Africa the latest to participate. Although the picture is not one of universal progress, it is the greatest advance in the condition of the world's population ever achieved in such a brief span of time.

Richard A. Easterlin is a professor of economics at the University of Southern California, Los Angeles. He holds an honorary doctorate from Lund University, Sweden. He is a member of the American Academy of Arts and Sciences and a former Guggenheim Fellow. He was president of the Population Association of America in 1978 and of the Economic History Association in 1980. His most recent book is Growth Triumphant: The Twenty-First Century in Historical Perspective *(1996).*

NOTE: The author is grateful to the University of Southern California for providing financial support.

THE purpose of this article is to survey human development worldwide since 1800, with special attention to the less developed world in the past half-century. I start with a short discussion of the concept of human development, proceed to indicators of various aspects of human development, and conclude with a few summary observations.

THE CONCEPT OF HUMAN DEVELOPMENT

Early in the post–World War II period, there was a tendency to focus on well-being in purely material terms—the goods and services at one's disposal—here called the "level" of living, following Davis (1945). This conception led naturally to use of the economists' measure of real gross domestic product (GDP) per capita as the primary measure of well-being. Critics expressed concern that GDP per capita failed to reflect a number of important aspects of human welfare, and they pointed to some notable disparities in the ranking of countries based on GDP per capita compared with other possible indicators of well-being such as length of life and education (Morris 1979; United Nations 1952; United Nations Research Institute for Social Development 1970). Many of these critics feared that if policymakers focused on GDP per capita, they would be unduly biased toward economic growth as a policy objective, rather than striving for balanced human development.

A recent product of this social indicators movement has been the U.N. human development index (HDI), now reported on an annual basis (United Nations Development Programme 1999). The HDI combines GDP per capita, life expectancy at birth, and a composite measure of education based on literacy and school enrollment into an overall index number. Some experimental work also seeks to include human rights in this broad measure of human development.

My approach here is influenced by the progressive broadening of the measure of human development. It is also affected by what people themselves say about their sources of well-being. In the early 1960s, social psychologist Hadley Cantril (1965) carried out an intensive survey in 12 countries, developed and less developed, asking open-ended questions about what people wanted out of life.[1] The results are instructive. In every country, material circumstances, especially level of living, are mentioned most often, being named, on average, by about three-fourths of the population. Next are family concerns—cited by about half—such as a happy family life and good relations with children and relatives. These are followed by concerns about one's personal or family health, which typically are named by about one-third of the people. After this, and about equal in importance, at around one-fifth of the population, are matters relating to one's work (a good job) and to personal character (emotional stability, personal worth, self-discipline, and so on). Perhaps surprisingly, concerns about broad international or domestic issues, such as war, political or civil liberty, and social equality, are not often mentioned, being named, on average, by fewer than 1 person in 20. Abrupt changes in the latter circumstances do affect people's sense of well-being at the time they occur, but ordinarily they are taken as given, and it is the things that occupy most people's everyday life that are typically in the forefront of personal concerns—making a living, marriage and family circumstances, and the health of oneself and one's family. Education—one of the principal components of the U.N. HDI—is not often mentioned, no doubt because it is largely a thing of the past for most adults, but it does show up in connection with aspirations for one's children. It seems reasonable to suppose that if Cantril's 1960s survey were replicated today, the results would be much the same, despite the economic changes that have since occurred, because of the similarity he found at that time between concerns in developed and less developed countries.

In the space available here, I try to assemble some rough indicators of the evolution of various dimensions of human development without attempting to combine them into a single measure. I include the three components of the HDI—GDP per capita, life expectancy, and education. I also add the fertility rate, as an indicator of women's status, and two measures of the prevalence of political democracy. The regional classification is that of the United Nations Population Division.[2] World and regional values are averages of country means weighted by population so as to approximate better the condition of people generally in various regions of the world. The present measures are far from exhaustive, but they are sufficient to suggest some of the immense changes in people's lives that have taken place in the course of the past two centuries.

LEVEL OF LIVING

The quantity of goods consumed by the average person has multiplied in the period since 1800 at a rate never before known. In most countries, it is possible to identify an approximate turning point after which living levels begin to advance at a previously unprecedented pace. Before the turning point, GDP per capita grows at best at a very low rate, usually about 0.2 percent per year; after the turning point, at a rate of 1.5 percent or more.[3] At 0.2 percent, it takes 350 years for GDP to double; at 1.5 percent, only 46 years.

The rate of improvement has risen noticeably over time. Whereas a 1.5 percent growth rate is typical of the historical experience of Western Europe and the United States, the growth rate in the less developed world since 1950 has averaged 2.5 percent, with rates in the various less developed regions other than sub-Saharan Africa ranging from 1.6 percent to 3.8 percent (Table 1, column 1). In less than half a century throughout the less developed world, average living levels have grown two- to fivefold except in sub-Saharan Africa (Table 1, column 2). One way of appreciating the rapidity of change is to note how it drives a wedge between the experiences of successive generations. An annual growth

TABLE 1

**MAJOR AREAS OF THE WORLD: GROWTH RATE OF REAL GDP PER CAPITA
(c. 1950-95), SHARE OF WORLD POPULATION, AND GDP PER CAPITA
AS A PERCENTAGE OF DEVELOPED COUNTRIES AVERAGE (c. 1995)**

	(1) Annual Growth Rate (percentage)	(2) Ratio: Per Capita GDP at End to Beginning	(3) Share of World Population (percentage)	(4) 1995 GDP per Capita (percentage of developed areas)
1. More developed areas	2.7	3.1	20	100
2. Less developed areas	2.5	2.9	80	18
a. China	3.8	5.0	21	17
b. India	2.2	2.5	17	10
c. Rest of Asia	3.7	4.6	21	23
d. Latin America	1.6	1.9	9	36
e. Northern Africa	2.1	2.4	2	18
f. Sub-Saharan Africa	0.5	1.2	11	8

SOURCES: In columns 1 and 2, lines 1 through 2b refer to the period 1952-95 and are calculated from Maddison 1998, 40; lines 2c-2f are for 1950-92, calculated from Maddison 1995, apps. A, C, and D. Northern Africa is a weighted average of Egypt and Morocco, which together account for over half of the region's population; sub-Saharan Africa is a weighted average of the rates for seven countries accounting for about half of the region's population (see 206). The sources for column 4 are the same; lines 1 through 2b are ratios for 1995, lines 2c-2f, for 1992. The values in 2e and 2f are based on all countries in each region. Column 3 is the medium variant projection for 2000 in United Nations 1998. For the regional classification used here and subsequently, see n. 2.

rate of 2.5 percent means that a parent would, on average, have less than half of what a child has at the same point in the life cycle; a grandparent, less than a fifth of what a grandchild has. Is it any wonder that intergenerational frictions often accompany modern economic growth?

The growth rates since 1950 of the developed areas have also been higher than in the historical past, actually exceeding slightly that of the less developed world (Table 1, column 1). As a result, the gap in living levels between the two remains very high. On average, living levels today in the less developed world are less than a fifth of those in the developed world, and in India and sub-Saharan Africa, they are a tenth or less (Table 1, column 4). Although living levels have improved greatly in most parts of the less developed world, they are still far short of those in more developed areas.

The transformation of living levels accompanying modern economic growth has been qualitative as well as quantitative. By comparison with the conveniences and comforts widely available in developed economies at the end of the twentieth century, everyday life two centuries ago was more akin to what we in America know today as "camping out." In late-eighteenth-century United States, which even then was a relatively rich society, among the rural population (95 percent of the total), housing consisted of "one story log houses and frame houses with one or two rooms and an attic under the rafters. . . . Cellars and basements were practically unknown and frequently there was no flooring except the hard earth. The fireplace with a chimney provided heating and cooking" (Brady 1972, 64). Toilet facilities consisted of outdoor privies. Water and wood had to be fetched. A few windows with shutters but no glass provided ventilation and daylight; candles supplemented the fireplace for light in the evening. The only methods of food preservation were curing and pickling. Transportation consisted of a horse and wagon.

The qualitative change from that world to the United States' current panoply of consumer goods—cars and planes, electrical appliances and running water, telecommunications and computers, pharmaceuticals and health care, and the phenomenal array of food and clothes—is literally incredible.[4] Although the followers in modern economic growth are not as far along as the United States, their rate of change is often much higher than that of the leaders in the past. For example, Japan experienced an annual growth rate of real GDP per capita of 5.7 percent from 1958 to 1987. Consumer durables such as electric washing machines, electric refrigerators, and television sets, found in few Japanese homes at the start of the period, became well-nigh universal, and car ownership soared from 1 percent to about 60 percent of households in only three decades (Yasuba 1991). What a difference to be a Japanese child raised in the 1980s rather than the 1950s!

LENGTH OF LIFE AND HEALTH

In the course of the past two centuries, life expectancy at birth, like GDP per capita, is typically marked by a sharp increase in the rate of improvement. The leading countries are again those of Western Europe and its overseas offshoots, but the turning points are later than those for living levels, typically falling in the last quarter of the nineteenth century. However, rapid improvement in life expectancy spreads more quickly to the less developed world, with marked advances occurring since the 1950s, usually concurrently with the rapid advance of living levels (Table 2).

In the less developed world, the rate of improvement in life expectancy, like that in GDP per capita, is much more rapid than in the historical experience of the leaders. In the early 1950s, life expectancy at birth in the less developed world other than Latin America was, on average, below that of Western Europe in the 1870s. Only four and a half decades later, life expectancy in most less developed areas outside of sub-Saharan Africa had reached the 60- to 69-year range, a level reached in the developed world only after eight decades of improvement. Even in sub-Saharan Africa, life expectancy, which started much lower than in other less developed areas, increased by 12 years up to the late 1980s. According to current U.N. estimates and projections using epidemiological models that take account of the spread of HIV infection there, life expectancy in sub-Saharan Africa is currently leveling off and will

TABLE 2
YEARS OF LIFE EXPECTANCY AT BIRTH,
MAJOR AREAS OF THE WORLD, 1950-55 AND 1990-95

	(1) 1950-55	(2) 1990-95	(3) Change, (2)–(1)
1. More developed areas	66.6	74.1	7.5
2. Less developed areas	40.9	61.9	21.0
a. China	40.8	68.4	27.6
b. India	38.7	60.3	21.6
c. Rest of Asia	39.4	62.0	22.6
d. Latin America	51.4	68.1	16.7
e. Northern Africa	41.8	62.2	20.4
f. Sub-Saharan Africa	35.3	47.0	11.7

SOURCE: United Nations 1998, 12, 546-66.

continue to do so through 2010, but it is expected then to resume its marked upward trend (United Nations 1998, 12).

In the 1960s, some experts came to adopt a "stationary state" expectation about the future of life expectancy in developed countries. Analysts at the National Center for Health Statistics, for example, cautioned in 1964 that "the death rate for the United States has reached the point where further declines as experienced in the past cannot be anticipated" (U.S. Department of Health, Education, and Welfare 1964). The reason was that historically—as in the less developed countries today— the great declines in mortality were due to reductions in infectious disease, which benefited especially those at younger ages. Further declines were seen as foundering on the hard rock of the degenerative diseases of older age, especially heart disease and cancer. As reasonable as this view seemed at the time, it was very shortly undercut by events. After 1968, a new decline in U.S.

mortality set in at a pace not much different from that prevailing from 1900 to 1964, as marked gains began to be made in reducing older-age mortality due to heart disease. Similar declines in mortality rates occurred in other countries leading in life expectancy. Thus the current improvement in life expectancy in the developed countries reflects chiefly progress on diseases previously viewed as the ineluctable result of aging, especially cardiovascular disease.

The marked upturn in life expectancy that started in the late nineteenth century is due to a technological breakthrough, but a quite different one from the industrial revolutions underlying modern economic growth (Easterlin 1999; Mokyr and Stein 1997; Preston and Haines 1991; Schofield, Reher, and Bideau 1991). It arises from major advances in the control of communicable disease—first via preventive methods and then via therapeutic techniques. In the first part of the nineteenth century, there was no knowledge of the causes of disease, very little of the mode of transmission, and almost none of how to treat disease. An example of health care knowledge at that time is the case of a Philadelphia tallow chandler in the fall of 1826, described by medical historian Charles Rosenberg (1979). The chandler "complained of chills, pains in the head and back, weakness in the joints and nausea":

Before seeing a regular physician, he was bled till symptoms of fainting came on. Took an emetic, which operated well. For several days after, kept his bowels moved with Sulph. Soda, Senna tea, etc. He then employed a Physician who prescribed another Emetic, which operated violently and whose action was kept up by drinking bitter tea. (13)

One can reasonably wonder about the value of the principal treatments for disease prevailing at that time—the use of emetics, cathartics, diuretics, and bleeding. A similar state of knowledge existed in the mid-twentieth century in many less developed areas and persists to some extent even to the present time (Caldwell et al. 1990).

The contrast with health knowledge in the developed countries today is illustrated by the prevailing methods of control of some of the major infectious diseases that evolved chiefly during the twentieth century. By the early 1930s, technology had been put into place that prevented the transmission of disease by a number of techniques: immunization for diphtheria and smallpox; dissemination of personal hygiene knowledge; mosquito control for malaria and yellow fever; and supervision of water and food for cholera, dysentery, and typhoid fever (Winslow 1931). Of these methods, only vaccination against smallpox was in use in the first part of the nineteenth century and, even then, not very widely—most of the developments just listed date from the last part of the nineteenth century or later. These preventive methods were responsible for much of the sharp upturn in life expectancy. Effective methods for the cure of major diseases did not become generally available until the 1940s, when penicillin and a long list of successor antibiotics and other drugs came along (Beeson 1980). In the less developed world, much the same preventive methods have been responsible for life expectancy improvement to date, although the concurrent availability there of antimicrobial therapeutic measures means that these have played a somewhat larger role than in the history of the leaders.[7]

There can be little doubt that health status improved in parallel with the advance of life expectancy as infectious disease was brought under control, because the same techniques that lowered deaths due to infectious disease also reduced the incidence and prevalence of such disease and thereby the extent of sickness in the population. Comprehensive evidence of the improvement in health is hard to come by, because of insufficient morbidity data, but the advance is clearly suggested by the dwindling (and often disappearing) number of cases in the United States in the twentieth century of reportable diseases such as typhoid fever, malaria, diphtheria, whooping cough, and smallpox (U.S. Bureau of the Census 1975). The reduction and elimination of the debilitating effects of such diseases meant that fewer people went through life with immune, cardiovascular, and other bodily systems permanently damaged by these diseases, and thus raised life-cycle resistance to disease in the population generally (see Mercer 1990). In the less developed world, similar improvements in health have been occurring and are sometimes credited with making a significant contribution there to higher economic productivity (Easterlin 1996, 89-91).

FAMILY CIRCUMSTANCES

The fertility rate, though not often used as a measure of human development, is surely symptomatic of a major change in family life and women's roles. This point is made eloquently by British social welfare scholar R. M. Titmuss (1966) in commenting on the impact of the fertility decline on English working-class women:

The typical working class mother of the 1890's, married in her teens or early twenties and experiencing ten pregnancies, spent about fifteen years in a state of pregnancy and in nursing a child for the first years of its life. She was tied, for this period of time, to the wheel of childbearing. Today, for the typical mother, the time so spent would be about four years. A reduction of such magnitude in only two generations in the time devoted to childbearing represents nothing less

than a revolutionary enlargement of freedom for women. (91)

The onset of rapid fertility decline started in the late nineteenth century in a number of western European countries (Easterlin 1996, chap. 8). It is currently spreading throughout the world (Table 3). Compared with the historical experience of the West, fertility in today's less developed areas, like mortality, typically starts from higher initial levels and declines more rapidly. In most countries, the timing of the onset of the rapid decline in fertility is close to that in mortality. Writing in the 1950s, demographers, generalizing chiefly from European experience, termed this "the demographic transition," a shift from initially high to eventually low levels of mortality and fertility. They saw the fertility decline as typically lagging the mortality decline, with a consequent temporary surge in population growth. Although there are exceptions to this pattern, this generalization is largely borne out by recent experience in less developed countries, where fertility declines have typically followed those in mortality by a decade or two. Currently, population growth rates are falling in all regions of the less developed world, confirming that the post–World War II "population explosion" was a transient phenomenon, as envisaged in demographic transition theory (United Nations 1998, 436).

There has been qualitative as well as quantitative change in childbearing behavior—a shift in the nature of fertility control. In the past, fertility

TABLE 3

**TOTAL FERTILITY RATE, MAJOR AREAS OF THE WORLD,
1950-55 AND 1990-95 (Births per woman)**

	(1) 1950-55	(2) 1990-95	(3) Decline, (2)–(1)
1. More developed areas	2.8	1.7	1.1
2. Less developed areas	6.2	3.3	2.9
a. China	6.2	1.9	4.3
b. India	6.0	3.6	2.4
c. Rest of Asia	6.1	3.4	2.7
d. Latin America	5.9	3.0	2.9
e. Northern Africa	6.8	4.0	2.8
f. Sub-Saharan Africa	6.5	5.9	0.6

SOURCE: United Nations 1998, 12, 516, 518.

was chiefly limited unintentionally by physical conditions such as malnutrition and by customs or practices motivated by concerns other than family size. Examples of such practices are prolonged breastfeeding, timing of entry into marriage, and abstinence, which were typically motivated by concerns for the health of mother of child.

Given these physical and social constraints on fertility, and levels of child mortality so high that only one out of two children survived to adulthood, most parents in the past (other than members of some elites) made little deliberate effort to restrict childbearing. In surveys of less developed countries in the 1960s, most respondents, often as many as 90 percent, reported never having attempted to limit family size—even after the questioner provided a detailed enumeration of a number of contraceptive practices (Easterlin, Pollak, and Wachter 1980). Behavioral evidence for Europe from the period prior to the fertility decline points to a similar absence of intentional limitation of family size at that time (Knodel 1977).

The great reduction in fertility in the twentieth century was accomplished by the adoption of intentional family size limitation by couples through the use of contraception or induced abortion. In the historical experience of European countries, the contraceptive methods chiefly employed to deliberately limit family size were abstinence, withdrawal, and the use of condoms. Even as late as 1970, a European survey found one-half to three-quarters of the reproductive-age population in a number of countries using withdrawal as the principal form of contraception (United Nations 1976). In today's less developed countries, the fertility decline has benefited from new techniques of contraception that have appeared since the 1960s—the oral pill, the intrauterine device, implants, and sterilization.

These developments in the nature of fertility control imply another significant shift in way of life. No longer do most parents simply have as many children as they can. Rather, they deliberately limit their family size by adopting practices that were previously nonexistent or, if known, were rarely used intentionally to reduce the number of offspring.

SCHOOL ENROLLMENT AND LITERACY

When one turns to education as a standard-of-living indicator, the picture of world leadership is somewhat different from that portrayed by the previous measures. Although western Europe and its offshoots are again in the forefront, England no longer leads the way in the nineteenth century, as it did in the movement toward higher GDP and life expectancy; rather, the mantle shifts to Scandinavia, the German states, and the United States. If early-nineteenth-century levels of education are measured by, say, the percentage of the school-age population enrolled in primary school in 1830, then Germany is first at 77 percent, followed by Scandinavia, 66 percent; the United States, 56 percent; England, 41 percent; France, 39 percent; and Japan, about 30 percent. Most countries elsewhere in the world had a trivial fraction of the school-age population enrolled in primary school at that time.[8] One cannot help but notice that the pattern of the early spread of industrialization outward from England was to areas where education, and thus the ability to learn new methods of production, was already relatively high in the world.

It would be a mistake to read the previous enrollment figures in light of education today. In the nineteenth century, school years and school days were shorter, and the curriculum was quite different. Numeracy probably lagged behind literacy. But if one were to tell a story of human development that focused on the emergence and spread of formal schooling, it would be rather different from that given by the economic historians' tale of industrialization or the demographers' story of life expectancy improvement. Unfortunately, that history of education has yet to be written. What one can say with some assurance is that the early-nineteenth-century differences cited previously are the product of trends that reach as far back as the sixteenth century, well before the onset of modern economic growth, trends that are connected in part to the Protestant Reformation with its emphasis on the need for each individual to be able to read the Bible herself (Cippola 1969; Easterlin 1981; Melton 1988; UNESCO 1957).

On a worldwide scale, the pattern for education is much like that for the other dimensions of human development. Taken collectively, Western Europe and its offshoots are the leaders, while throughout much of the less developed world, the move to universal formal schooling occurs chiefly in the twentieth century, particularly since World War II (Table 4). Again, as with the other indicators, the rapidity of change in the less developed areas is much greater than was true in the historical experience of the West.

TABLE 4

**ADULT LITERACY RATE, MAJOR AREAS
OF THE WORLD, 1950 AND 1995 (Percentage)**

	(1) 1950	(2) 1995	(3) Change, (2)–(1) (percentage points)
1. More developed areas	93	98	5
2. Less developed areas	40	70	30
a. China	48	82	34
b. India	19	52	33
c. Rest of Asia	24	72	48
d. Latin America	57	86	29
e. Northern Africa	12	53	41
f. Sub-Saharan Africa	17	56	39

SOURCES: UNESCO 1957; World Bank 1999.

POLITICAL DEMOCRACY

The striking record of human improvement so far depicted is marred when one turns to political democracy. The relevance of democracy to well-being is put as follows by Alex Inkeles (1991): "Democratic systems give people a greater sense of freedom and, I would argue, more actual freedom, to influence the course of public events, express themselves, and realize their individual human potential" (x).

I use two measures in complementary fashion here to describe the spread of democratic institutions— one relating primarily to the executive branch of government, and one, to the legislative branch. The executive branch measure gives weight chiefly to two things: procedures for executive recruitment and limits on the power of the chief executive. Such limits might arise from a legislature, but they could also be due to a political party or parties not wholly controlled by the nation's leader or to some other groups, such as the church or military (Gurr, Jaggers, and Moore 1991). The measure for the legislative branch, legislative effectiveness, indicates whether a legislature exists and how important a role it plays in political decision making (Banks 1971). Both measures are based on the judgments of scholars with specialized knowledge of the political histories of the individual countries.

For the developed areas, the long-term trend since 1800 has seen a marked expansion in political democracy, although not without setbacks. In 1800, significant constraints on the chief executive were rare, and the development of effective legislatures was confined to a few countries. By the 1990s, indicator values for the executive and legislative branches were averaging near their maximum values (Table 5).

The world picture with regard to the spread of democracy in the last half-century is much less positive than that conveyed by the long-term trends in the developed areas. In the

TABLE 5
INDICATORS OF POLITICAL DEMOCRACY, MAJOR AREAS OF THE WORLD,
1950-59 AND 1990-94 (From minimum of 0 to maximum of 1.0)

| | (1) | (2) | (3) | (4) | (5) | (6) |
| | Executive Branch | | | Legislative Branch | | |
	1950-59*	1990-94	Change, (2)–(1)	1950-59*	1990-94	Change, (5)–(4)
1. More developed areas	.72	.92	.20	.81	.85	.04
2. Less developed areas	.33	.34	.01	.52	.56	.04
a. China	0	0	0	.20	.33	.13
b. India	.90	.80	−.10	1.00	1.00	0
c. Rest of Asia	.32	.34	.02	.53	.50	−.03
d. Latin America	.32	.69	.37	.70	.73	.03
e. Northern Africa	.08	.04	−.04	.27	.32	.05
f. Sub-Saharan Africa	.25	.14	−.11	.46	.35	−.11

SOURCES: The measure for the executive branch is that of "institutionalized democracy," as reported in Jaggers and Gurr 1995. This measure is the sum of four component measures and varies from 0 to 1.0 in 0.1 increments. The components are measures of the competitiveness of political participation (ranging from 0 to 0.3), competitiveness of executive recruitment (0 to 0.2), openness of executive recruitment (0 to 0.1), and constraints on the chief executive (0 to 0.4). See Gurr, Jaggers, and Moore 1991 for further discussion. The measure for the legislative branch is that of "legislative effectiveness" as given in Banks 1971, [1992] 1995. The measure is scaled here as follows: 0 = no legislature exists; 0.3 = ineffective legislature; 0.7 = partially effective legislature; 1.0 = effective legislature. See Banks 1971, xvii, for discussion.

*For northern and sub-Saharan Africa, 1960-69 or years in that decade for which a country's data are available.

less developed world, other than India and Latin America, the development of democratic institutions is at a fairly low level (Table 5, lower panel). Only in Latin America has there been noticeable improvement since the 1950s, and then only with regard to the executive branch. The contrast with the previous human development indicators is striking. The indicators of political democracy here do not follow the typical pattern, where the progress of less developed areas in the last four or five decades has been more rapid than in the history of the developed countries. One might like to believe, following Lipset (1959) and Barro (1997), that economic growth stimulates democracy. Given the unprecedented growth of GDP per capita in the less developed world since 1950, however, it is troubling to see so little evidence of increased political democracy in the present measures.

Against the background of such limited political democracy in the less developed world generally, India stands out as a sharp exception. The contrast with China is notable. When human rights are added to the human development comparison, China's relative success in economic growth, health, and fertility reduction must be weighted against India's remarkable record of political democracy. India's feat has been accomplished with a population much more heterogeneous linguistically than most and with income and literacy levels lower than those of the United Kingdom and the United States in the first half of the nineteenth century, when those countries' democratic attainment was less than India's today.

CONCLUDING OBSERVATIONS

Consider a world of a billion and a half people—impoverished, illiterate, and decimated by infectious disease—whose numbers will triple in the next half-century. What will be its fate? Not many, I suspect, would forecast an unprecedented improvement in conditions of life. Yet this is just what has happened over the last half-century in today's less developed areas other than sub-Saharan Africa. While population has, in fact, tripled, real GDP per capita has multiplied from two- to five-fold and life expectancy has soared into the 60- to 69-year range. Literacy has risen sharply, and in some areas, the virtual eradication of illiteracy is within sight. The sharp upsurge in the rate of population growth caused by mortality reduction is now receding as the second phase of the demographic transition—fertility decline—sets in. Fertility rates have already declined by 40 percent or more, portending significant changes in women's roles. Only in the area of political democracy is there little sign of widespread improvement. But in the political realm, the shift from colonial rule to independence in a number of countries must be recognized as an important advance.

None of this is to say that the situation is one of unmitigated progress.

Especially in the newly emerging nations of sub-Saharan Africa, the latecomers to the world scene, the picture remains mixed and in some countries is darkened by the terrible burden of widespread HIV infection. But even in sub-Saharan Africa, life expectancy has improved noticeably, and this gain is projected to be largely sustained. Important strides have been made, too, with regard to the reduction of illiteracy, and there are also signs of incipient fertility decline.

One might point to measures that give a more equivocal reading of world human development than the present ones. Feelings of subjective well-being, for one, have changed little over the past half-century in those developed countries for which measures exist, despite significant advance in the objective measures reported here (Easterlin 1974, 1995). Some would argue that there has been serious environmental degradation, although the historical evidence for this appears ambiguous (Simon 1995, pt. V). The present survey, however, has focused on the current consensus of human development indicators stressed by the United Nations. For these, the story is clearly one of the increasing globalization of human development. As we enter the new millennium, the human condition is a world apart from that of two centuries ago.

Notes

1. In a face-to-face interview, the respondent was asked to give his view of the best of all possible worlds for himself—"his wishes and hopes as he personally conceives them and the realization of which would constitute for him

the best possible life" (Cantril 1965, 22). A similar question elicited views on the worst possible life. A respondent could, and often did, name a variety of concerns—living level, health, and so on. One example of the care with which the survey was conducted is Cantril's description of the problem "of translating the original questions from English into the various languages used. . . . considerable time was spent with experts to be sure the translation contained the precise nuances wanted. One of the methods often utilized in this translation process was to have someone who knew the native language, as a native, for example, an Arab, and who also was completely fluent in English translate our questions into Arabic. Then someone whose native language was English but who had a perfect command of Arabic would translate the Arabic back into English so a comparison could be made with the original question and, through discussion and further comparisons, difficulties could be ironed out" (26).

2. More developed areas comprise Northern America, Japan, Europe, Australia, and New Zealand; less developed, all others. Caribbean nations are included with Latin America; Melanesia, Micronesia, and Polynesia, under "Rest of Asia" (which excludes Japan).

3. Evidence for GDP and subsequent human development indicators relating to the historical experience of developed countries is given in greater detail in Easterlin 1996, 2000.

4. This decade has seen the appearance of several valuable studies providing remarkable detail on the change in American consumption in the twentieth century (Brown 1994; Cox and Alm 1999; Lebergott 1993, 1996).

5. The statement about similarity in rate of change before and after the 1960s is based on the age-adjusted mortality rate, which weights age-specific mortality declines on the basis of each age group's share in the population. The measure of life expectancy at birth gives disproportionate weight to the youngest ages (Lee and Skinner 1999) and thus fails to reflect as fully the death-rate declines at older ages.

6. The transition economies of Eastern Europe, some of which experienced notable declines in life expectancy, especially among males, in the first part of the 1990s, appear now to be recovering (World Health Organization 1999a).

7. Because the emergence of drug-resistant strains of malaria parasites and the associated rise in malaria prevalence have been widely publicized by the media, it is worth noting the statement in the World Health Organization's 1999 report that, "notwithstanding these serious setbacks, a return to the previously high malaria-related mortality rates within this vast sector of the human population [the world other than sub-Saharan Africa] has never been remotely approached" (1999b, 50).

8. Enrollment figures are from Easterlin 1981, 18-19, except Japan, which is based on Hanley 1990, 69, and Taira 1971, 375, and is for the late pre-Meiji period. Historical literacy estimates are generally consistent with those for school enrollment (Cipolla 1969, 115; UNESCO 1957, 58; Yasuba 1987, 290).

References

Banks, Arthur S. 1971. *Cross-Polity Time Series Data*. Cambridge: MIT Press.

———. [1992] 1995. *Cross-National Time Series Data Archive*. Binghamton, NY: Center for Social Analysis.

Barro, Robert J. 1997. *Determinants of Economic Growth: A Cross-Country Empirical Study*. Cambridge: MIT Press.

Beeson, Paul B. 1980. Changes in Medical Therapy During the Past Half Century. *Medicine* 59(2): 79-99.

Brady, Dorothy S. 1972. Consumption and the Style of Life. In *American Economic Growth: An Economists' History of the United States*, ed. Lance E. Davis, Richard A. Easterlin, and William N. Parker. New York: Harper & Row.

Brown, Clair. 1994. *American Standards of Living, 1918-1988*. Cambridge, MA: Blackwell.

Caldwell, John C., Sally Findley, Pat Caldwell, Gigi Santow, Wendy Cosford, Jennifer Braid, and Daphne Broers-Freeman, eds. 1990. *What We Know About the Health Transition: The Cultural, Social, and Behavioral*

Determinants of Health. Canberra, Australia: Australian National University, Health Transition Centre.

Cantril, Hadley. 1965. *The Pattern of Human Concerns*. New Brunswick, NJ: Rutgers University Press.

Cipolla, Carlo M. 1969. *Literacy and Development in the West*. Baltimore, MD: Penguin Books.

Cox, W. Michael and Richard Alm. 1999. *Myths of Rich and Poor: Why We're Better Off Than We Think*. New York: Basic Books.

Davis, Joseph S. 1945. Standard and Content of Living. *American Economic Review* 35(1): 1-15.

Easterlin, Richard A. 1974. Does Economic Growth Improve the Human Lot? In *Nations and Households in Economic Growth: Essays in Honor of Moses Abramovitz*, ed. Paul A. David and Melvin W. Reder. New York: Academic Press.

———. 1981. Why Isn't the Whole World Developed? *Journal of Economic History* 41(1): 1-19.

———. 1995. Will Raising the Incomes of All Increase the Happiness of All? *Journal of Economic Behavior and Organization* 27(1): 35-47.

———. 1996. *Growth Triumphant: The Twenty-First Century in Historical Perspective*. Ann Arbor: University of Michigan Press.

———. 1999. How Benevolent Is the Market? A Look at the Modern History of Mortality. *European Review of Economic History* 3(3): 257-94.

———. 2000. The Worldwide Standard of Living Since 1800. *Journal of Economic Perspectives* 14(1): 7-26.

Easterlin, Richard A., Robert A. Pollak, and Michael L. Wachter. 1980. Toward a More General Economic Model of Fertility Determination: Endogenous Preferences and Natural Fertility. In *Population and Economic Change in Developing Countries*, ed. Richard A.

Easterlin. Chicago: University of Chicago Press.

Gurr, Ted Robert, Keith Jaggers, and Will H. Moore. 1991. The Transformation of the Western State: The Growth of Democracy, Autocracy, and State Power Since 1800. In *On Measuring Democracy: Its Consequences and Concomitants*, ed. Alex Inkeles. New Brunswick, NJ: Transaction.

Hanley, Susan B. 1990. The Relationship of Education and Economic Growth: The Case of Japan. In *Education and Economic Development Since the Industrial Revolution*, ed. Gabriel Tortella. Valencia: Generalitat Valenciana.

Inkeles, Alex, ed. 1991. *On Measuring Democracy: Its Consequences and Concomitants*. New Brunswick, NJ: Transaction.

Jaggers, Keith and Ted Robert Gurr. 1995. Polity III: Regime Change and Political Authority, 1800-1994 [computer file]. 2d ICPSR version. Boulder, CO: Keith Jaggers; College Park, MD: Ted Robert Gurr [producers]. Distributed by Inter-university Consortium for Political and Social Research, Ann Arbor, MI.

Knodel, John. 1977. Family Limitation and the Fertility Transition: Evidence from the Age Patterns of Fertility in Europe and Asia. *Population Studies*, 31 July, 219-49.

Lebergott, Stanley. 1993. *Pursuing Happiness*. Princeton, NJ: Princeton University Press.

———. 1996. *Consumer Expenditures: New Measures and Old Motives*. Princeton, NJ: Princeton University Press.

Lee, Ronald and Jonathan Skinner. 1999. Will Aging Baby Boomers Bust the Federal Budget? *Journal of Economic Perspectives* 13(1): 117-40.

Lipset, Seymour Martin, 1959. Some Social Requisites of Democracy: Economic Development and Political Legitimacy. *American Political Science Review* 53(1): 69-105.

Maddison, Angus. 1995. *Monitoring the World Economy 1820-1992*. Paris: Development Centre of the Organisation for Economic Co-operation and Development.

———. 1998. *Chinese Economic Performance in the Long Run*. Paris: Development Centre of the Organisation for Economic Co-operation and Development.

Melton, James van Horn. 1988. *Absolutism and the Eighteenth Century Origins of Compulsory Schooling in Prussia and Austria*. New York: Cambridge University Press.

Mercer, Alex. 1990. *Disease, Mortality, and Population in Transition*. Leicester, UK: Leicester University Press.

Mokyr, Joel and Rebecca Stein. 1997. Science, Health, and Household Technology: The Effect of the Pasteur Revolution on Consumer Demand. In *The Economics of New Goods*, ed. Timothy F. Bresnahan and Robert J. Gordon. Chicago: University of Chicago Press.

Morris, Morris David. 1979. *Measuring the Condition of the World's Poor: The Physical Quality of Life Index*. New York: Pergamon.

Preston, Samuel H. and Michael R. Haines. 1991. *Fatal Years: Child Mortality in Late Nineteenth Century America*. Princeton, NJ: Princeton University Press.

Rosenberg, Charles E. 1979. The Therapeutic Revolution: Medicine, Meaning, and Social Change in Nineteenth-Century America. In *The Therapeutic Revolution*, ed. Morris J. Vogel and Charles E. Rosenberg. Philadelphia: University of Pennsylvania Press.

Schofield, Roger, David Reher, and Alain Bideau. 1991. *The Decline of Mortality in Europe*. Oxford: Clarendon Press.

Simon, Julian L., ed. 1995. *The State of Humanity*. Cambridge, MA: Blackwell.

Taira, Koji. 1971. Education and Literacy in Meiji Japan: An Interpretation. *Explorations in Economic History* 8(4): 371-94.

Titmuss, Richard M. 1966. *Essays on the Welfare State*. London: Unwin University Press.

United Nations. 1952. *Preliminary Report on the World Social Situation*. New York: United Nations.

———. 1976. *Fertility and Family Planning in Europe Around 1970*. New York: United Nations.

———. 1998. *World Population Prospects: The 1998 Revision*. Vol. 1, *Comprehensive Tables*. New York: United Nations.

United Nations Development Programme. 1999. *Human Development Report 1999*. New York: Oxford University Press.

UNESCO. 1957. *World Illiteracy at Mid-Century*. Paris: United Nations Educational, Scientific, and Cultural Organization.

United Nations Research Institute for Social Development. 1970. *Contents and Measurement of Socio-Economic Development: An Empirical Enquiry*. Geneva: United Nations Research Institute for Social Development.

U.S. Bureau of the Census. 1975. *Historical Statistics of the United States, Colonial Times to 1970*. Bicentennial ed., pt. 2. Washington, DC: Government Printing Office.

U. S. Department of Health, Education, and Welfare. 1964. *The Change in Mortality Trend in the United States*. National Center for Health Statistics, 3d ser., no. 1. Washington, DC: Government Printing Office.

Winslow, Charles-Edward Amory. 1931. Communicable Diseases, Control Of. In *Encyclopaedia of the Social Sci-*

ences, ed. Edwin R. A. Seligman. Vol. 4. New York: Macmillan.

World Bank. 1999. *World Development Report 1998/99: Knowledge for Development.* New York: Oxford University Press.

World Health Organization. 1999a. *Health for All Database.* Copenhagen: World Health Organization.

———. 1999b. *The World Health Report 1999: Making a Difference.* Geneva: World Health Organization.

Yasuba, Yasukichi. 1987. The Tokugawa Legacy: A Survey. *Economic Studies Quarterly* 38(4): 290-308.

———. 1991. Japan's Post-War Growth in Historical Perspective. *Japan Forum,* 1 Apr., 57-70.

ANNALS, *AAPSS*, **570**, July 2000

Globalization
in Southeast Asia

By PETER A. COCLANIS and TILAK DOSHI

ABSTRACT: The authors attempt to accomplish four interrelated tasks in this article: (1) to develop a plausible and defensible approach to studying globalization; (2) to define Southeast Asia; (3) to delimit and historicize the globalization process in Southeast Asia; and (4) to describe and analyze the economic performance of Southeast Asia over the past 30 years or so, paying particular attention to the region before, during, and after the events of 1997.

Peter A. Coclanis is George and Alice Welsh Professor and chairman of the History Department at the University of North Carolina at Chapel Hill. He is the author of numerous works in U.S. and international economic history. Tilak Doshi is chief Asia economist for the Unocal Corporation. He has published widely in both petroleum economics and the economy of Southeast Asia. The authors have collaborated on several occasions previously, most recently on an essay entitled "The Economic Architect: Goh Keng Swee," in Lee's Lieutenants: Singapore's Old Guard, *edited by Lam Peng Er and Kevin Y. L. Tan (1999).*

L EXUSES and olive trees; jihads vs. McWorlds:[1] the vague and amorphous concept known as globalization has evoked some inspired binary images from the chattering classes over the past decade or so. Alas, as globalization qua process has evolved in tandem with postmodernism qua sensibility, a good number of opaque, if not unfathomable, binary representations have appeared as well. To Roland Robertson (1992), for example, globalization suggests "the twofold process of the particularization of the universal and the universalization of the particular" (177-78). More obscure still is the approach offered by the reliably enigmatic literary theorist Fredric Jameson (1998), for whom globalization is "an untotalizable totality which intensifies binary relations between its parts—mostly nations, but also regions and groups, which, however, continue to articulate themselves on the model of 'national entities' (rather than in terms of social classes, for example)." Jameson, however puzzling, is just getting warmed up: "But what we now need to add to the other qualifications implicit in the formulation—binary or point-to-point relations already being rather different from some plural constellation of localities and particulars—is that such relations are first and foremost ones of tension and antagonism, when not outright exclusion: in them each term struggles to define itself against the binary other" (xii). And so on. If much of this stuff can be characterized as "globaloney," to use Claire Booth Luce's punchy term, which has recently been recycled by economist Paul Krugman, we believe that there is nonetheless something identifiable and analytically valuable about the concept of globalization (Krugman 1998, 73). In this article on globalization in Southeast Asia, we shall try to lay out precisely what and, in so doing, will both delimit and historicize this process. We will even throw in an apposite Southeast Asian binary of our own: Davos Man versus the *orang ulu*.[2]

In a very broad way, we all instinctively know or at least think we know what globalization is. The problem is pinning down the concept in analytical terms. Rather than looking to Louis Armstrong for inspiration here—when asked about the definition of jazz, the great trumpeter famously responded that "if you gotta ask, you'll never know"—let us take a shot at specification. Despite the vaporous quotations cited previously, there has in fact been some very useful writing on globalization and its effects. According to one, the globalizers have "given a cosmopolitan character to production and consumption in every country." As a result,

all old-established national industries have been destroyed or are daily being destroyed. They are dislodged by new industries, whose introduction becomes a life and death question for all civilized nations, by industries that no longer work up indigenous raw material, but raw material drawn from the remotest zones; industries whose products are consumed, not only at home, but in every quarter of the globe. In place of the old wants, satisfied by the productions of the country, we find new wants, requiring for their satisfaction the products of distant lands and climes. In place of the old local and national seclusion and self-sufficiency, we have intercourse in every direction, universal interdependence of nations. And as in material, so also in intellectual production. The intellectual creations of individual nations become common property.

Moreover, the globalizers "by the rapid improvement of all instruments of production, by the immensely facilitated means of communication, [draw] all, even the most barbarian, nations into civilization. The cheap prices of [their] commodities are the heavy artillery with which [they batter] down all . . . walls."

A good start, if a bit wordy and a touch dramatic. Oh, yes, a bit on the venerable side, too: the preceding quotations are not from William Greider or Edward Luttwak but from Marx and Engels's *Communist Manifesto*, written over 150 years ago (Marx and Engels [1848] 1998, 39-40; Greider 1997; Luttwak 1999). These two scientific socialists certainly captured the spirit of globalization, even if they used different lingo: the group we refer to earlier as globalizers they prefer to call the bourgeoisie.

However powerful Marx and Engels's descriptive language—language that they employ to "burst asunder" the "integument" of globalization, er, capitalism—other, more rigorous or at least testable and thus falsifiable definitional approaches are possible. For example, in defining globalization, one can emphasize change and process and, in so doing, stress increases in the absolute size of transnational flows of labor, capital, products, services, and the like

or, more fruitfully, increases in the relative importance of these flows. Krugman, for one, often looks to the relationship between the rate of growth in world trade and the rate of growth in world production as a proxy measure of globalization; that is, if the former is consistently higher than the latter, the process called globalization is occurring (Krugman 1998, 73). Far be it from us to criticize definitional concision—in principle, we all are for parsimony—but reducing globalization to a quantifiable ratio of one sort or another is a bit exiguous even for our tastes. Rather, we prefer to interpret long-term growth in the relative importance of world trade, for example, as a manifestation and expression of deeper, more complex, and ultimately more meaningful qualitative changes in the structure, organization, and operation of economic life.

Along these lines, the Organization for Economic Cooperation and Development defines globalization as "the geographic dispersion of industrial and service activities (for example, research and development, sourcing of inputs, production and distribution) and the cross-border networking of companies (for example, through joint ventures and the sharing of assets)" (Bannock, Baxter, and Davis 1998, 176). Not elegant, perhaps, but rich in descriptive and even anatomical power. In this regard, social theorist Manuel Castells (1994) emphasizes interdependence, scale, scope, and simultaneity, defining the global economy as "an economy that works as a unit in real time on a planetary basis" (21). Thomas Friedman (1999), too, stresses the qualitative: globalization comes into existence when "everyone" feels the pressures, constraints, and opportunities attending the relative increase in importance of world trade, and the "democratizations" of technology, finance, and information associated with the same (59). Here, Friedman follows much the same path taken by Fernand Braudel, when the great French historian was working on the origins and spread of capitalism. In *Capitalism and Material Life* (1973) and elsewhere, Braudel stressed everyday people and everyday life: capitalism can be said to have come into existence in a particular place when a sufficient number of people were sufficiently affected by "capitalist" markets, behaviors, and mentalités as to render alternative "markets," behaviors, and mentalités increasingly unimportant, insignificant, or even obsolete (1973, xi-xv and passim). Can we not just substitute "globalization" for "capitalism," "global" for "capitalist" and fill in the blanks? Probably not, but by combining certain quantitative ratios—relative increases in transnational flows of one sort or another over a sustained period of time—with some of the qualitative measures discussed previously, we can rein in, if not capture completely, the wild conceptual beast known as globalization.

The mere mention of wild conceptual beasts offers a nice segue into Southeast Asia per se. Even as we write, there is considerable disagreement over the proper bounds of Southeast Asia, indeed, over whether or not a coherent, readily identifiable, culturally discrete geographical entity called Southeast Asia can even be said to exist. The very term "Southeast Asia," for example, became common only during World War II, when it was used with reference to the Japanese-occupied parts of Asia south of China. Prior to that time, the area—at least in the West—was either packaged generically and climatologically as Tropical Asia or Monsoon Asia or, instead, subdivided, spliced, and diced into subregions known as "Further India," the Malay Archipelago, Indochina, and the East Indies, along with a residual outlier: the Hispanicized Philippines. To the Chinese, on the other hand, the area east of India and south of China was known traditionally as *Nan-yang*, the (lands of the) Southern Ocean (Williams 1976, 3-11; Osborne 1990, 3-5).

In the academy, it was only with the publication of D.G.E. Hall's trailblazing *History of South-East Asia* in 1955 that the rubric in question began to resonate widely. It should be noted, moreover, that however broad his conceptual embrace, Hall (at least in the first edition) excluded one part of the region, the Philippines, from consideration. In later editions of his *History*, Hall did include the Philippines, however, and most scholars have more or less followed his lead ever since (Williams 1976, 3-40).

In retrospect, it is not difficult to understand the late entrance of Southeast Asia onto the nominal or even notional scene. For several centuries, much of the area had been under the political control, whether titular or real, of one or another of the

European imperial powers. Through both formal and informal means, these powers worked hard to establish and enforce close economic, political, and cultural ties between themselves and their respective colonies or in some cases groups of colonies. At the same time, these same powers worked formally and informally to impede, if not prohibit, similar ties between neighboring parts of the area organized under different European flags. As a result, the various constituent parts of what we now call Southeast Asia often had much closer links with European metropoles than they did with one another. To employ, albeit in a slightly different way, a concept associated with the distinguished Southeast Asianist Benedict Anderson: imperial logic militated against an "imagined community" in the region and, indeed, against even a commonly accepted regional name (Anderson 1983).

To be sure, we do not wish to imply that, but for what Giovanni Arrighi (1978) has called the geometry of imperialism, Southeast Asia and Southeast Asians would fit together hand in glove, or, given the area's climate, perhaps we should say foot in thong. The historical experiences of, let us say, Brunei and the Philippines, Myanmar and Singapore, Java and Laos are none of them particularly close. This said, the area's common geographical and climatic features, the innumerable contacts, migrations, and cultural exchanges between the area's peoples over the millennia, and the fact that the entire area was shaped to a greater or lesser degree by the same extraneous or at least extraregional forces—Indian and Sinic civilizations, Islam, and, more recently, the West—gives substance to the claim that Southeast Asia can legitimately and profitably be examined, analyzed, and interpreted as a discrete geopolitical area, if not an undifferentiated whole (Williams 1976, 24-52).

Thus far in this article, we have attempted to "unpack"—to use the debased currency of the academic realm—the meanings of two concepts: globalization and Southeast Asia. Our task now is to bring these two concepts together, which is more problematic than may appear on the surface. For example, one of the central narrative lines in recent years in both the business weeklies and even in professional journals in business and economics has been the purported incorporation of Southeast Asia into the "global market." Countless stories have appeared documenting either the rise of Singapore—one of the original Asian "tigers," along with Taiwan, South Korea, and Hong Kong—or, at some remove, the attendant ascent of regional "dragons" such as Thailand, Malaysia, and Indonesia. The unstated premise, the unarticulated assumption behind many of these stories is that these areas (and still others in the region, such as Vietnam and the Philippines) were experiencing something completely new. In the least adroit versions of the story, Southeast Asian economies are depicted as traditional, backward, and inefficient until a series of exogenous changes in transportation, communications, and production technology began to affect them in the 1970s and 1980s, courtesy of Western multinationals, thank you. More sophisticated narrators conceded that parts of the region were deeply involved in world markets, mainly as exporters of raw materials, as far back as the late nineteenth century, this time courtesy not of Western multinationals but rather of looser and less formal institutions and instruments associated with Western merchant capital.

Not everyone has accepted these views, of course. A cadre of specialists on the economic history of Southeast Asia has long argued that the region was a focal point for both trade and transnational flows of labor and capital for centuries prior to the age of high imperialism, which began in the second half of the nineteenth century. The early modern period offers a case in point. Focusing on Southeast Asia's key role in three great trades during this period—that of the Indian Ocean and the South China Sea, along with the more celebrated but quantitatively less significant "East India" trade with Europe—these scholars put the lie to glib contemporary assertions that Southeast Asia was somehow a latecomer to extraregional, dare we say "global," economic activity. Indeed, in recent years, some of these specialists have gone further still, pushing for a fundamental reinterpretation of world economic history during the early modern period, which reinterpretation places Southeast Asia not on the periphery but at the very center of international trade and exchange (Reid 1988-93; Frank 1998).

These revisionist scholars are not just reeling in the usual suspects either. For example, although they acknowledge both the symbolic and the real commercial importance of the Chinese eunich admiral Zheng He (Cheng Ho), whose seven expeditions through the South China Sea and Indian Ocean between 1405 and 1433 stand up well to comparison with anything done during the period known in the West as the Age of Discovery, they are more interested in broader trends, particularly in the scale and scope of production and exchange in the East vis-à-vis the West (Levathes 1994). These scholars differ considerably on many empirical details. Moreover, some make extremely bold, perhaps even rash, claims and adopt strident tones. Even after allowing for the same, however, in light of their overall findings, it is difficult for anyone to deny the fact that Southeast Asia was much more prominent in world trade during the early modern era than was previously assumed. Indeed, commodities, capital, and labor may have flowed in greater quantities and across greater distances to and from Southeast Asia between 1400 and roughly 1800 than to and from any other region in the world (Reid 1988-93; Frank 1998; Wong 1997).

Similarly, these scholars and others have demonstrated that throughout the nineteenth century—not just after 1850, when the British and French began to consolidate and formalize their imperium on the mainland—Southeast Asia was a principal arena in the global economic scheme. By the 1870s, the region's importance was obvious to all, as the "Victorian Internet"—the transoceanic telegraph cable—linked the region ever more closely to growing extraregional markets, particularly in Europe, and technological improvements and cost reductions in transoceanic navigation facilitated ever greater economic streams and flows (Standage 1998; Headrick 1988, 18-48, 97-144). As European, South Asian, and East Asian capital poured in, Southeast Asian commodities—rice, sugar, cotton, coffee, tin, teak, and rubber—poured out. Labor poured in, too, largely from South India and South China. Until the worldwide depression of the 1930s and World War II, much of Southeast Asia was as global as any part of the world. Indeed, many textbook cases of so-called open economies are drawn from the region: Burma, Malaya, and Thailand, to name but a few.

Once past the trials and tribulations of postwar decolonization and nation building, many parts of Southeast Asia attempted to reclaim their erstwhile prominence in the international economy. By the 1970s and 1980s, a number of areas had done so, leading to oh so much talk of tigers and dragons in both the East and the West. Does all of this mean that the authors of this article are craftily attempting to deprecate, depreciate, and debunk the au courant notion that "something happened" in the last decade or so? That Southeast Asia was as embedded in the global economy in 1600 or 1900 as it is in 2000? That Southeast Asia, to paraphrase country-and-western artist Barbara Mandrell, was global

when global wasn't cool? Hardly. All we have hoped to do in this section is to establish the fact that Southeast Asia has an economic history that began prior to the fall of communism and the triumph of neoliberalism, the fact that some parts of the region were central to the world economy well before Jamestown was settled in 1607, and the fact that the region's global importance has generally been underestimated since that time. One could, in fact, call this section "Southeast Asia Slouching Toward Globalization," in other words. This said, let us turn to the main business at hand: Southeast Asia's economic history since World War II, particularly over the past decade when globalization became a so-called fact on the ground.

GROWTH, INTEGRATION, AND THE 1997-98 FINANCIAL CRISIS

The 10 countries of modern Southeast Asia straddle a vast geographic area, bounded by Australia to the south, India to the west, China to the north, and the Pacific Ocean to the east, and are populated by some half a billion people. With the exception of Thailand, they were all European colonies at one time (and under Japanese rule in the early 1940s). Following independence in the decades after World War II, some have evolved into modern competitive democracies (Thailand, the Philippines) or have elected governments under single dominant-party rule (Malaysia, Singapore) or Communist governments (Laos and Vietnam). Indonesia, Malaysia, the Philippines, Singapore, Thailand, and

Vietnam constitute Southeast Asia's larger or more developed economies. The remaining four include the tiny oil-rich sultanate of Brunei and the region's three poorest members—Laos, Cambodia, and Myanmar (Burma). Little will be said of this latter group, due to lack of data as well as their marginal importance to our theme—the globalization of Southeast Asia.

Amid national exhaustion and bankruptcy of the former colonial powers at the end of World War II, the United States emerged as the new hegemon. It had long replaced Great Britain as the world's great maritime nation, and it alone commanded the economic resources for the postwar reconstruction of Europe and Asia. Moreover, as impresario of the new global economic system created with the establishment of the World Bank and the International Monetary Fund in Washington, D.C., the nation's leaders felt compelled to assume primary responsibility for promoting stable and sustainable international economic growth. Clearly, U.S. policy preferences in the postwar period should be viewed at least in part in the context of the depression of the 1930s, particularly as reactions against the destructive autarkic economic policies of that period. It is equally clear, however, that U.S. commitments in Asia in the postwar period were also sustained by the strategic imperatives of the Cold War. That is to say, without U.S. perceptions of an overarching strategic interest in the prosperity and stability of Asia as a bulwark against Asian communism, it is difficult to imagine that the remarkable

economic performance in Southeast Asia would have occurred as it did.

Modern, internationally oriented economic growth was thus established in Southeast Asia in the context of an open, multilateral trading system based on the General Agreement on Tariffs and Trade—the linchpin of the new international economic order.[3] Since the mid-1960s, one of the great changes of modern history began with the rapid growth of several Asian economies. Indeed, East Asia—including a large part of its Southeast Asian component—has grown faster on average than any other part of the world over the past three decades. Beginning with Japan, waves of rapid economic growth cascaded down first to the newly industrializing countries (NICs), or the Four Tigers—South Korea, Taiwan, Hong Kong, and their Southeast Asian counterpart, Singapore. Rapid growth soon followed in the so-called next-tier NICs, all in Southeast Asia: Indonesia, Malaysia, and Thailand. More recently, Vietnam and the Philippines joined the group of rapidly growing economies, after both carried out belated economic reforms in the late 1980s or early 1990s (World Bank 1993; Blomqvist 1997; Tan 1999).

In the three decades up to 1995, per capita income grew at an astonishing 7.2 percent annually in Singapore and about 5 percent in Indonesia, Malaysia, and Thailand, in contrast to South Asia's 1.9 percent and Latin America's 0.9 percent. Alone among the market economies of Southeast Asia, the Philippines performed poorly in per capita income growth: its average annual

TABLE 1
SOUTHEAST ASIA'S EXPORT-ORIENTED GROWTH

	Annual Percentage Growth in Gross Domestic Product		Trade as a Percentage of Gross Domestic Product		Annual Percentage Growth in Exports of Goods and Services		Manufactures as a Percentage of Total Merchandise Exports		Foreign Direct Investment (current millions of dollars)	
	1980-90	1990-97	1980	1996	1980-90	1990-97	1980	1996	1980	1996
Indonesia	6.1	7.5	54.0	51.0	2.9	9.2	2.0	51.0	1,093	7,960
Malaysia	5.2	8.7	113.0	183.0	10.9	14.0	19.0	76.0	2,333	4,500
Philippines	1.0	3.3	52.0	94.0	3.5	11.5	21.0	84.0	530	1,408
Singapore	6.6	8.5	440.0	356.0	10.8	13.3	47.0	84.0	5,575	9,440
Thailand	7.6	7.5	54.0	83.0	14.0	12.8	25.0	73.0	2,444	2,336
Vietnam	4.6	8.6	48.9*	82.0	—	26.9†	—	—	16	1,500
South Asia	5.7	5.7	21.0	30.0	6.4	12.4	53.0	76.0	464	3,439
Latin America	1.8	3.3	32.0	33.0	5.3	7.3	19.0	45.0	8,188	38,015
World‡	3.1	2.3	39.0	43.0	5.2	7.0	65.0	78.0	191,595	314,696

SOURCE: World Bank 1999.
*1985.
†Merchandise exports for 1990-96.
‡All values refer to weighted averages except foreign direct investment, which refers to simple sums.

growth rate of 1.2 percent over the 30-year period converged with the poor performance of its developing-country counterparts in South Asia and Latin America. Due to the excesses of the Marcos regime in its later years, and the decline in central authority during the following Aquino administration, moreover, the Philippines did not share in the region's high growth performance of the 1980s and early 1990s either (World Bank 1993; Lin 1988).

To put a sense of perspective on the globalization of Southeast Asia following decolonization, Table 1 quantifies some economic attributes that measure the region's recent growth performance and intensifying links to the world economy.

With the exception of the Philippines—the long-time "sick man of Southeast Asia"—Southeast Asia's economic growth has been exceptional, with annual rates in the 5-7 percent range for the decade 1980-90. Growth rates were even higher—averaging around 7-8 percent annually—during 1990-96, again with the exception of the Philippines. The Philippines has only recently begun to exhibit the rapid growth rates its counterparts in Southeast Asia have long enjoyed, averaging over 5 percent annually over the years 1994-97, as the government of President Ramos began to implement economic reforms that included deregulation, privatization, and the liberalization of the trade- and foreign-investment regimes.

Two factors prevented reunified war-ravaged Vietnam from participating in the economic boom in

Southeast Asia of recent decades: externally, the economic and political alignment with the Soviet Union, and the invasion and occupation of Cambodia in 1978; internally, the rigidity of Marxist-Leninist doctrine and state control over the economy. In late 1986, however, the sweeping events besetting the Soviet Union and Eastern Europe abroad and recurrent economic crises within the country forced drastic reversals in policy, signaled by fundamental reforms under the banner of *doi moi* (renovation). In the space of five years, Vietnam made a decisive break from a long history of war, central planning, and economic crises. Since then, it has registered among the region's most impressive growth rates in output and in exports, albeit from very low bases.

Although the policies and growth patterns of the Southeast Asian countries differ significantly, one commonality among them is that their economies have been significantly more open, measured by the ratio of total exports and imports of goods and services to gross domestic product (GDP), than are the economies of their counterparts in South Asia or Latin America (World Bank 1993; Lin 1988). Not surprisingly, Singapore and Malaysia, reflecting their long histories as open, trade-oriented economies, have trade (exports plus imports) that much exceeds the size of their domestic output, but the other Southeast Asian countries also have significantly more trade-oriented regimes than their counterparts in Latin America or South Asia. The openness of the region is further underlined by

the rapid growth in exports, significantly exceeding the global average, over the past two decades. (The data for Indonesia, which show a declining trade-to-GDP ratio between 1980 and 1996, and a relatively low rate of growth in exports, are misleading in that they reflect the fall in the value of oil exports.) The Southeast Asian adoption of a trade-oriented model of development, in contrast to the closed approach of Latin America, is evident in the rates of export growth achieved (World Bank 1993; Lin 1988).

The export-oriented growth experience of the Southeast Asian countries has not been a mere continuation of primary commodity export patterns that became established as a result of incorporation into the colonial order from the seventeenth century onward. Manufactured exports as a share of total exports from the region have grown rapidly over the past two decades. Southeast Asian countries have emerged as an important base for offshore production by multinational corporations. The export-oriented strategy of the key Southeast Asian countries typically began with the manufacture of low-skill, labor-intensive goods but gained momentum with the emergence of the semiconductor industry, which increasingly set up offshore assembly plants. By 1975, according to one estimate, East Asia—including key export processing zones in Malaysia and Thailand—employed over 90 percent of worldwide offshore electronic assembly plant workers (Radelet and Sachs 1997, 53).

Even more striking than the globalization of product markets of recent decades—and the trade flows that have sustained it—is the global integration of capital markets. While global trade has expanded twice as fast as world output in the second half of the twentieth century, foreign direct investments have grown four times as fast. Southeast Asia has been a particularly important destination for foreign direct investment, attracting considerable sums from outside the region, which have enhanced its export performance and contributed to its long-term growth potential. It is remarkable, and a testimony to the extent of the region's openness to global flows of capital and technology, that relatively small countries such as Thailand and Malaysia and even tiny Singapore have each attracted more foreign investment than all of South Asia together. (Of course, in the converse, it is also remarkable how closed the Indian subcontinent has been to the global economy.) Over this same period, the six key countries of Southeast Asia received foreign investments that amounted to over 70 percent of the total invested by foreigners in all of Latin America and the Caribbean and to over 7 times the total invested in all of South Asia.

The globalization of Southeast Asia in its economic dimensions, then, has been robust and intensive. With the exception of Myanmar, Laos, and Cambodia, the paradigmatic strategy for the market-based Southeast Asian economies is export-oriented growth, deepening integration into the global economy by encouraging foreign direct investment. This strategy contrasts sharply with the classic (now abandoned or repudiated) Indian and Latin American developmental models espousing state ownership of industry and the "commanding heights" of the economy, together with the encouragement of import substitution behind protectionist barriers (World Bank 1993).

Yet in 1997, after three decades of sustained and rapid growth—when Singapore had achieved developed-country status; when Indonesia, Malaysia, and Thailand were rapidly increasing the wealth of their citizenries; and when even Vietnam and the Philippines were beginning to be labeled "high performers"—financial crisis and economic recession struck with a fury that shocked observers and participants alike. With the financial shock wave emanating from its epicenter in Thailand—which floated the baht in July 1997 after a futile attempt to support the currency—the contagion spread with a speed that seemed incredible. By early 1998, the Indonesian rupiah was down more than 80 percent against the dollar, and the currencies of Thailand, Malaysia, and Philippines all fell by 30-50 percent. Within months of the baht flotation, the stock markets of all four saw losses of 60 percent or more in dollar terms. The "Asian flu," or what Paul Krugman (1999) has wryly called "bahtulism," had set in (xi).

On the eve of the crisis in 1996, when warning signs were already apparent in Thailand's financial and real estate sectors, no one could yet imagine that Thailand or Indonesia were only months away from going, cap in hand, to the International Monetary Fund for massive financial bailouts. To be sure, some analysts, most notably Alwyn Young (1992) and Paul Krugman (1994), were already raising questions about the "economic miracle" in Southeast Asia, particularly about the degree to which this "miracle" was based on capital and labor mobilization rather than on increased factor productivity. And clearly, the region was no stranger to financial instability or recession: Indonesia and the Philippines suffered financial shocks in 1983, Thailand in 1984, and Malaysia and Singapore saw economic downturns in 1985. However, in contrast to previous occasions, the depth of the 1997-98 downturn—in currencies, equity values, and output—and the simultaneity of the impact across key Southeast Asian economies set this crisis apart. Indeed, the massive losses of wealth built up in previous years and the hardships imposed on millions of people—in societies that lacked institutionalized welfare safety nets—constituted a watershed for Southeast Asia (Crafts 1998; Corden 1999; Mallet 1999).

Much has already been written on the Asian financial crisis. From the perspective of the globalization process in Southeast Asia, some key attributes of the crisis stand out. From the early 1990s, a rising share of global capital flows has consisted of short-term portfolio funds. Today, both lending and equity markets are globally integrated, and as a result, there has been a delocalization of finance as global funds have become increasingly important as ready sources of capital and credit. The decades of rapid economic growth in Southeast Asia led to, in the words of

economist Max Corden (1999), "an euphoria stage of the investment and borrowing boom" (37). Thus, while, on the supply side, large funds scoured the globe for short-run opportunities, the economic boom in Southeast Asia led, on the demand side, to a binge of corporate borrowing. Increased capital inflows fueled rapid credit expansion, lowered the quality of credit, and inflated asset prices, which encouraged further capital inflows in a frenzied boom—evident in escalating property prices and increased construction in the cities and in rising equity values in the stock markets of Southeast Asia.

Contributing in a significant way to the financial crisis were the formal and informal currency pegs that discouraged both lenders and borrowers from hedging. Highly leveraged corporate sectors and large unhedged short-term debt made countries such as Thailand and Indonesia highly vulnerable to changes in market sentiments. By late 1996, pressures on the baht had emerged, and they intensified through the first half of 1997. This occurred against a background of an unsustainable current-account deficit (caused by a slowdown in export growth, which in turn was related to the baht's peg to an appreciating U.S. dollar), rising short-term and unhedged foreign debt in the corporate sector, and increasingly apparent financial-sector weaknesses. Weaknesses in bank and corporate governance and the lack of market discipline, with lax and poorly enforced prudential regulations, encouraged excessive risk taking. There existed close and often corrupt relationships between governments, financial institutions, and corporate borrowers, which worsened the problems. Weak accounting standards, poor disclosure practices, and lack of prudential oversight reflected such crony arrangements. The lack of appropriate commercial norms of accounting and risk assessment hid growing weaknesses until it was too late (Corden 1999; Crafts 1998).

With mounting exchange rate pressures, and ineffective interventions by Thailand's Central Bank, the baht was floated on 2 July 1997 and promptly collapsed. With astonishing rapidity, the contagion of sharply negative market sentiments, rapid withdrawals of foreign private capital, bank runs, and drastic economic downturns spread to Indonesia (and South Korea in northeast Asia). The financial shock and its immediate aftermath led to one of the most fundamental changes to have occurred in modern Southeast Asia: the demise of President Suharto's regime of 32 years in an Indonesia that towers over the rest of the region in geographical size and sheer weight of population (over 200 million people). Malaysia and the Philippines, less exposed to short-term foreign debt than their neighboring counterparts, were less affected but nevertheless experienced steep falls in currency and stock market values and in economic activity.

If global economic integration, domestic economic deregulation, and rapid advances in technology—especially information and communication technologies—are the three great pillars of modern globalization,

then Southeast Asia can certainly be said to have manifested them in its postwar economic history. The postwar decades of rapid material advance led to an ever deepening integration of Southeast Asia into the global economy. Market-oriented reform, partly as a response to the requirements of the deepening integration into competitive global markets, was carried out in the Southeast Asian economies, albeit at different speeds and comprehensiveness in each of them. Economic reforms involved not only trade liberalization but other complementary steps as well: domestic economic deregulation for attracting foreign investments, and privatization of public-sector enterprises.

Globalization is leading to a push for ever greater transparency in the government and corporate sectors. Securities and corporate analysts, rating agencies, and the business media gather and provide data and analysis to track economic and business performance with ever more powerful analytic tools and ever faster channels of communication. The revolution in information and communication technologies, combined with the phenomenal growth in the global capital market since the mid-1990s, has profoundly affected—negatively in the recent financial crisis—and will continue to affect the economies of Southeast Asia.

Globalization took on a virulent form in the Asian financial crisis, and it constitutes a profound challenge to the region's governments and corporate sector. Indeed, as Lawrence Summers (1999) points out, managing international economic integration may be the preeminent challenge facing policymakers around the world. In a world of capital mobility, governmental capacity to tax capital or regulate industry has eroded. This constriction in the state's capacity to carry out discretionary macroeconomic policy may well be perceived as a positive development in modern political economy. By requiring credible commitments to make policy and regulatory behavior of the state transparent, international capital markets—and the associated technological infrastructures in information and communications—have raised the domestic political costs of incompetence, inefficiency, corruption, and fiscal irresponsibility for governments everywhere (Friedman 1999, 83-193).

The Asian financial crisis has clearly shown that short-term capital flows were excessive and destabilizing to both borrowers and lenders alike. Thailand's foreign corporate debts, short-term and unhedged, were a particularly risky form of global integration. Yet it would be a pity if the lessons learned from the events of 1997-98 led policymakers to impede capital flows from global markets to Southeast Asia. In this regard, Malaysia's response to the crisis—the establishment of capital controls and the expenditure of much rhetoric regarding the "conspiracies" associated with Western capitalism—seems a dubious case in point. If anything, the recent events in Southeast Asia point to the importance of establishing robust domestic financial sectors that keep pace with rapid economic growth and integration into global capital markets.

The mainstream economics explanation of the growth experience of Southeast Asia has been based on the "Washington consensus": that is, the pursuit of economic policies based on outward orientation, macroeconomic prudence, and domestic liberalization. This means, in common parlance, first, trade a lot; second, avoid inflation and maintain sensible and stable exchange rates and interest rates; and third, promote competition and, in general, let the private sector thrive. The crisis events of Southeast Asia qualify the basic message of the Washington consensus with an important rider: that it is important to sequence liberalization of domestic capital markets to match the development of adequate regulatory and supervisory capacity of financial regulators. Are the governments in Southeast Asia equal to the challenge of establishing appropriate rules and institutions for effective systems of corporate governance, incentive-compatible property rights, and transparent accounting and prudential standards in both public and private sectors? The answer to this question will largely determine the extent to which Southeast Asia emerges from its recent turmoil stronger and better able to confront the challenges of inevitable globalization in all its manifestations.

Notes

1. The references in the text are taken from the titles of recent books by Thomas L. Friedman (1999) and Benjamin R. Barber (1995).

2. "Davos Man" refers, of course, to the global economic and business elite, who participate in the World Economic Forum, held every February at a mountain retreat in Davos, Switzerland. *Orang ulu* is a term used in Malaysia and Indonesia to refer to "traditional," country people.

3. Note that much of the data included here is drawn from publications prepared by the World Bank, the Asian Development Bank, and similar institutions. For good recent overviews of Southeast Asia's economic trajectory over the last 30 years, see, for example, Blomqvist 1997; Tan 1999. Older works by scholars such as Bela Balassa, Anne Krueger, and Seiji Naya are still useful as well, particularly for establishing the framework and context for Southeast Asia's modern growth experience.

References

Anderson, Benedict R. O'G. 1983. *Imagined Communities: Reflections on the Origins and Spread of Nationalism*. London: Verso.

Arrighi, Giovanni. 1978. *The Geometry of Imperialism: The Limits of Hobson's Paradigm*. Trans. Patrick Camiller. London: NLB.

Bannock, Graham, R. E. Baxter, and Evan Davis. 1998. *Dictionary of Economics*. New York: John Wiley.

Barber, Benjamin R. 1995. *Jihad vs. McWorld*. New York: Times Books.

Blomqvist, Hans C. 1997. *Economic Interdependence and Development in East Asia*. Westport, CT: Praeger.

Braudel, Fernand. 1973. *Capitalism and Material Life, 1400-1800*. Trans. Miriam Kochan. New York: Harper & Row.

Castells, Manuel. 1994. European Cities, the Informational Society, and the Global Economy. *New Left Review*, Mar.-Apr.: 18-32.

Corden, Max. 1999. *The Asian Crisis: Is There a Way Out?* Singapore: Institute of Southeast Asian Studies.

Crafts, Nicholas. 1998. East Asian Growth Before and After the Crisis. Working paper WP/98/137, International Monetary Fund.

Frank, Andre Gunder. 1998. *ReOrient: Global Economy in the Asian Age*. Berkeley: University of California Press.

Friedman, Thomas L. 1999. *The Lexus and the Olive Tree: Understanding Globalization*. New York: Farrar, Straus & Giroux.

Greider, William. 1997. *One World, Ready or Not: The Manic Logic of Global Capitalism*. New York: Simon & Schuster.

Hall, D.G.E. 1955. *A History of South-East Asia*. New York: St. Martin's Press.

Headrick, Daniel R. 1988. *The Tentacles of Progress: Technology Transfer in the Age of Imperialism, 1850-1940*. New York: Oxford University Press.

Jameson, Fredric. 1998. Preface. In *The Cultures of Globalization*, ed. Fredric Jameson and Masao Miyoshi. Durham, NC: Duke University Press.

Krugman, Paul. 1994. The Myth of Asia's Miracle. *Foreign Affairs* 73: 62-78.

———. 1998. *The Accidental Theorist and Other Dispatches from the Dismal Science*. New York: W. W. Norton.

———. 1999. *The Return of Depression Economics*. New York: W. W. Norton.

Levathes, Louise. 1994. *When China Ruled the Seas: The Treasure Fleet of the Dragon Throne, 1405-1433*. New York: Oxford University Press.

Lin, Ching-yuan. 1988. East Asia and Latin America as Contrasting Models. *Economic Development and Cultural Change* 36, suppl. (Apr.): S153-S197.

Luttwak, Edward. 1999. *Turbo-Capitalism: Winners and Losers in the Global Economy*. New York: HarperCollins.

Mallet, Victor. 1999. *The Trouble with Tigers: The Rise and Fall of South-East Asia*. London: HarperCollins.

Marx, Karl and Frederick Engels. [1848] 1998. *The Communist Manifesto: A Modern Edition*. London: Verso.

Osborne, Milton. 1990. *Southeast Asia: An Illustrated Introductory History.* 5th ed. North Sydney, Australia: Allen & Unwin.

Radelet, Steven and Jeffrey Sachs. 1997. Asia's Bright Future. *Foreign Affairs* 76: 44-59.

Reid, Anthony. 1988-93. *Southeast Asia in the Age of Commerce 1450-1680.* 2 vols. New Haven, CT: Yale University Press.

Robertson, Roland. 1992. *Globalization: Social Theory and Global Culture.* London: Sage.

Standage, Tom. 1998. *The Victorian Internet: The Remarkable Story of the Telegraph and the Nineteenth-Century's On-Line Pioneers.* New York: Walker.

Summers, Lawrence H. 1999. Distinguished Lecture on Economics in Government: Reflections on Managing Global Integration. *Journal of Economic Perspectives* 13: 13-18.

Tan, Gerald. 1999. *The End of the Asian Miracle? Tracing Asia's Economic Transformation.* Singapore: Times Academic Press.

Williams, Lea E. 1976. *Southeast Asia: A History.* New York: Oxford University Press.

Wong, R. Bin. 1997. *China Transformed: Historical Change and the Limits of European Experience.* Ithaca, NY: Cornell University Press.

World Bank. 1993. *The East Asian Miracle: Economic Growth and Public Policy.* New York: Oxford University Press.

———. 1999. *World Development Report 1998/99: Knowledge for Development.* New York: Oxford University Press.

Young, Alwyn. 1992. A Tale of Two Cities: Factor Accumulation and Technical Change in Hong Kong and Singapore. In *NBER Macroeconomics Annual 1992.* Cambridge: MIT Press.

Regulating Immigration in a
Global Age: A New Policy Landscape

By SASKIA SASSEN

ABSTRACT: This article argues that transformations in the state and the interstate system, particularly those brought on by globalization, have produced new constraints and opportunities in the handling of immigration. This becomes evident through a critical examination of three key features of current immigration policy in the United States and, to variable degrees, also in other highly developed countries. These three features are the handling of immigration as (1) a process autonomous from other processes and policy domains; (2) a unilateral, sovereign matter; and (3) operating in a context where the state is a given, untouched by the massive domestic and international transformations that are increasingly reconfiguring states and the interstate system. The author argues that immigration policymaking needs to recognize interaction effects, develop multilateral approaches, and factor in the changed character of unilateral sovereign authority.

Saskia Sassen is professor of sociology at the University of Chicago and Centennial Visiting Professor at the London School of Economics. Her most recent books are Guests and Aliens *(1999) and* Globalization and Its Discontents *(1998). Her books have been translated into 10 languages. Two of her books,* The Global City *and* Cities in a World Economy, *are being reissued in 2000 in updated editions. She is a member of the Council on Foreign Relations and a visiting fellow of the American Bar Foundation.*

NOTE: This article is based on the author's project "Making Immigration Policy in a Global Economy: From National Crisis to Multilateral Management" (on file at the Department of Sociology, University of Chicago). The author thanks the Twentieth Century Fund (now The New Fund) for its support.

IMMIGRATION policy is deeply embedded in the question of state sovereignty and the interstate system. The state itself has been transformed by the growth of a global economic system and other transnational processes. These have brought on conditions that bear on the state's regulatory role and its autonomy. As a result, it is no longer sufficient simply to assert the sovereign role of the state in immigration policy design and implementation; it is necessary to examine also the transformation of the state itself and what that can entail for migration policy and the regulation of migration flows and settlement. A similar argument can be made with respect to the interstate system.

The major implication for immigration policy is that these developments have had an impact on the sovereignty of the state and its capacity for unilateral action. The reality of economic globalization has forced states to learn how to be more multilateral. This is most clearly evident in the activities of the World Trade Organization (WTO) and in the handling of global financial crises. Both the impact on the state's sovereignty and the state's participation in the new global economic system have transformed the state itself, have affected the power of different agencies within it, and have furthered the internationalization of the interstate system through a proliferation of bi- and multilateral agreements. Yet immigration policy in most of the highly developed countries has not been marked by major innovations as we have seen in other policy realms.

Here I examine three of the key features of the immigration policy framework in the highly developed countries in light of these transformations in the state and the interstate system, particularly those brought on by globalization. These three key features are (1) the handling of immigration as if it were a process autonomous from other processes and policy domains; (2) the handling of immigration as a unilateral sovereign matter; and (3) taking the state as a given, untouched by the massive domestic and international transformations within which the state operates.

This is, clearly, a somewhat stylized account of the major features of immigration policy. It abstracts and, in so doing, leaves out multiple details. But it gets close to the heart of the matter. Let me address each of these features by noting their growing incompatibility with the broader transformation under way and what needs to be done.

MORE RECOGNITION OF INTERACTION EFFECTS

Elsewhere (1988, 1999b) I have argued strenuously that international migrations are not autonomous processes and, further, that some of the actors in the international migration story are not usually recognized as such. Among these actors are, for instance, (1) multinational corporations, through their role in internationalizing production, with the associated displacement effects on local small-scale producers and the establishment of linkages between the capital-receiving and capital-sending countries involved; (2) governments, through their military operations, with the associated displacements of people and ensuing flows of refugees and migrants; (3) International Monetary Fund austerity measures, through their role in mobilizing the poor into a desperate search for survival strategies that include migration, whether domestic or international, as one option; and (4) most recently, free-trade agreements, through their strengthening of cross-border flows of capital, services, and information, which include as one key component the cross-border circulation of professional workers.

A key issue in the case of immigration policy is the absence of any recognition that immigration may often be one of the trade-offs in these processes. There are a whole range of trade-offs, positive and negative, in all of these flows—in direct foreign investment, in offshore manufacturing, in International Monetary Fund austerity measures, in free-trade agreements. Frequently, these trade-offs are recognized and formalized into the policy framework. But immigration is never seen as one of the trade-offs—it simply is not on the map. Immigration policy continues to be characterized by its formal isolation from other major policy arenas. But is it possible to handle immigration as an autonomous event? Migrations are embedded in larger dynamics, and they often are initiated through the actions of key actors in receiving countries, whether governments or corporations. If an immigration flow is initiated partly as a result of a receiving country's policies in other, nonimmigration domains, would not immigration policy gain from recognizing such interaction effects? What is gained by not recognizing interaction effects?

Factoring in interaction effects is complicated, certainly much more complicated than pretending that immigration is simply the result of poverty and the acts of individual emigrants. One version of such a recognition of interaction effects is to attach immigration impact statements to policies that involve overseas actions likely to have significant impacts on local people and local forms of livelihood. A major example of this is, of course, the introduction by U.S. agribusiness of large-scale commercial crops for export into a region in another country where small holders were the local norm. The displacement of small holders and their subsequent transformation into a supply of wage labor for large-scale commercial agriculture sets the stage for labor migrations. This is a pattern that we have seen repeat itself in many parts of the world, including the Caribbean and Mexico, two important source countries for immigrants to the United States. (See, for example, Zolberg 1990 on military actions and refugees.)

While the concept of immigration impact statements might seem impractical and resemble an academic exercise, it is worth noting its evolution. More than ten years ago, when I first wrote about this (1988), such a concept was simply not conceivable even as a subject for discussion. By 1992, the debate around the North American Free Trade Agreement (NAFTA) regularly included evaluations of the immigration impact, particularly Mexican migration to the United States. In an important and pathbreaking research report by the immigration office in the U.S. Department of Labor, we can find one of the first formal recognitions of the impact of U.S. activities overseas on the formation of migration flows (U.S. Department of Labor 1989). Minor as they may seem, these two cases represent an important opening in the wall of autonomy built around immigration policy. When we look close to the ground, we can see that the politics of immigration are opening up to the recognition of interaction effects.

Economic globalization brings with it an additional set of factors for immigration policy. It intensifies, multiplies, and diversifies these interaction effects. If we accept, as I have argued, that immigration flows are partly embedded in these larger dynamics, then we may eventually confront the necessity of a radical rethinking of what it means to govern and regulate immigration flows. Such a radical policy rethinking has been worked out with respect to trade through the Uruguay Round of the General Agreement on Tariffs and Trade (GATT) and the creation of the WTO. Such a policy rethinking is also becoming evident regarding military operations, with the growing weight of international cooperation, U.N. consent, and multilateral interventions. And it is being done for telecommunications policy and other areas that require compatible standards around the world.

What is important to emphasize here is that many of these areas are extremely complex, that the policy reformulation could not have been foreseen even a decade ago, and, perhaps most important, that the actual changes in each of these domains forced the policy changes. From where I look at the immigration reality—which is the freedom of the scholar rather than the day-to-day constraints of immigration policymakers and analysts—the changes brought about by the growing interdependencies in the world will sooner or later force an equally significant policy reformulation for immigration.

What is now experienced as a crisis in the state's control over its borders may well be the sign that we need to redraw the map within which we confront the difficult question of how to regulate and govern immigration flows in an increasingly interdependent world. Taking seriously the evidence about immigration produced by vast numbers of scholars and researchers all over the world could actually help because it tends to show us that these flows are bounded in time and space and are conditioned on other processes; they are not mass invasions or indiscriminate flows from poverty to wealth.

MORE MULTILATERALISM
AT THE REGIONAL LEVEL

As for the second feature of the immigration policy framework, unilateral sovereign action, globalization has had a particular type of impact in forcing states to learn to be more multilateral in other domains. First, the increase in international economic activity has brought with it an increase in multilateral economic agreements. Global trade requires convergence in manufacturing and operational standards; global markets in finance require transparency and international standards for accounting and financial reporting (see, for example, various chapters in Olds et al. 1999 and Smith, Solinger, and Topik 1999).

A second important issue is the declining effectiveness and clout of unilateral state action. Because a growing number of processes are today cutting across borders and even becoming transnational, governments are increasingly at a disadvantage in addressing some of today's major issues unilaterally (Ruggie 1993). This is not the end of national states; rather, it means that the "exclusivity and scope of their competence" (Rosenau 1992) have changed—that there is a narrowing range within which the state's authority and legitimacy may exclude other actors from involvement in international issues. The other actors can be other states or nonstate actors; for example, nongovernmental organizations have a growing role in economic development and environmental policy.

A third issue is the shrinking of the range of cross-border policy arenas that can be examined from the exclusive confines of the interstate system narrowly defined. We are seeing a growing institutionalization and formalization of systems of governance, especially for global finance and business, which are not state centered (Dezalay and Garth 1996; Sassen 1996). Emerging is a supranational, often semi-privatized framework that does not fit comfortably in older forms of the interstate system. This does not signal the end of the interstate system as an important space for cross-border processes. Rather, the interstate system is no longer the only major institutionalized space for cross-border activities. A growing number of cross-border economic activities can now take place without involving governments (Sassen 1996; Bonilla et al. 1998). This has forced the interstate community to include nonstate actors in international negotiations or international responses, and it has forced this community to be more international in its approach rather than confining itself to being simply a collection of national interests.

Reality has forced new conditions and new practices on the interstate system. This contributes to internationalizing the interstate system and may well set an important precedent for handling other policy issues, including immigration, in a more multilateral manner.

The increasing tension between the growing pressures toward multilateralism and internationalism, on the one hand, and the ongoing insistence on unilateral action when it comes to immigration issues, on the other, have been partly resolved, in my analysis, through the growth of de facto, rather than de jure, bi- and multilateralism in the handling of specific aspects of international migrations (Sassen 1999a).

This is most evident and advanced in the case of Western Europe where the necessity of multilateral approaches to immigration has been forced onto governments by the requirements of formalizing an economic union. It is also evident in the negotiations between the European Union (EU) and the Central European countries to institute measures aimed at ensuring that asylum seekers stay in the country of first asylum in Central Europe and not move on to the EU, as well as measures aimed at streamlining the apprehension and return of unauthorized immigrants in Central Europe to prevent them from going on to the EU. These are all conditions that require multilateral action, no matter the rhetoric on unilateral sovereign powers.

Where the effort toward the formation of transnational economic spaces has gone the furthest and been most formalized, it has become clear that existing frameworks for immigration policy are problematic (Papademetriou and Hamilton 1996). Current immigration policy in developed countries is increasingly at odds with other major policy frameworks in the international system and with the growth of global economic integration. There are, one could say, two major epistemic communities: one concerning the flow of capital and information; the other, immigration. Both of these "communities" are international, and each enjoys widespread consensus in the community of states.

There are strategic sites in today's global economy where it becomes clear that the existence of two very different regimes for the circulation of capital and the circulation of immigrants poses problems that cannot be solved through the old rules of the game, where the facts of transnationalization weigh in on the state's decisions regarding immigration. The EU and the national governments of member states have found the juxtaposition of the divergent regimes for immigration flows and for other types of flows rather difficult to handle. To deepen its integration by implementing open borders, the EU has been forced to address the fact that it will have to accept the cross-border mobility of non-EU-origin residents. The EU experience in this regard shows us with great clarity the moment when states need to confront the contradictions in their design of formal policy frameworks (Hollifield 1992).

The other major regional systems in the world are far from that moment and may never reach it because they are far simpler than the EU. Yet they contain less formalized versions of the juxtaposition of border-free economies and border controls to keep immigrants out. NAFTA is one such instance, as are, in a more diffuse way, various initiatives for greater economic integration in the Western Hemisphere. A recent proposal to check trucks at the border between Mexico and the United States as part of drug-trade policing, with an immigration control component, ran into enormous complaints from parties connected to Mexico-U.S. trade, who argued that it would have disastrous consequences for free trade in the region. This illustrates at a micro-level the tension between these two different regimes for cross-border flows. (See also Castro 1999.)

A CHANGED STATE IN A CHANGED ENVIRONMENT

As for the third feature of the immigration framework, taking the state as a given, a number of transformations signal that the state itself may well have changed in some of its characteristics and that it is subject to judicial scrutiny to an extent not known before. To keep on formulating immigration policy as if the state were the same, a sort of background factor, may not be the most enlightened or effective way to proceed. Further, to make expanded police action a key part of new immigration measures and to exempt those actions from judicial review at a time when judicial review and individual rights have also strengthened is a formula for expanding litigation against the state rather than making the state more effective in its attempt to regulate immigration (Sassen 1999b).

The state has been altered in several of its key features. There are the changed international environments within which states operate today, as discussed previously, and there is the transfer of state functions to supranational organizations, to the private corporate sector through privatization and deregulation, and to the citizenry through the expansion of judicial review and administrative law (Aman 1998; Rosenau 1997).

There is an incipient unbundling of the exclusive authority of the state over its territory. Further, some components of sovereignty have been relocated to supranational entities, most importantly the EU and the WTO. There is no doubt that some of the intellectual technology that governments have and that allow them to control their subjects and their territory has now shifted to nonstate institutions. This is illustrated by the new privatized transnational regimes for cross-border business and the growing power of the logic of the global capital market over national economic policy (Sassen 1996).

This is well illustrated in the new special regimes for the circulation of service workers within the framework of the General Agreement on Trade in Services (GATS) and NAFTA. These regimes have been uncoupled from any notion of migration, even though they represent in fact a version of temporary labor migration. Whether in NAFTA or in GATS, these are regimes for labor mobility that are in good part under the oversight of supranational entities such as the WTO that are, in practice, quite autonomous from governments. We can see here the elements of a privatization of certain aspects of the regulation of cross-border labor mobility. It becomes part of the larger institutional reshuffling of some of the components of sovereign power over entry and can be seen as an extension of the general set of processes whereby state sovereignty is partly being decentered onto other non- or quasi-governmental entities for the governance of the global economy.

In some ways, this can be seen as yet another instance of the privatization of that which is profitable and manageable. The privatization of what were once public sector firms is clearly a growing trend in a growing number of countries. But we are also seeing the privatizing of what was once government policy in several emergent cross-border legal and regulatory regimes for international business, notably the rapid growth of international commercial arbitration and the growing importance of credit rating agencies. In addition, we can, as I have argued elsewhere, see NAFTA and GATS as containing a venue for the privatizing of components of immigration policy that are characterized by high-value added (that is, persons with high levels of education and/or capital), manageability (they are likely to be temporary migrants and working in leading sectors of the economy and hence visible and subject to effective regulation), and benefits (given the new ideology of free trade and investment). At the limit, governments might be left with the supervision of what might be represented as the difficult and low-value-added components of immigration: poor, low-wage workers; refugees; and dependents. This can clearly have a strong impact on what comes to be seen as the category "immigrant," with the attendant policy and broader political implications.

The invocation of international covenants, particularly human rights instruments, to make national policy signals yet another type of relocation of government functions: a relocation of some components of the legitimation process out of the national state and into international agreements. This is a move away from statism—the absolute right of states to represent their people in international law and international relations—toward a conceptual and operational opening for the emergence of other subjects and actors in international law (Soysal 1994; Jacobson 1996; Franck 1992). The international human rights regime has been a key mechanism for making subjects out of those hitherto invisible in international law: first-nation people, immigrants and refugees, women. This has brought about a growing number of instances where one sector of the state is in disagreement with another. It is perhaps most evident in the strategic role that the judiciary has assumed in the highly developed countries when it comes to defending the rights of immigrants, refugees, and asylum seekers.[1]

Finally, the growth of administrative law and the judicialization of politics also represent a move away from statism, but on the domestic level. When it comes to immigration, the courts have been used both in Western Europe and in the United States to contest decisions taken by the legislatures. The strengthening of police authority in the regulation of immigration is not going to escape litigation. It is an aspect of immigration policy that does not sit comfortably in the context of individual rights and civil society, which are such important features in these countries.

The state itself has been transformed by this combination of developments. This is partly because the state under the rule of law is one of the key institutional arenas for the implementation of these new domestic and new international regimes—

whether the global rights of capital or the human rights of all individuals regardless of nationality. And it is partly because the state has incorporated the objective of furthering a global economy, as is evident in the ascendance of certain government agencies—for example, in the U.S. Treasury—and the decline of others, such as those linked to the social fund.

Economic globalization and the human rights regime have altered the terrain within which international relations between states take place, and they have contributed to the formation or strengthening of an international civic arena, from the world of international business to that of international nongovernmental organizations. Immigration today increasingly intersects with these new worlds and is partly embedded in them, in turn partly escaping sovereign state control. These are transformations in the making as we speak. My reading is that they matter. It is easy to argue the opposite: the state is still absolute; all of these are minor wrinkles. But it may well be the case that the transformations mark the beginning of a new era. Scholarship on mentalities has shown how difficult it is for people to recognize systemic change in their contemporary conditions. Seeing continuity is much simpler and often more reassuring.

CONCLUSION: ACTING ON THE NEW POLICY LANDSCAPE

Crucial to the possibility of innovative thinking on the immigration front is the need to get over the sense of an immigration control crisis, which prevails today in many of the highly developed countries—even though many scholars disagree on the existence of a crisis. One of the questions raised by these developments concerns the nature of the control by the state in regulating immigration. The question is not so much about the effectiveness of a state's control of its borders—we know it is never absolute. It is, rather, about the substantive nature of this control given the new economic regime, international human rights agreements, the extension of various social and political rights to resident immigrants over the past twenty years, the multiplication of political actors involved with the immigration question, and so forth (Hollifield 1992; Weil 1998). While a national state may have the power to write the text of an immigration policy, it is likely to be dealing with a complex, deeply embedded, and transnational process that it can only partly address or regulate through immigration policy as conventionally understood.

The fact that today there are a growing number of constraints on the state's capacity to handle the immigration reality should not be seen as a control crisis. The type of analysis developed in this article opens up the immigration policy question beyond the familiar range of the border and the individual as the sites for control. It signals that international migrations are partly embedded in conditions produced by economic internationalization both in sending and in receiving areas. We need a more comprehensive evaluation of what the arenas are and who the actors are in the world of immigration today.

The perception of crisis is in some ways unwarranted, even though states have less control than they would like because immigration is caught in a grid of other dynamics. When we look at the characteristics of immigrations over time and across the world, it is clear that they are highly patterned flows, embedded in other dynamics that contain equilibrating mechanisms; that they have a duration (many immigrations have lasted for twenty years and then come to an end); and that there is more return migration than we generally realize (for example, Soviet engineers and intellectuals who went back to Moscow from Israel; Mexicans who returned after becoming legal U.S. residents through the 1986 Immigration Reform and Control Act amnesty program, feeling that now they could move repeatedly between the two countries). We also know, from earlier historical periods when there were no controls, that most people did not leave poorer areas to go to richer ones, even though there were plenty of such differences in Europe within somewhat reasonable travel distances. Finally, we know, from a diversity of types of evidence, that most people do not want to emigrate to a foreign country and that many who have emigrated would rather be circular migrants than permanent immigrants. (For a full discussion of these various aspects, see Sassen 1999b).

A key issue is whether national states have the capacity to pursue a broader international agenda, one that goes beyond the furthering of economic globalization and that addresses questions of equity and mechanisms for a better distribution of resources, allowing more people in poor countries to make a living. The past two decades show us, first, that international cooperation and multinational agreements are on the rise. About 100 major treaties and agreements on the environment have gone into effect since 1972, though not all remain in force. According to the WTO, there are currently 76 free-trade agreements in place. There is now also more multilateral collaboration on crime; most recently, the Financial Action Task Force has been formed to confront new types of crime in the realm of finance made possible by digitalization. The complexity of the task is enormous since different countries have very different traditions in terms of surveillance and permissibility (for example, with respect to bribery). The WTO, the EU, and even such bodies as the Financial Action Task Force confront enormously complex policy issues that require innovation. Clearly, multilateral approaches to cross-border issues are growing.

Second, while the international role of the state in the global economic arena has to a large extent focused on furthering deregulation, strengthening markets, and pushing for privatization, most states contain agencies and interests that go in other directions. For instance, the participation of national states in the global environmental arena has frequently led to the signing of multilateral agreements that aim at supporting measures to protect the environment. That is not to say that they are effective, but they do create a framework that legitimates both the international pursuit of a common good and the role of national states in that pursuit (Ruggie 1993). They represent a countervailing force to the fact that the role of the state in the international economic arena seems to be largely confined to pursuing the goal of maximizing the profitability of certain economic sectors and actors, not even all sectors and actors, in its own economy.

Third, it is important to recognize that the state participated in the implementation of the new global economic order. Global capital has made claims on national states, and these have responded through the production of new forms of legality. The new geography of global economic processes, the strategic territories for economic globalization, had to be produced both in terms of the practices of corporate actors and the requisite infrastructure and in terms of the work of the state in producing or legitimating new legal regimes. Representations that characterize the national state as simply losing significance fail to capture this very important dimension. I view deregulation not simply as a loss of control by the state but also as a crucial mechanism with which to negotiate the juxtaposition of the interstate consensus to pursue globalization and the fact that national legal systems remain the major or crucial instantiation through which guarantees of contract and property rights are enforced. Can national states also participate in the implementation of other cross-border frame-

works to govern other cross-border dynamics, such as those concerning development and immigration?

The actual participation of more and more states in multilateral negotiations and the growth of international regimes with various levels of formalization to handle economic, environmental, and even military issues set the stage for more multilateralism in the handling of international migrations. Exploring such options today is a more reasonable proposition than 10 years ago, because it has the potential of harmonizing the handling of migration with the handling of other cross-border flows. Indeed, the tenor of the times has already pressured states into more bi- and multilateral collaboration than the formal rhetoric of statism signals. Aman (1998) notes, in his work on the impact of globalization on administrative law, that it is in the interest of the state to play an increasingly active role at the global level. The participation of national states in new international legal regimes of this sort may contribute to the development of transnational frameworks aiming at promoting greater equity.

I am arguing for a new role for the state in immigration policy: more international and more multilateral, including the participation of nonstate actors. At the heart of this type of multilateralism I see the necessity for sending and receiving countries to work together in the handling of international migration flows; the fact that some countries are both receiving and sending migrants also calls for more collaboration on the part of the various parties involved. This architecture of multilateralism would be centered on regions and on the major cross-border migration flows that they contain.

Further, in the longer term, it is more likely that stronger legal regimes will develop on a global basis if the global issues involved have a national regulatory counterpart (Aman 1998). In the case of immigration policy, this means a far broader range of innovations in terms of both the new international environments within which states operate and the new domestic environments within which issues relating to individual rights and civil society have become stronger.

Given the ineffectiveness of much immigration policy and given the undesirability of expanding police methods to control immigration, how much can be lost by innovating in immigration policy? There has been an enormous amount of policy innovation when it comes to the economy and even the environment and international military frameworks. We need to explore and realize the policy options and constraints that emerge from the actual features of international migrations and from the new global and domestic landscape for policymaking.

Note

1. At the limit, this means that the state is no longer the only site for sovereignty and the normativity that comes with it and, further, that the state is no longer the exclusive subject for international law. Other actors, from nongovernmental organizations and minority populations to supranational organizations, are increasingly emerging as subjects of inter-

national law and actors in international relations (Sassen 1996).

References

Aman, Alfred C., Jr. 1998. The Globalizing State: A Future-Oriented Perspective on the Public/Private Distinction, Federalism, and Democracy. *Vanderbilt Journal of Transnational Law* 31(4): 769-870.

Bonilla, Frank, Edwin Melendez, Rebecca Morales, and Maria de los Angeles Torres, eds. 1998. *Borderless Borders*. Philadelphia: Temple University Press.

Castro, Max, ed. 1999. *Free Markets, Open Societies, Closed Borders?* Miami: University of Miami, North-South Center Press.

Dezalay, Yves and Bryant Garth. 1996. *Dealing in Virtue: International Commercial Arbitration and the Construction of a Transnational Legal Order.* Chicago: University of Chicago Press.

Franck, Thomas M. 1992. The Emerging Right to Democratic Governance. *American Journal of International Law* 86(1): 46-91.

Hollifield, James F. 1992. *Immigrants, Markets, and States.* Cambridge, MA: Harvard University Press.

Jacobson, David. 1996. *Rights Across Borders: Immigration and the Decline of Citizenship.* Baltimore, MD: Johns Hopkins University Press.

Olds, Kris, Peter Dicken, Philip F. Kelly, Lilly Kong, and Henry Wai-Chung Yeung, eds. 1999. *Globalization and the Asian Pacific: Contested Territories.* London: Routledge.

Papademetriou, Demetrios G. and Kimberly A. Hamilton. 1996. *Converging Paths to Restriction: French, Italian, and British Responses to Immigration.* Washington, DC: Carnegie Endowment for International Peace, International Migration Policy Program.

Rosenau, J. N. 1992. Governance, Order, and Change in World Politics. In *Governance Without Government: Order and Change in World Politics*, ed. J. N. Rosenau and E. O. Czempiel. New York: Cambridge University Press.

Rosenau, James N. 1997. *Along the Domestic-Foreign Frontier: Exploring Governance in a Troubled World*. New York: Cambridge University Press.

Ruggie, John Gerard. 1993. *Multilateralism Matters: The Theory and Praxis of an Institutional Form*. New York: Columbia University Press.

Sassen, Saskia. 1988. *The Mobility of Labor and Capital: A Study in International Investment and Labor Flow*. New York: Cambridge University Press.

———. 1996. *Losing Control? Sovereignty in an Age of Globalization*. New York: Columbia University Press.

———. 1999a. Beyond Sovereignty: De-Facto Transnationalism in Immigration Policy. *European Journal of Law and Immigration* 1: 177-98.

———. 1999b. *Guests and Aliens*. New York: New Press.

Smith, David A., Dorothy J. S. Solinger, and Steven C. Topik, eds. 1999. *States and Sovereignty in the Global Economy*. London: Routledge.

Soysal, Yasemin Nuhoglu. 1994. *Limits of Citizenship: Migrants and Post-national Membership in Europe*. Chicago: University of Chicago.

U.S. Department of Labor. Bureau of International Affairs. 1989. *The Effects of Immigration on the U.S. Economy and Labor Force*. Immigration and Policy Research Report no. 1. Washington, DC: Government Printing Office.

Weil, Patrick. 1998. *The Transformation of Immigration Policies: Immigration Control and Nationality Laws in Europe: A Comparative Approach*. Florence: European University Institute.

Zolberg, Aristide R. 1990. The Roots of U.S. Refugee Policy. In *Immigration and U.S. Foreign Policy*, ed. R. Tucker, Charles B. Keely, and L. Wrigley. Boulder, CO: Westview Press.

ANNALS, *AAPSS*, **570**, July 2000

Labor Versus Globalization

By GEORGE ROSS

ABSTRACT: The transnationalization of markets places labor movements everywhere in newly troubling situations. In vastly different ways in different regions of the globe, union movements and supporters have long sought to control and humanize capitalism within the frameworks of nations. For a brief moment after World War II, they seemed finally to have succeeded. Recent transnationalizing tendencies have made economic borders substantially more permeable and have undercut the capacities of nations to regulate within them, however. This leaves labor in postindustrial societies with declining resources, weakened organization, and few new ideas. Labor movements in other parts of the world stand in different relationships to current market changes from those in the West, indeed sometimes in contradiction to them. This makes desperately needed transnational labor cooperation extremely difficult. Successful responses are few and far between for the moment, and capital has seized the initiative.

George Ross is director of the German and European Studies Center and Morris Hillquit Professor in Labor and Social Thought at Brandeis University. At Harvard University, he is also senior associate (former acting director) of the Minda de Gunzburg Center for European Studies and executive director of the European Union Center. His most recent books are Brave New World of European Labor *(1999) (with Andrew Martin et al.) and* Jacques Delors and European Integration *(1995).*

LABOR versus globalization is the most recent version of the general history of free labor organization versus capitalist industrialization.[1] At the core of this history are relationships between labor organizations and the markets that surround them. Markets are volatile social processes that change very quickly. Labor movements are hard-won organizations that are slow to develop and change. To take the Western example, as capitalism emerged, capitalists reorganized the labor process and the labor market surrounding it. Free labor, undoubtedly the most significant innovation underlying economic modernity, was thereby created. For workers, this meant the loss of traditional protection and the necessity to confront a whole new set of circumstances. The labor movement emerged in response to local changes, in almost as many forms and fashions as there were local cultures, industries, and firms. But local capital could threaten to relocate and expand labor markets, invariably with strong legal and political support. Given the mobility of capital, therefore, labor was almost always obliged to play catch-up. As labor responded locally, capital became more national, making labor markets national as well. Labor itself then had to become national. This process took well over a century in most Western countries, and, with some exceptions, it was not until the post–World War II period that it succeeded.[2]

Globalization should thus be seen, from labor's point of view, as a dramatic new manifestation of a chronic problem, that of markets' expanding beyond labor's capacities to affect them. As this has happened, unions and workers' other organizations have consistently had to enlarge their strategic domain to keep workers from being played off against each other, undermining wage and labor standards. But for trade unions, as for national states, the regulation of markets becomes considerably more difficult as markets are extended across national boundaries. Regulating and constraining markets require legitimate and authoritative jurisdictions. Beyond national boundaries, there exist no jurisdictions comparable to the national state.

The term "globalization" is ambiguous. It refers to multiple processes, and they are all too often schematized and described hyperbolically as *the* independent variable of our era (see, among many, Thurow 1992; Luttwak 1993). Trade has been growing faster than output, with exports of the 24 countries of the Organization for Economic Cooperation and Development (OECD) increasing at an average annual rate close to twice that of gross domestic product (GDP) (6.3 compared with 3.7 percent between 1960 and 1989). The share of imports and exports in those countries' GDPs correspondingly increased over the same period (from 37.6 to 56.3 percent) (OECD 1991, tabs. 3.1 and 4.8). Foreign direct investment (FDI) grew 3.0 times more rapidly than output and 2.5 times faster than exports and domestic investment between 1986 and 1990. The annual growth rate and the world's stock of FDI quadrupled between 1980 and 1991. By

1990, total sales (domestic and export) of transnational corporations (TNCs) reached $5.5 trillion, 2.5 times the $2.2 trillion total value of exports of goods and services (excluding trade within TNCs), making TNCs central players in the world economy (United Nations 1992, v). Financial integration increased even more rapidly than trade, FDI, and TNC sales, however. Portfolio outflows rose 14 times from 1980 to 1991, from $15.0 billion to $205.3 billion. Rapid as this seemed, it was dwarfed by the growth of transactions in foreign exchange markets, from a negligible daily trading volume in the late 1950s to about $1 trillion in the early 1990s—50 times the daily value of international trade (United Nations 1992, 61).

WORLDS OF LABOR IN THE GOLDEN AGE

These different and unevenly developing trends vary greatly in their regional impact.[3] Labor protest against globalization has come first and foremost from those advanced capitalist societies where globalization is occurring against a historical background of labor movement nationalization. In the decades after 1945, national political economies in the West thrived in a virtuous circle of growth and change. Successful firms were often willing to pay higher wages, grant greater job security, and seek trade union help to obtain cooperation in work and to deepen the market for expensive consumer goods to those who actually produced them.

The Golden Age model tied production and macroeconomic policy into a balanced national system. Keynesianism, facilitated by the optimism created by high growth, gave states legitimate new roles. Full employment, a union dream, briefly became a reasonable goal. Governments redistributed portions of the system's profitability to expanded social programs. In this situation, unions became allies of employers and governments. Strong unions could prevent downward pressure on wages and prices, help keep wage levels in line with productivity growth, and prod the demand needed for full employment.

Labor success in these years began with organizing wage earners but also involved soliciting solidarity from others. Unions advocated redistributing income, wealth, and authority, aims that brought them into the political arena. Rules to define and actualize labor citizenship in the workplace were in part the result of legislation. Governments developed macroeconomic policies favorable to full employment and growth. Unions thus advocated including workers as partners in major public decisions and demanded that they themselves be recognized as the organized manifestations of larger labor movements.

The Golden Age was a rare win-win situation for capital and labor in the West. Labor organizations caught up with capital and, as a result, regulated markets overlapped with national boundaries. This brief moment was the product of negotiated common interests rather more than tariff protection.

International trade was important, but what counted most to the key actors—capital, labor, the state, and politicians—was national trade. And underlying this unusual (relative) confluence of interests was enhanced confidence in national statist solutions to economic and social problems (see Marglin and Schor 1990; Sassoon 1998).

Labor outside the West

What was happening outside the West in these years? Our planet was already well globalized by the Golden Age. By the later 1960s, a few non-Western societies had reproduced many of the economic and social strengths of Europe and North America. In Japan, for example, labor organizations, contractualism, and state social policies were weak, along with liberal democracy more generally. Japan's successful modernization did involve strong labor-capital coordination in large firms and in quasi-tripartite general ways for the economy as a whole. The arrangements were very different from those in the West, however: large employers committed to life-long employment rather than shorter-term negotiated job security arrangements, for example, with quasi-company unions in big firms and little labor organization outside them. Moreover, in Japan—along with most of the newly industrializing countries (NICs), where unions, if they existed, were often tightly controlled by semi-authoritarian states—trade protection was a key tool to promote export-led development. Protectionism was also a strong tool in Central and Latin America, where authoritarian regimes and import-substitution development strategies made labor conditions very difficult.

Labor also existed in the so-called Second and Third Worlds, if for both the Golden Age was but a distant fantasy. In the socialist world, coordination and cooperation between elites and labor occurred in authoritarian ways from a political center, via transmission-belt labor organizations. The whole socialist system, composed of numbers of nonsovereign nations around a Soviet center, was walled off from the world of capitalist markets. In the Third World, societies were engaged in the early stages of transition to free labor markets and market societies. This meant that labor involved in modern labor forces and markets was a relatively small part of working populations. Third World societies faced particular burdens as latecomers in the tentacular global capitalist system that already existed. Economic and political relationships with stronger Northern capitalist systems constrained their development paths. They also had to make their ways in a geopolitical context marked by the Cold War.

Labor's flawed internationalism

How were these many different worlds of labor connected? If labor movements had always advertised themselves as internationalist, labor's Golden Age globe was profoundly national. Different national labor movements had different relationships to domestic and international markets and conflicts of interest. This created problems in generating transnational labor perspectives. Significant transnational labor organizations were international confederations of national union organizations, themselves usually confederations of sectoral union organizations. Such structures virtually guaranteed that these organizations would reflect national union preferences.

The Golden Age was also the high Cold War period, and large transnational labor organizations were deeply imprinted by political concerns. The World Federation of Trade Unions was a front for Soviet political objectives, while the International Confederation of Free Trade Unions, vastly more autonomous, was nonetheless a valued, often heavily subsidized, ally for Western (which often meant American) Cold War causes. The Catholic World Confederation of Labor, with its own ideological baggage, was squeezed between two giant armies.[4] Cold War confrontation took on particular importance in the Third World when, after initial confrontations in Europe, superpowers turned toward shaping the political allegiances of decolonizing and other non-Western nations. For Third World unions, this often meant strident Cold War politicization. The Soviets and Americans spared no expense to promote their forms of unionism in non-Western settings.

THE MAELSTROM: LABOR
AND GLOBALIZATION TODAY

Labor in Europe and North America has reacted most strongly to today's globalization. The disinte-

gration of Golden Age growth models began in the late 1970s. Decisions most important to unions moved from national arenas upward toward transnational arenas, whether economic or political. At the same time, they also moved downward toward subnational arenas, transferring matters from places where unions could be effective toward those where they were weaker. Perhaps the most damaging change of all occurred in Western macroeconomic policy outlooks, however. Keynesianism was abandoned to promote price stability. In Europe, this contributed to unemployment at Great Depression levels: 11 percent across European Union (EU) countries by the mid-1990s, a catastrophe for unions. In the United States, similar trends created an expansion in the American low-wage labor market.[5] One commonality, however, was a dramatic loss of good semiskilled industrial jobs, which were disappearing in Europe at twice the (already substantial) rate in the United States (see Wood 1994).

Intensified economic internationalization was bound to increase the vulnerability of Western unions because it ended the relative insulation of postwar national political economies. Spillovers from increasing trade, globalized financial markets, and corporate regime shopping reduced the effectiveness of national policies. Other national regulatory capacities declined, while the costs of national policies running counter to international market logics rose. Capital found new options to exit from national contexts and new ways of expanding the spatial scope of markets.

Labor, in contrast, is more deeply entrenched in national arrangements than ever, a consequence of its own Golden Age accomplishments. The effectiveness of unions in setting labor standards had been contingent on their ability to engage in multi-employer collective bargaining by providing both positive and negative incentives (for example, protection against competitive wage bidding and strikes embracing whole sectors). In the new era, employers (and economists) argue that such bargaining obstructed flexible adaptation to new technologies and rapidly changing international market opportunities. As such arguments have been translated into reality, unions have lost leverage. Decentralization of bargaining makes union organization above the firm—at national and sectoral levels—harder to sustain. Even beyond this, within the European Single Market and Economic and Monetary Union (EMU), on the one hand, and the North American Free Trade Agreement (NAFTA), on the other, even those collective bargaining systems that remain most centralized are likely to become components of a decentralized regional bargaining structure.

Challenges from globalization have been amplified by longer-run changes in the labor force. Tertiarization, feminization, and "precarization" diminish resources on which unions depend, particularly the strength in numbers and identity given them by blue-collar workers of the "old working class." The degree to which such deindustrialization is accelerated by competition from new entrants to the industrialized world or by intensified competition is significant (Rodrik 1997). There has also been job reduction in advanced economies because of new electronic technologies. The loss in manufacturing jobs is evident (OECD 1994, pts. 1, 2). In Europe and North America, service sector jobs have risen to 60-70 percent of total employment.

Such changes pose other threats to labor organizations. The "old working class," with its base in manufacturing, was largely male. The growing female labor force participation that began in the earlier postwar period continues. Women work fewer hours than men do, and, even when they work longer hours, they do so for shorter periods over their working life. Thus women have been filling a larger portion of growing atypical employment—part-time, fixed-term, and temporary agency jobs—than men have. Part-time and temporary jobs are also disproportionately held by young people, while women and young people under age 25 are found more often than men in low-paying work (OECD 1996, 72-74, tab. 3.2). The resulting conflicts of interest between the declining traditional working class and growing labor force components make it difficult to redefine union identities in terms that could encompass both.

Political clout has always been an essential labor tool to organize, raise money, enforce labor standards, and get rules guaranteeing employer good faith in bargaining. It is important as well in capturing the attention of economic policymakers. In return, unions could offer electoral support to friendly parties. It is manifest today that labor's supply of political clout is in vertiginous decline. Class voting has diminished. There has been divorce, or at least separation, between center-left parties and trade unions. Center-left and social democratic governments have taken the lead in implementing globalizing policy shifts, privatizing, deregulating, restructuring, de-indexing wage growth, cutting back the public sector, making the labor market flexible, and encouraging entrepreneurs. In certain cases—the United Kingdom and the United States come to mind—there has even been a serious deterioration in unions' legal rights. The growing deafness of political and administrative classes to union claims is evident everywhere, particularly in the realm of economic policy.

Western labor movements stand in a different relationship to globalization from labor in most of the rest of the world. As they have set up regional trading blocs, North America and Europe have themselves reacted differently, however. Economic transnationalization in North America has been largely an issue of market building, most recently with NAFTA. Economic transnationalization within the EU is more advanced than in NAFTA, having moved from a customs-free area toward a unified single market in the 1980s and a single currency in the 1990s (in EMU).[6]

In Europe, employers automatically calculate transnationally, and national governments have given up regulatory and macroeconomic policy prerogatives. European integration has also given unions incentives to develop Europe-wide capacities. EU institutions allow much more political regulation than do other regional blocs, not to speak of the global economy, facilitating cross-border union communication and action. Transnational governance is limited, however, by the treaty of the EU, which focuses predominantly on market integration and liberalization. Areas that most concern labor, such as pay and rights to organize and strike, are currently excluded, while social policy issues more generally remain the prerogative of EU member states.

Because industrial relations and social policy are left in EU member states' hands, European unions still act primarily in national arenas. In EU decision-making procedures, the intergovernmental Council of Ministers has the last word, making pressure on national governments a more promising way for unions to influence decisions than working at the European level. These disincentives to invest in European structures reinforce the chronic obstacles to transnational labor action posed by institutional, cultural, and language differences. Conflicts of interest, perceived and real, between national unions, often paralleling those of their governments within the EU, are further obstacles.

European integration thus gives national unions reason to transnationalize, but multiple factors also induce them to stay home. Paradoxically, both have happened. A thickening network of transnational union activities has developed through the European Trade Union Confederation (ETUC), which was founded in

1973. The new Europeanization of the later 1980s triggered changes in the ETUC's leadership, organization, and capabilities, and, by the 1990s, the confederation had become a limited but genuine participant in European policy formation, with growing significance to its member organizations.

The ETUC has had a number of modest successes. As a result of legislative activity from Brussels in which the ETUC participated, a range of new regulatory instruments on workplace health and safety, equality between men and women, and working hours now exists. The ETUC has also participated in "social dialogue" in the "negotiated legislation" that the 1991 Maastricht Treaty established.[7] The first "negotiated legislation" was on parental leave, and it has been followed since by deals on the rights of part-time workers and the contractual obligations of employers in shorter-term work contracts. Perhaps the most significant piece of new law has set up European Works Councils. Because of these works councils, several tens of thousands of trade unionists from all national branches of Europe's largest firms meet and cooperate transnationally.[8]

The ETUC was originally formed from national union confederations and, as it modernized, invited transnational sectoral federations into its highest instances. It remains weak organizationally compared to its constituents but is much stronger than it was a decade ago. It still has little capacity to mobilize workers per se, however, and there has been precious little trans-European labor mobilization. The ETUC is a provider of linkages between its constituent organizations, which themselves can mobilize but almost exclusively on the national level, and it is a conduit for information about Europe, its dangers, and its possibilities (Leisinck 1995; Martin and Ross 1999).

The resultant pattern of union Europeanization is ambiguous, however. It is much too weak at the sectoral level, for example. Moreover, EMU is changing the strategic environment. In many contexts, the idea of national social pacts has returned, in which national unions and employers collaborate, in one form or another, to seek greater national competitiveness. This process could renationalize union concerns and close off opportunities for the ETUC to continue the strategies that it has been pursuing. National agreements to make economies leaner and meaner could lead to a general race to the bottom. The ETUC is in a position to provide some coordination between its national constituents' strategies, however. In this role, the ETUC could also enter into new coalitions with European institutions interested in fostering upward emulation, particularly through use of the new employment clause in the Amsterdam Treaty of 1997. It could also help to maximize the positive possibilities of the supply-side proposals that European elites now favor, while arguing for greater demand-side action. All will depend upon the capacity of the ETUC to be proactive and creative.

The ETUC also faces the challenge of integrating (and to some extent actually establishing) unions in the post-socialist societies of Central and Eastern Europe now applying for membership in the EU. These largely new unions are weak. Accession to the EU provides incentives for Central and Eastern European nations to make more space for them, but the occasionally savage market arrangements that have come into being work against this (ILO 1997). The ETUC cannot make strong unions emerge in these areas on its own, but it can provide significant assistance. The results, like everything in the general area of union responses to globalization, are hard to predict, but a serious transnational union movement extending well to the east of the old Cold War boundaries is conceivable.

The North American situation is different. NAFTA, a regional economic bloc roughly analogous to the EU, is a more recent creation, coming into effect only in 1993. NAFTA is highly asymmetrical, two small and dissimilar economies attached to the United States, with its huge market and superpower economy. Moreover, NAFTA is a simple free-trade area with none of the unifying, sovereignty-pooling, and institution-building ambitions of the EU. NAFTA will reshape its three constituent markets primarily through the workings of market mechanisms over time. These will have an impact on labor and, in consequence, stimulate labor responses.

The logic of the interdependence of NAFTA's member markets has been surgically removing Canada's protected branch-plant economy. The challenge to labor, particularly

Canada's in its largest industrial province, Ontario, has been great. Many good jobs have been lost, and, although total employment levels have been restored since, whether these lost jobs have been permanently replaced by new good jobs remains to be seen. On the other hand, the low value of the Canadian dollar (which Canadian governments have encouraged) plus the relative labor cost advantage that Canada provides from its good public social services still make Canada a desirable place for American firms to locate. This may be a mixed blessing, however, since American capital now views Canada as a giant shopping mall for buyouts. Mexico's place in NAFTA, on the other hand, is clearly to serve as a low-wage location for outsourcing U.S. production.

NAFTA includes a North American Agreement on Labor Cooperation, the so-called Labor Side Agreement. This does not pretend to promote transnational harmonization and regulation. Instead, it enjoins each member to promote, in its own way, a set of general principles, including labor rights, standards, equal pay for equal work, health and safety, and equal treatment for migrant workers (Stone 1995). Only health and safety, child labor, and minimum wage provisions are legally enforceable, however. If a NAFTA country decides that another is not applying its own laws in these areas, it can complain to the Commission for Labor Cooperation (comprising a secretariat and NAFTA's ministers of labor), after which long and complex consultation, hearings, and evaluations are held. One scholar concludes that "NAFTA, which imposes no substantive cross-border labor regulations, comes close to a no-regulation regime. Accordingly, this model solves none of the problems that globalization poses for labor" (Stone 1995, 1208).

NAFTA could stimulate labor behavior that makes it even more difficult to face problems. NAFTA unifies nothing but markets, leaving labor movements nationalized and with few recourses except those that exist nationally. This in itself is an incentive to seek protection from globalization from governments and political elites through protectionism. In NAFTA's short history, this has been quite evident, with both Canadian and U.S. unions seeking to reverse the agreement and reimpose external barriers, the Canadians against the Americans and the Americans against the Mexicans. U.S. unions have even managed to lobby successfully to block the extension of fast-track negotiating authority (Shoch in press). NAFTA results are not yet in, but they could contribute to a no-win situation where labor either loses politically in its efforts to gain protection and is further weakened or wins some protection at the cost of placing its own society at competitive disadvantage.

There may be other options. A union based in one of the NAFTA member countries can undertake transnational action itself. Thus it may try to organize workers and/or their union in another NAFTA country to confront a common problem such as whipsawing, when a multinational employer tries to use one against the other. It can try to use its power in one country where labor standards can be enforced to pressure employers to behave better in another, for example. It can promote coordinated action in the other country as well. American unions have tried this with Mexico, with mixed success. A union can also initiate or support a fair labor standards campaign with transnational nongovernmental organizations (NGOs) and/or political forces, involving widespread publicity and tactics like boycotts.

Western labor movements are playing catch-up with capital, as they always have. This time, however, because they had caught up so much in the era of national economic development immediately preceding the current era of globalization, they must play catch-up with declining resources and influence. It is quite possible that the regional economic blocs where they now find themselves will be more important to their futures than abstract globalization processes. Clearly, regional blocs and larger transnationalization processes present significant threats.

Labor in other parts of the world is less prepared and less endowed. Latin America, a hugely varied region, faced transnationalization in the 1980s within the ruins of import-substitution models of development that were caught by new pressures for liberalization coming from the North. International diplomacy, credit markets, and the mandates of multilateral trade organizations created high levels of debt plus difficult relations with the International Monetary Fund, the World Bank, private debtors, and new austerity. Because these changes coincided with a return to democracy, the period has been more for establishing legal and organizational frameworks for free labor movements than for anything else, against a very volatile economic background. The result has been union movements that are weak at the enterprise level, inclined to do politics at the top, and likely to line up behind their governments in transnational matters.

Regionalization is also an issue in Latin America. Mercosur, a fledging regional trading bloc involving southern Latin America, is a customs-reducing zone with common market ambitions but without transnational institutional pretensions. Unions within the member countries have formed a consortium to press for the inclusion of labor protection clauses in the Mercosur agreements. Their Social Charter, which includes much from the International Labor Organization (ILO) conventions on labor rights and standards, has so far been refused by governments, however (Stone 1999; ILO 1997, 157-64).

The labor situation elsewhere complicates the picture even more. There is a fledgling regional association in Asia (Asian Pacific Economic Cooperation [APEC]), but its identity and purpose remain unclear. Within the region, there is a huge disparity of economic practices, no unifying model of labor relations, and general labor weakness (ILO 1997, 165). Japan is in the throes of a long economic crisis. In Asia's NICs, in the throes of major change after recent international market crises, union movements are feeble and often dependent upon national regimes.

Indeed, it has been only recently that labor relations in some of the NICs have begun to emerge from the shadows of authoritarian political power.

The situation is bleakest in those parts of the world where modernization is just beginning. In Africa, for example, participation in international trade liberalization has come as a by-product of rigorous structural adjustment policies imposed by the International Monetary Fund and the World Bank. The effects have involved actual declines in living standards and in the number of workers in the formal labor market. Given political uncertainty across most of the continent and other huge problems (disease pandemics, in particular), this world of labor is certain to be ill treated by globalization for some time.

In some areas of Asia—including certain of the remaining Communist regimes—aggressive strategies of low-labor-cost production are in full bloom. Child labor, sweatshops, and oppressive domestic outwork proliferate. Regimes in countries pursuing such strategies usually interpret imprecations for higher labor standards and rights as protectionist efforts to stifle development, and they often mobilize their own labor movements (such as they are and often dependent upon governments) to make their point.

This situation creates perplexing dilemmas. Labor movements and governments in more advanced capitalist settings have tried to insert social clauses in bilateral and multilateral trade agreements, but progress has been very slow. Perhaps the best example of this is what has happened at ministerial meetings of the recently established World Trade Organization (WTO). In 1996, there was a concerted campaign to include a minimal social clause covering core social rights (freedom of association, bargaining, striking; forced labor; discrimination in employment; child labor) in WTO proceedings, backed by numerous NGOs, the ILO, the International Confederation of Free Trade Unions, and the ETUC. Governments from the West supported the campaign, but ferocious opposition from developing countries argued that the proposal would deprive them of legitimate comparative market advantages. Western multinationals and business associations opposed the clause as well, fearing the consequences for free trade. The WTO refused to accept the proposal, although it will be brought up again.

The overlapping conflicts of interest in the debate on social clauses illustrate the problems of labor and globalization. A coalition of Western economic interests and less developed countries is very difficult to defeat. This, in turn, means that Western governments, who negotiate such matters, do not place social clauses at the top of their priority lists, even if they will give them lip service. Outcomes here are therefore unpredictable. What is most likely is a long and multitargeted campaign conducted by labor organizations, the ILO, and, quite as important, those highly mobilized NGOs that are labor's allies. The immediate future probably lies in mobilization by "transnational advocacy networks" involving a wide range of different actors around campaigns of deep issues of principle, in particular core labor rights seen as basic human rights (Keck and Sikkink 1998). Labor's transnational union organizations, obliged to reconfigure after the Cold War, have focused on such matters. They are perhaps labor's best hope in the medium term. Today, however, they are still largely tied up in their past patterns of behavior.

LABOR'S MANY WORLDS: TOWARD WHAT FUTURE?

"Globalization" is a term that confuses as much as it clarifies. It denotes a bundle of very different trends pointing in different directions and moving at different speeds. "Labor" is also a misleading term. If there is an emerging transnationalized labor market, there are multiple labors and multiple worlds of labor. Labor has developed within nation-states and today faces globalization in largely nationalized postures. Labor's nationalization was a logical catch-up strategy as markets grew outward from local settings toward national boundaries. Nationalization—the use of national political and regulatory resources to constrain the boundaries of markets to overlap with actual national geographical frontiers—leaves labor deeply committed to the nation as its home, however. This is the nub of labor's problems today.

There is no magic bullet for labor in this situation. Catching up nationally meant gathering in and organizing different groups with different interests and persuading them that they had broader things in common than organizing struggle for these common goals. This took more than a century in itself. Unions are unlikely to chase an expanding market into a transnational no-union zone successfully overnight, therefore, for two fundamental reasons. First, the common denominator of cultural and linguistic commonalities that helped bring together workers within nations does not exist transnationally. Instead, there are different national labors, which will be very difficult to transcend. Quite as important, the sovereign institutions of governance that exist at the national level and that might be pressured to regulate markets nationally do not exist transnationally.

Labor is thus far perhaps the major loser from globalization, and its progress in coping with globalization has been limited and slow. National labor movements, which will have to be the base of transnational labor action, are being weakened. It is difficult to see how they will be able to build the transnational unity of purpose needed to confront globalizing trends in time to counteract this decline. At present, there are huge tasks of transnational organization to undertake. Only international union cooperation and organization can take the lead. They either do not yet exist or, in the form of ongoing organizations from the Golden Age, have barely begun to reconfigure their missions. There is much to be done, therefore, but few candidates for doing it and a rapidly ticking clock. Still, it did take a century for labor to cope with national markets. We should at least give it a few decades, rather than a few years, to find ways to catch up with international capital.

Notes

1. At the outset, I refer readers to ILO 1997. This report contains a wealth of pertinent information and analysis on this article's subject.

2. Even then there were cases, the United States being one, in which national industrial relations systems backed by adequate juridical substance were much less national then commentators usually admitted. There might be regional situations where unionism was precarious, like the American South, or economic sectoral situations where unionism was discouraged or limited.

3. They have been most significant in the triad areas (Europe, North America, Australasia, and the industrialized Far East).

4. The International Confederation of Free Trade Unions was also active in creating transnational sectoral organizations, the International Trade Secretariats, which, because they were closer to the economic ground, were more useful in establishing communication and cooperation between national sectoral unions.

5. The United States thus maintained general employment levels, but at the expense of a proliferation of poorly paying jobs, expanding poverty, and greater income inequality.

6. I use the acronym "EU" for convenience, even though "Europe" has had several titles in its short existence.

7. Maastricht set up a process designed to encourage the growth of peak European producer groups. It allowed them to negotiate on specific issues, and, if they could agree, their agreement would become European law.

8. The works councils, in the best of circumstances, could promote the development of genuinely transnational unionism. Alternatively, they could foster a transnational microcorporatism that would further weaken national unions.

References

ILO (International Labor Organization). 1997. *World Labor Report: Industrial*

Relations, Democracy and Social Stability, 1997-1998. Geneva: ILO.

Keck, Marget and Katherine Sikkink. 1998. *Activists Beyond Borders: Advocacy Networks in International Politics*. Ithaca, NY: Cornell University Press.

Leisinck, Peter, ed. 1995. *The Challenges to Trade Unions in Europe: Innovation and Adaptation*. Cheltenham: Edward Elgar.

Luttwak, Edward. 1993. *The Endangered Dream: How to Stop the United States from Becoming a Third World Country and How to Win the Geo-economic Struggle for Industrial Supremacy*. New York: Simon & Schuster.

Marglin, Steven and Juliet Schor, eds. 1990. *The Golden Age of Capitalism*. Oxford: Clarendon Press.

Martin, Andrew and George Ross, eds. 1999. *The Brave New World of European Unions*. New York: Berghahn.

OECD (Organization for Economic Cooperation and Development). 1991. *Historical Statistics 1960-1989*. Paris: OECD.

———. 1994. *OECD Jobs Study*. Paris: OECD.

———. 1996. *OECD Employment Outlook, July*. Paris: OECD.

Rodrik, Dani. 1997. *Has Globalization Gone Too Far?* Washington, DC: Institute for International Economics.

Sassoon, Donald. 1998. *One Hundred Years of Socialism*. New York: New Press.

Shoch, James. In press. Rising from the Ashes of Defeat: Organized Labor and the 1997 and 1998 "Fast-Track" Fights. *Politics and Society*.

Stone, Katherine Van Wezel. 1995. Labor and the Global Economy: Four Approaches to Transnational Labor Regulation. *Michigan Journal of International Law* 16(4): 987-1028.

———. 1999. To the Yukon and Beyond: Local Laborers in a Global Labor Market. *Journal of Small and Emerging Business Law* 3(1).

Thurow, Lester. 1992. *Head to Head: The Coming Economic Battle Among Japan, Europe, and America*. New York: Morrow.

United Nations. 1992. *World Investment Directory*. Vol. 3. New York: United Nations.

Wood, Adrian. 1994. *North-South Trade, Employment and Inequality: Changing Fortunes in a Skill Driven World*. Oxford: Clarendon Press.

ANNALS, AAPSS, 570, July 2000

The Student Anti-Sweatshop
Movement: Limits and Potential

By JAY R. MANDLE

ABSTRACT: This article analyzes the student anti-sweatshop movement in the United States and its efforts to employ codes of conduct to
secure improved conditions for workers in the international apparel
industry. After discussing the globalization of that industry, the
article examines the content of the codes of conduct that have been
suggested by the student movement, on the one hand, and the members of the Apparel Industry Partnership, on the other. It concludes
with a critique of the strategy of relying on codes of conduct and suggests that the pursuit of workers' rights should be sought in a
strengthened International Labor Organization.

*Jay R. Mandle is the W. Bradford Wiley Professor of Economics at Colgate Univer-
sity. He is coauthor, with Louis Ferleger, of* No Pain, No Gain: Taxes, Productivity and
Economic Growth *(1992) and* A New Mandate: Democratic Choices for a Prosperous
Economy *(1994). He has written extensively on the economic development of the
English-speaking Caribbean and the process of globalization.*

THE student anti-sweatshop movement is fueled by a powerful sense of ill-gotten gains. The earnings achieved by universities when they license their logos for use on sweatshirts, baseball caps, T-shirts, jackets, and jerseys stand in stark contrast to the incomes earned by the workers producing that apparel. The Union of Needletrades, Industrial and Textile Employees (UNITE) has calculated that whereas a major university may receive as much as $1.50 for each $19.95 baseball cap sold, workers in the Dominican Republic producing those caps earn only about $0.08. It is this discrepancy that stirs moral outrage. In an open letter to their respective campuses, leaders of the student movement wrote, "We were as shocked as you to find out that baseball caps with our schools' logos were made in a sweatshop," and demanded that they be informed "where our college logo apparel is produced and that it is produced under decent conditions" (UNITE n.d., 2, 1).

THE INTERNATIONAL APPAREL INDUSTRY

The concern with university-licensed apparel is best understood in the context of the apparel industry generally, an industry that in recent years has become increasingly globalized. The specific segment of the U.S. apparel industry that has relocated production to Third World nations is the sector that does not have to concern itself with rapidly changing consumer tastes. The latter, garments with a high fashion content, tend to remain close to their retail markets because demand tends to be variable, and producing abroad risks accumulating unmarketable inventories (Singer 1997, 125-26). In contrast is the university-licensed apparel market. Not subject to continuous variations in style, these products can be produced overseas without a concern that a gap in time between production and sale will result in the accumulation of undesired apparel.

Total employment internationally in the clothing industry was stable between 1980 and 1992, at close to 4.9 million employees. But this stability masks the fact that these were years of dramatic change in the geographic pattern of employment. Over 850,000 jobs were lost in the developed world. That number was matched by growth in the Third World, more than four-fifths of which occurred in Asia. The Asian countries where clothing employment growth was most dramatic—totaling 500,000 jobs—were Bangladesh, Thailand, Indonesia, and the Philippines. Among the developed countries, the United States lost the highest number of clothing jobs, though the percentage decrease in such employment was higher in the other countries that saw big decreases in clothing employment—France, Germany, and the United Kingdom—as well as Latin America (ILO 1996, 36-37).

This pattern of industrial relocation clearly reflected a search for inexpensive labor. Data on wage rates, however, are scarce. The industrial trade newspaper *Women's Wear Daily* did publish information on apparel worker wages per hour late in 1996 for 19 relatively poor countries. The wages reported were indeed low. Hourly wage rates, converted to U.S. dollars, were lowest in Bangladesh and Myanmar at $0.10-$0.18. They ranged between $0.20 and $0.68 for China, Pakistan, Vietnam, India, Sri Lanka, and Indonesia. In Asia, only in the Philippines and Thailand did the hourly wage rate approximate $1.00. Wages were higher in the Central American countries for which data were provided. For the most part, wages fell between about $1.00 an hour and somewhat less than $2.00, though the wage rate in Costa Rica was reported at $2.38 (Labor Costs 1996).

The question that arises is why the labor force in Latin America and Asia can be induced to work for the very low wage rates reported by *Women's Wear Daily*. In economic theory, wages fall within a range limited by the marginal productivity of labor at the high end and the wages offered by the next best alternative available to workers at the low end. Employers will not pay workers more than the last worker hired contributes to the firm's revenue, while employees will not accept wages lower than they could secure in alternative employment. The actual wage rate paid within that range depends upon the relative bargaining strength of the two sides.

Employment alternatives available to workers are in part determined by their country's level of economic development. In the case of the countries under consideration here, none has experienced the structural transformation characteristic of modern economic growth. Unlike economically developed countries where the percentage of the labor force employed in agriculture typically is around 5 percent, in this group of countries that percentage is much higher. For the Asian countries, the labor force percentage in agriculture ranges from China's 72.2 percent to Sri Lanka's 35.6 percent. In Central America, the range is from 67.8 percent for Haiti to 20.4 percent for Costa Rica. Asia's weighted mean agricultural labor force comes to about two-thirds of the employed workforce; in Latin America, the proportion is about one-third (World Bank 1999, tabs. 2.3 and 2.4).

The problem is that the agriculture sector everywhere tends to be a sector with low relative levels of labor productivity. Because of this, work in agriculture pays low wages, but, particularly in Asia, this sector creates most of the employment opportunities. That in turn means that clothing has to offer only a somewhat higher wage than the very low one that is paid in agriculture in order to recruit its labor force.

That tendency for the clothing industry to pay its workers only slightly more than agriculture might have been at least partially offset if clothing workers had been able to engage in collective bargaining. But for the most part, employers in the clothing industry have not had to contend with union representation. In the apparel industry, according to the International Labor Organization (ILO), "today many workers fail to engage in collective bargaining because there is no recognized trade union at their place of work" (ILO

1996, 107). Clothing workers have not had access to the market power that unionization would have provided them. In the absence of organized labor, individual workers have to secure work essentially as price takers. They either accept the going wage or seek work elsewhere. Thus it was that the clothing industry was able to secure its labor force at very low wages and it was Asia that attracted the clothing industry.

Although everywhere in Asia and Central America, wages in the clothing industry were low, the picture with regard to changes in those wages over time was mixed. Two countries with very large increases in employment, Bangladesh and India, experienced reduced wages, while other Asian countries—Sri Lanka, Indonesia, the Philippines, and Thailand—saw compensation increase dramatically. The pattern is similarly mixed in Central America. Wages declined in Guatemala and Costa Rica, but, in contrast, wages increased in Honduras by more than one-third between 1980 and 1992. In Mexico, virtual wage stagnation was experienced (ILO 1996, tab. 5.1).

What is noticeable, at least for the large Asian countries, is that it was only the least developed countries (as measured by gross domestic product per capita), Bangladesh and India, that experienced decreased wages in clothing. In the others, at higher levels of economic development, wages increased, although they remained, of course, at low levels. At the same time, the extent of job creation in clothing itself does not appear to be a determinant in the movement of wages. There is no positive association between the growth in employment and increased wages. What this suggests is that while the clothing industry sought out low-cost labor, the movement in the wages it paid over time depended upon larger labor market processes. What seems to have happened in the relatively developed countries of Asia is that the price of labor was bid up in clothing because wages were rising in other sectors of the economy as the process of growth proceeded. In short, clothing was attracted to low-wage labor markets, but the trend in the wages it offered over time was determined by the alternative employment options created in the development process.

THE MOVEMENT

The anti-sweatshop movement came to life after a series of disclosures in 1995 and 1996 brought to light shocking labor conditions in the apparel industry. Sweatshops were found producing for The Gap in Central America, Kathie Lee Gifford's Wal-Mart clothing line in Honduras, and Nike shoes in Indonesia. Further unfavorable public notice resulted from a Department of Labor raid on the El Monte compound in Southern California at which 72 undocumented immigrant workers were in a condition of peonage (Ross 1997, 26-29). In response, in August 1996 on the initiative of the Clinton administration, the Apparel Industry Partnership (AIP) was created to address the issue of sweatshops. Members included prominent apparel firms, nonprofit organizations working in the field, and two unions—UNITE and the Retail, Wholesale and Department Store Union. AIP issued an interim report in April 1997 and a final agreement in November 1998. In that agreement, members of AIP agreed to create a nonprofit organization, the Fair Labor Association (FLA), "to oversee monitoring of compliance" with the Workplace Code of Conduct that had been agreed to in April 1997 (Apparel Industry Partnership 1999, 1).

A draft of a Collegiate Code of Conduct for firms producing licensed merchandise was issued as part of the agreement. In the draft, standards for the licensed apparel industry were proposed concerning working hours, overtime compensation, and health and safety conditions. The code would prohibit the use of child labor, forced labor, discrimination, and harassment and abuse. The draft agreement also included a provision according to which "licensees shall recognize and respect the right of employees to freedom of association and collective bargaining" (Collegiate Code of Conduct 1998, 2).

The proposals in the draft concerning wages, benefits, and monitoring drew the opposition of the union members of the AIP, resulting ultimately in the two unions and the Interfaith Center on Corporate Responsibility's quitting the group. Instead of the living wage that the unions wanted, the clause in the draft called upon licensees to pay, "as a floor, at least the minimum wage required by local law or the local prevailing industry wage, whichever is higher, and shall provide legally mandated benefits" (Collegiate Code

of Conduct 1998, III.B.1). With regard to compliance and monitoring of the agreement, the provisions of the draft emphasized self-monitoring and self-enforcement, in contrast to the independent external overview sought by the dissenters. According to the draft, company names and locations were to be made available to the Collegiate Licensing Company, but only on a confidential basis (Collegiate Code of Conduct 1998, IV.A.4). Although the draft declared that its adherents were committed to "conducting periodic announced and unannounced visits . . . to survey compliance with the Code," the results of these visits were to remain private. Further, only a sampling of the production facilities were to be investigated, and then by as yet unnamed inspectors (Collegiate Code of Conduct 1998, V.A).

Mark Levinson of UNITE defended his union's withdrawal from the AIP by saying, "This agreement is not very good. How can you talk about eliminating sweatshops without making a commitment to pay a living wage?" Alan Howard, also speaking for UNITE, declared that "the monitoring is badly flawed. We don't think it's very independent monitoring and the companies pick their monitors and the factories to be monitored so there won't be surprise inspections" (Greenhouse 1998, 2). Michael Shellenberger, a spokesman for Global Exchange, summarized the objections to the agreement when he said, "This is a step backwards. These companies will be able to market their products as sweatshop-free—without actually making changes to sweatshop practices abroad" (Dobnik 1998, 5; United Students Against Sweatshops 1999).[1]

Notwithstanding these objections, the Collegiate Code of Conduct draft won the endorsement of 17 universities, including Duke and Notre Dame, pioneers with regard to university codes of conduct. By midsummer, that number had swelled to more than 100. At the same time however, other schools had refrained from signing on, arguing that the draft provisions were inadequate. Included in this group were the University of Michigan, the University of Wisconsin, and the University of California (Appelbaum and Dreier 1999, 77).

The dissenters won at least a partial victory when, in April 1999, the University of California announced revisions to the code it had adopted the previous year. Clauses were added to require firms to adhere to applicable environmental laws and local and national health and safety laws and to recognize the right of employees to collective bargaining. Perhaps most important, from the point of view of the critics of the original document, the University of California added a provision concerning a living wage. According to the revised code, the standard for wages should be the market wage, legal minimum wage, or a level of compensation "which constitute a 'living wage,' whichever provides greater wages and benefits" (University of California 1999, C.1). No definition of the term "living wage," however, was provided in the document.

WORKERS IN POOR AND RICH COUNTRIES

John Cavanagh, an activist in the anti-sweatshop movement, writes that "today governments are more compromised than ever in succumbing to corporate demands, and trade union movements around the world are much weaker." With that the case, the power to counter the strength of multinational corporations requires "new coalitions of citizen movements coordinating not only across labor, environmental, consumer and other social sectors, but also across geographic borders" (Cavanagh 1997, 40). That is what the anti-sweatshop movement is attempting to do with codes of conduct. It hopes to provide an external counterweight to assist workers in poor countries in dealing with multinational corporations.

The problem is that the underlying assumption in Cavanagh's formulation that common interests actually unite workers in poor countries and developed nations has not been shared by the American Left, including most particularly the union movement. On the contrary, there is a strong feeling in the United States that the interests of workers in poor and rich countries are in conflict with each other. This view of the matter is what leads analysts like Thomas Palley, the assistant director of public policy (economics) at the AFL-CIO, to advocate protectionist tariffs against imports produced with the use of inexpensive labor.[2] It is this same problem that Randy

Shaw (1999) indirectly addresses when he writes in support of a living wage that "Americans are more likely to support corporate pressure campaigns and become actively involved in fighting third-world sweatshops if they view raising workers' wages abroad as diminishing the corporate incentive for exporting domestic jobs" (123). Overlooked in Shaw's discussion is the fact that it is hard to expect the support of Third World workers for a program that reduces the incentives for U.S. firms to create jobs overseas. The reason is that it is just such employment creation that is a mechanism by which wages in poor countries are bid up.

This is not to deny the possibility of the discovery of a community of interests that, in fact, will permit an alliance to be developed in the way that Cavanagh envisions. But it is not automatically achieved. Creating a community of interests involves the necessity of very carefully weighing the trade-offs that, in fact, do exist between the interests of workers in poor and rich countries. Labor market circumstances in poor countries only too obviously result in the willingness of workers to accept employment at wage levels that would be rejected by their counterparts elsewhere. With that comes downward pressure on the wages of the workers in developed-country industries that compete with companies located in the Third World. Doing nothing to promote increased wages in poor countries is unconscionable. Furthermore, raising those wages would lessen some of the downward pressure on wages in the developed

countries. But at the same time, too great an increase in this regard, though benefiting metropolitan workers, would result in a reduction in Third World employment, an obviously unacceptable alternative.

This risk of harming workers in poor countries in the name of helping them is inherent in the living-wage proposal. The attractiveness of that proposal lies in the fact that existing minimum wages in poor countries frequently leave their recipients in dire poverty (Brakken 1999, 5-6; Sweatshop Watch 1999b, 1). Its reasonable assumption is that all employed workers, even those working at minimum wages, should earn incomes that are adequate for a life above desperation. This is what motivates the United Students Against Sweatshops (1999) when it says, "The FLA should define what is essential to meet a worker's basic needs and engage in an original cost-of-living study in the areas where there are manufacturing sites. The FLA should commit in advance to paying workers these wages which meet their basic needs, once those levels are determined" (3). But while all of this is valid, it remains the case that too great an increase in wages could wipe out jobs because of the resulting increased costs of production.

What is disturbing about the living-wage methodology discussed by Sweatshop Watch and Global Exchange is that there is no evident sensitivity to the risk that raising wages might result in job loss. The possible implications of a living wage for reduced employment receive no attention in, for example, Sweatshop

Watch's methodological paper on the subject (Sweatshop Watch 1999b). Because this is so, the advocates of the proposal are defenseless against the charge that what it represents is in reality hidden protectionism, motivated by the desire to defend American jobholders against low-wage competitors. The fact that UNITE provides active support for the anti-sweatshop movement might further be used to support the charge. Such an indictment in all likelihood does a disservice to the motives of those in the student movement. But at the same time, their insensitivity to the down-side risks of their ideas exposes them to the charge of naïveté, only slightly less damning an indictment than that of defending the workers of a wealthy country in preference to those of a poor nation.

In addition to its demand for a living wage, the anti-sweatshop movement would like to ensure that the right to collective bargaining contained in the Collegiate Code of Conduct is made a reality. It would attempt to do so by writing into codes of conduct language barring harassment, providing unions with free access to employees, and requiring union recognition by licensees (Sweatshop Watch 1999a). The fact is, however, that even with stipulations such as these, it is very hard to believe that codes of conduct, no matter how stringent the language, will succeed in producing union representation. No written document can make certain that employers will recognize unions as negotiating partners or will engage in good-faith bargaining with them.

The most likely response by employers to such codes would be formal acceptance of the right to organize but opposition to unions in practice nevertheless. If this were the case, it would be left to private monitors to discover these breaches and set in motion the withdrawal of the right of the offending firm to produce licensed merchandise. It takes little imagination to envision the delays and evasions that would be resorted to in the process. This is especially likely in an industry like clothing, where the ability of firms to move from one country to another is substantial.

WORKERS' RIGHTS

Yet it is this last demand, the right of unions to organize and bargain collectively, that most legitimately can make a claim as having the highest priority for implementation. Collective bargaining provides a mechanism by which workers can influence the wage they receive. Even if, with the presence of a union, the levels achieved initially were low, and the advance from the present rates minimal, a process at least would have been installed whereby in the future, if not at present, a higher wage might be negotiated.

Businesses, however, have a strong vested interest in resisting enhanced worker bargaining power. In most circumstances, even when the instruments of electoral democracy are in place, the owners of firms are able to use their wealth to influence the political environment in a direction hostile to union rights. The difficulty that presents itself is how to provide what is institutionally necessary to make sure that union rights are protected in practice.

It is here that international standards and monitoring are called for. But these standards should not be confined to an individual industry, nor should they be monitored by private institutions. To be effective, they would have to be universal, sanctioned by international law. If trade can be subject to a body of codified and enforceable rules, as in the case of the World Trade Organization, there is no reason that labor relations cannot similarly be put under such an international discipline. For this to be accomplished, there would have to be international agreement on union rights and the establishment of international machinery to ensure compliance.

Even if it is difficult at this moment in history to be optimistic that such an institutionalization of collective bargaining rights might occur, it certainly does not seem far-fetched to hope that a movement such as the student anti-sweatshop movement would adopt this goal as fundamental to its agenda. To do so, however, the movement will have to distance itself from the protectionist position adopted by the Left in the United States. It will have to accept that labor market circumstances differ by country and that those differences provide a basis for international trade, not a reason to curtail it, as the AFL-CIO economists would have us do. Low wages in poor countries provide those nations with comparative advantages in the production of goods using labor-intensive methods of production. It is in their

interests as well as our own that we buy those relatively inexpensive goods from them and concentrate our own production in more high-tech industries. At the same time, what should be unacceptable anywhere is a denial of labor bargaining rights. That is, though wages will differ according to a nation's level of development, such differences provide no justification for denying any workers—in rich or in poor countries—the ability effectively to participate in the labor market by utilizing collective bargaining.

A much enhanced and empowered ILO would be the obvious candidate among existing international organizations to administer such a union-rights regime. Of the 176 conventions passed by the ILO since its inception in 1919, 7 of the more recent ones have come to be recognized as core labor standards. The content of these 7 is what is mentioned when there is discussion of attaching a social clause to trade agreements. Two of the 7 specifically address the right to organize and bargain collectively. The first of these, concerned with the right to organize, was accepted by the ILO in 1948 (C87), and the second, dealing with collective bargaining and the right to organize, was passed in 1949 (C98) (International Confederation of Free Trade Unions 1999, 1-2).

These are the conventions that could set the standard to which all countries would be held accountable. The Convention on the Freedom of Association and Protection of the Right to Organize (C87) is very detailed in specifying that all workers have the right to belong to organizations of their own choosing, that they have the right to set their own rules and select their own leaders, and that their organizations should not be vulnerable to government's interference with or efforts to disband a functioning union. The Convention on the Right to Organize and Collective Bargaining (C98) protects individual workers from anti-union discrimination in either hiring or dismissal and stipulates that an employer will not be permitted to establish nominal unions that in reality are under the employer's control. Collective bargaining is explicitly endorsed. The convention calls for countries to take measures "to encourage and promote the full development and utilisation of machinery for voluntary negotiation between employers or employers' organizations and workers' organizations, with a view to the regulation of terms and conditions of employment by means of collective agreements" (ILO 1999).

The ILO is a U.N. organization in which each delegation is composed of representatives of business, labor, and the government. At present, there are 174 member states. In its procedures, individual countries are called upon to ratify conventions that are passed by a majority of the ILO members. There are supervisory mechanisms present in the organization, but by no means does the ILO possess strong enforcement powers. This is particularly true concerning conventions that, though passed by the organization, have not been ratified by individual countries. In that case, the abstaining country can claim exemption from even the limited enforcement that the ILO is capable of implementing.

Neither of the two core conventions on trade union rights has been adopted by the United States. Indeed, of the seven core labor standards, only one (C105, Abolition of Forced Labor, adopted in 1957 and ratified in 1991) has been accepted by the United States. Nothing therefore could be more obvious than endorsement of at least C87 and C98 by this country as a sine qua non for the implementation of a worldwide enforcement and monitoring system concerning labor rights.

For the student anti-sweatshop movement to mount a campaign that has real long-term hope of raising the living conditions of impoverished clothing workers, it will have to accept that there is more to the problem than entrepreneurial greed. Wages are lowest where worker alternatives are most limited. Growing employment in clothing does not always result in rising wages, but the chances of its doing so are greatest when that expansion occurs in a country where economic development is proceeding. When that occurs, wages in clothing rise because opportunities elsewhere expand. What students therefore should advocate is the spread of development and the policies associated with that spread. That is the process that best enables workers to secure higher wages.

In the context of economic growth, the ability of clothing workers to secure improved standards of living could be assisted by a greatly strengthened union movement internationally. Codes of conduct are not sufficient to ensure the objective. The enforcement mechanism available in that approach is limited, given the evasion capability of employers. Rather, the agenda in this regard should be to look to a globally enforced code of conduct with regard to union rights, to be administered by the ILO. In this regard, the seven core labor standards are important, but the two conventions concerning labor rights are essential. Students could well initiate the effort to internationalize trade union rights and, by doing so, help eliminate sweatshops by lobbying to obtain U.S. ratification of ILO Conventions 87 and 98 and by working to strengthen that organization.

Notes

1. Criticisms have come from the other side as well. Some corporate producers reject it as too demanding. According to a report in the *New York Times*, the FLA "has encountered problems attracting corporate members." Objections center on the risk that they might be embarrassed if monitors uncover violations and their reluctance to absorb the costs involved with compliance and their being assessed for the costs of monitoring (Greenhouse 1999, 1-2).

2. Palley (1998) writes that there should be a "social tariff" on goods from countries with a "low wage structure," the purpose of which "is to compensate for low wages and lack of commitment to social goals regarding the environment, worker health and safety and social welfare" (172).

References

Apparel Industry Partnership. 1999. Frequently Asked Questions About the Apparel Industry Partnership. Available at http://www.lchr.org/sweatshop/faq.htm. Accessed 1 Sept. 1999.

Appelbaum, Richard and Peter Dreier. 1999. The Campus Anti-Sweatshop Movement. *American Prospect* Sept.-Oct., 71-78.

Brakken, Eric. 1999. *Critical Analysis of the Fair Labor Association*. Available at http://www.asm.wisc.edu/asas/. Accessed 1 Sept. 1999.

Cavanagh, John. 1997. The Global Resistance to Sweatshops. In *No Sweat: Fashion, Free Trade and the Rights of Garment Workers*, ed. Andrew Ross. New York: Verso.

Collegiate Code of Conduct. 1998. The Collegiate Code of Conduct for CLC Licensees [30 Nov. 1998 Task Force Draft]. Available at http://www.news.wisc.edu/misc/code.html. Accessed 14 Aug. 1999.

Dobnik, Verena. 1998. Employees Sign Sweatshop Pact. Associated Press, 5 Nov. Available at http://www.cleanclothes.org/codes/AIP-3.htm. Accessed 14 Aug. 1999.

Greenhouse, Steven. 1998. Plans to Curtail Sweatshops Rejected by Union. *New York Times*, 5 Nov. Available at http://www.cleanclothes.org/codes/AIP-3.htm. Accessed 14 Aug. 1999.

———. 1999. 17 Colleges Join Against Sweatshops. *New York Times on the Web*, 16 Mar. Available at http://graphics.nytimes.com/images/. Accessed 15 Aug. 1999.

International Confederation of Free Trade Unions. 1999. *Internationally-Recognized Core Labour Standards in the United States: Report for the WTO General Council Review of the Trade Policies of the United States*. Available at http://www/ocftu.org/english/els/escl99wtousa.html. Accessed 2 Sept. 1999.

ILO (International Labor Organization). 1996. *Globalization of the Footwear, Textiles and Clothing Industries*. Geneva: International Labor Organization.

————. 1999. *ILOEX: The ILO's Database on International Labour Standards*. Available at http://ilolex.ilo.ch:1567/scripts/convde.pl?C98. Accessed 14 Aug. 1999.

Labor Costs: Where and How Much? 1996. *Women's Wear Daily*, 31 Dec. Available at http://www.nlsearch.com. Accessed 12 Aug. 1999.

Palley, Thomas I. 1998. *Plenty of Nothing: The Downsizing of the American Dream and the Case for Structural Keynesianism*. Princeton, NJ: Princeton University Press.

Ross, Andrew. 1997. Introduction. In *No Sweat: Fashion, Free Trade and the Rights of Garment Workers*, ed. Andrew Ross. New York: Verso.

Shaw, Randy. 1999. *Reclaiming America: Nike, Clean Air, and the New National Activism*. Berkeley: University of California Press.

Singer, Sally. 1997. Rat-Catching: An Interview with Bud Konheim. In *No Sweat: Fashion, Free Trade and the Rights of Garment Workers*, ed. Andrew Ross. New York: Verso.

Sweatshop Watch. 1999a. *Code of Conduct for University Trademark Licenses: Working Model*. Available at http://www.sweatshopwatch.org/swatch/codes/code.html. Accessed 14 Aug. 1999.

————. 1999b. *A Working Living Wage Methodology*. Available at http://www.sweatshopwatch.org/swatch/wages/formula.html. Accessed 5 July 1999.

UNITE (Union of Needletrades, Industrial and Textile Employees). N.d. *A UNITE Report on Campus Caps Made by BJ&B in the Dominican Republic*. Available at http://www.uniteunion.org/sweatshops/schoolcap.html. Accessed 14 Aug. 1999.

United Students Against Sweatshops. 1999. *Position Statement on the Fair Labor Association, March 31, 1999*. Available at http://www.asm.wisc.edu/usas/fla-state.htm. Accessed 14 Aug. 1999.

University of California. 1999. *Code of Conduct for Trademark Licensees, August 3, 1998, as Amended April 26, 1999*. Available at http://www.sweatshopwatch.org/swatch/codes/ucas/revision.html. Accessed 1 Sept. 1999.

World Bank. 1999. *World Development Indicators 1999*. Washington, DC: World Bank.

ANNALS, *AAPSS*, **570**, July 2000

The Bark Is Worse Than the Bite: New WTO Law and Late Industrialization

By ALICE H. AMSDEN and TAKASHI HIKINO

ABSTRACT: In spite of (or because of?) the successful industrialization of leading latecomers under a set of institutions that had deviated from free-market norms, by the 1990s the global economic order had formed around rather orthodox neoliberal principles. At close examination, however, the new rules of the World Trade Organization, a symbol of neoliberalism, are flexible and allow countries to continue to promote their industries under the banner of promoting science and technology. The success formula of late industrialization—allocating subsidies in exchange for monitorable, result-oriented performance standards—is still condoned. The problems bedeviling latecomers today are not formal legal constraints but informal political pressures exerted by North Atlantic economies in favor of radical market opening. Latecomers lack a vision to guide them in responding to this pressure.

Alice H. Amsden is professor of political economy at the Massachusetts Institute of Technology. Her forthcoming book, to be published in 2000, is The Rise of the Rest: Latecomers' Challenge to the West.

Takashi Hikino is associate professor of economics at Kyoto University. His recent books include Big Business and the Wealth of Nations *(1997), edited with Alfred D. Chandler, Jr., and Franco Amatori, and* Policies for Competitiveness *(1999), edited with H. Miyajima and T. Kikkawa.*

A FTER World War II, some late industrializers outside the North Atlantic economies overcame oligopolistic entry barriers and penetrated mid-technology industries that required relatively advanced skills. In 1965, developing countries supplied less than one-twentieth of world manufacturing output. By 1995, they supplied nearly one-fifth (Amsden forthcoming).

The rise of "the rest"—comprising the most successful late industrializers—changed the face of the world economy. Ranging from China, Korea, and Taiwan to Brazil, Turkey, and India, late industrializers challenged the fundamental principles of liberal political economy.[1] Instead of relying on market forces, "the rest's" rise involved extensive subsidization of manufacturing industry. At the same time, new institutions arose everywhere that tied subsidies to monitorable performance standards, thereby reducing "government failure" (Amsden forthcoming). Late industrializers effectively created a new growth model based on a control mechanism other than the "invisible hand." They thereby shifted the center of gravity in their economies away from primary product-based assets toward knowledge-based assets, the essence of economic development.

Given a more liberal global environment under the aegis of a new World Trade Organization (WTO), the question is whether or not even less industrialized countries can follow in the footsteps of the pioneering latecomers and also use subsidies and performance standards to accelerate growth. By the same token, the question is whether or not the pioneers themselves can continue using their success formula to penetrate deeper into high-technology industries.

In terms of WTO law, the answer in both cases is yes. As argued later in this article, the WTO and the General Agreement on Tariffs and Trade (GATT), the predecessor of the WTO, have much in common in terms of industrial policy, the major differences being that the WTO forbids export subsidies (except by the poorest countries) and restricts tariffs for import surges to eight years. Other types of safeguards, for balance-of-payments disequilibria, for example, may be used in perpetuity. Whatever else the WTO stands for, and whatever else the future will bring in terms of more liberal investment rules and more binding intellectual property rights, the WTO as now constituted is an institution that promotes science and technology. In the name of science and technology, countries in a position to exploit the WTO's rules can continue to support their own industries, to target national champions for government assistance, and to advance the general cause of their national competitiveness.

What has changed since the world's axis tilted more toward liberalism is not in the realm of law but in the realm of politics, or vision. By 2000, the rhetoric of latecomer countries had become largely liberal, and even the most obvious deviants from liberalism had no explicit alternative vision to guide their policymaking, so strong was the global influence of North Atlantic behavioral norms.

PERFORMANCE STANDARDS

Given the absence of adequate knowledge-based assets, late-industrializing countries have had to use subsidies in order to make mid-technology industries sufficiently profitable to attract investors to undertake a "three-pronged" investment: in plants of minimum efficient scale; in distribution networks; and in managerial and technological capabilities (Chandler 1990). Nevertheless, whereas subsidies may be a necessary condition for industrial expansion, they are not a sufficient one. Countries must also allocate subsidies in a disciplined manner, under what may be called a reciprocal control mechanism.

A control mechanism is a set of institutions that disciplines economic behavior based on a feedback of information that has been sensed and assessed. The control mechanism of the North Atlantic revolved around the principle of market competition, which disciplined economic actors and allocated resources efficiently. The "invisible hand" thus transformed the chaos and selfishness of free-market forces into general well-being (Mandeville [1714] 1924). The control mechanism of "the rest" revolved around the principle of reciprocity, which disciplined subsidy recipients and thereby minimized government failures. Subsidies were allocated to make manufacturing profitable—to convert moneylenders into financiers and importers into industrialists—but did not become giveaways. Recipients of subsidies were subjected to

monitorable performance standards that were redistributive in nature and result-oriented. The reciprocal control mechanism of "the rest" thus transformed the inefficiency and venality associated with government intervention into collective good.

In the cotton textile industries of East Asia, for example, the privilege of selling in the protected domestic market was made conditional on the fulfillment of export targets. Similarly, Brazilian industries had to match imports with an equivalent value of exports or comply with some sort of trade-balancing arrangement. In the automobile assembly and consumer electronics industries throughout "the rest," the right to sell locally under tariff protection was tied to the localization of parts and components manufacture, thereby contributing to the growth of national small and medium-sized vendors. A condition for receiving the soft loans of development banks was the employment of nonfamilial professionals in responsible positions, such as chief financial officer and quality control engineer. Development bank credit for heavy industries committed borrowers to contributing their own capital (under debt-equity ratio requirements) and constructing plants of minimum efficient scale. In India, price controls in the pharmaceutical industry encouraged cost-saving innovation and exporting in exchange for loosely enforced foreign patent laws. In Korea, a lucrative license to establish a general trading company depended on exports meeting criteria related to value, geographical diversity, and product complexity. As industries in "the rest" upscaled, performance standards increasingly pertained to research and development (R&D). Chinese science and technology enterprises were granted a special legal status in exchange for meeting performance standards with respect to technically trained employment and new products in total sales. Small Taiwanese firms were cherry-picked to locate in science parks, which obliged them to spend a certain percentage of their sales on R&D and employ advanced production techniques.

"The rest" rose, therefore, in conjunction with getting the control mechanism right. Whatever prices existed, whether as a consequence of market forces, technocratic choice, or political intervention, these were taken as given by policymakers concerned with industrial expansion. Around existing prices a set of rules and institutions was constructed to attract resources into manufacturing and make those resources conform with performance standards that were result-oriented.

TECHNO-STANDARDS: THE BRAZILIAN MIRACLE

In this section, we briefly review some of the performance standards stipulated by Brazil's development bank, BNDES. We do so to indicate the depth and breadth of measures to minimize "government failure" (see Amsden forthcoming for documentation). BNDES's techno-standards were stipulated in clients' contracts. All clients were required to reach a certain debt-equity ratio and liquidity ratio, thereby enjoining them to use a share of their own capital in any government-supported project. Clients were also prohibited from distributing their profits to stockholders of a controlling company. Companies were not allowed to make new investments of their own or change their fixed capital without BNDES approval. If a company required financial restructuring, it was forced by BNDES to divest itself of non-production-related assets.

Raw material requirements were designed first to develop natural resources and then to protect the environment. In the case of pulp and paper producers, BNDES made it mandatory for them to have a guaranteed source of local raw materials in order to minimize the need to import. They were also ordered to reforest a certain number of acres within a specified time period. In the iron and steel sector, a repeated contractual requirement was that clients had to provide the development bank with details about reforestation projects as well as figures on sales over time of pig iron in the domestic and foreign markets. If the bank did not accept a company's pig-iron-selling patterns, the company was obliged to renegotiate a contract with the bank. There were also instructions about meeting vegetable carbon pollution standards.

Loan conditions concerning administration, national equipment, technology, and other subjects tended to be firm-specific. The conditions were often detailed, intrusive, and formulated in such a way that a client had to comply before it received a loan. Among the bank's primary concerns were that firms be managed efficiently; that family-owned firms hire professionals in top administrative positions who were independent and not family retainers; that ownership of a firm not change during a loan period; that companies develop their own technology; and that firms source their engineers and machinery locally, whenever possible. In exchange for subsidies in the form of preferential credit, the BNDES thus imposed performance standards that forced its clients to be result-oriented.

THE FLEXIBILITY
OF WTO LAW

The question that faces countries that aspire to development today is whether or not, in an era in which the rules of the WTO govern trade, the approach adopted by "the rest" toward industrialization remains viable. Our affirmative answer to this question is based on the fact that, apart from performance standards in the form of export subsidies, there is nothing in WTO law that prevents other countries from promoting their nascent industries and subjecting them to performance standards.

The WTO, like the GATT, enables members to protect themselves from two types of foreign import competition: competition from aggregate imports that destabilizes their balance of payments (Article XVIII)[2] and competition that threatens their individual industries, due either to an import surge (Article XIX on temporary safeguards) or to an unfair trade practice (Article VI on anti-dumping and countervailing duties). The GATT placed no formal limits on the duration of a safeguard, whereas the WTO limits the duration of safeguards to eight years and improves their transparency.

Under the GATT, voluntary export restraints (VERs) were the premier safeguard. While they had been used most prevalently by North Atlantic countries, they had also been relied upon by "the rest" to protect strategic industries. Korea, for example, used a form of VER to ban imports of automobiles and electronics from Japan, its most serious competitor. This agreement (to which Japan was not even a consenting party) began to function in the 1980s and remained in effect until 1999, long enough to allow these industries to build up their knowledge-based assets (Taiwan and China were neither GATT members nor early signatories to the WTO and thus could protect these and other industries more openly, the electronics industry in Taiwan being a case in point). VERs are banned under the new WTO because they are "discriminatory": their effect varies by country. The advantage of eliminating VERs was that they are nontransparent. The disadvantage was that they serve a useful purpose, and "unless a superior means of serving that purpose is provided, then countries will find ways of their own to do it, and those ways are likely to be even worse" (Deardorff 1994, 57).

As predicted, countries in "the rest" have raised tariffs in lieu of using VERs or other cumbersome safeguards. Despite the fact that the level of tariffs fell after the Uruguay Round of trade negotiations, developing countries have bound many of their tariffs at fairly high levels (or have left them altogether unbound) as the starting point for their entry into the WTO. In the event of an import threat, they can raise their tariffs to these high levels and keep them there for at least eight years.

While developing countries have committed to a significant increase in their tariff bindings in the Uruguay Round (albeit at levels generally well above currently applied rates), they are still unlikely to invoke Article XIX (on safeguards) because they have both the unfettered right to raise tariffs to their bound levels and virtual carte blanche authority to impose new tariffs or quotas for balance of payments reasons. (Schott 1994, 113)

Raising tariffs in an emergency has become the recourse even of countries whose policy regime has been liberalized. For example, when a new free-trade Mexico confronted stiff foreign competition in 1995, tariffs were increased from the prevailing rates of 20 percent or less to 35 percent on clothing, footwear, and manufactured leather products if they were imported from nonpreferential sources. These sectors were already protected to a certain degree through anti-dumping duties and a relatively restrictive use of marking and origin requirements (Organization for Economic Cooperation and Development 1996, 106).

Marking and origin requirements are forms of non-tariff measures (NTMs) that restrict trade. In the Uruguay Round of negotiations, however, "achievements in the area of NTMs had been less than had been expected" (Raby 1994). Mexico's affiliation to the North Atlantic Free Trade Area (NAFTA), a free-trade agreement, is itself a form of managed trade that violates orthodox free-market principles. Members of free-trade agreements can protect themselves against all other countries except one another, and unlike members of a customs union, they need not have common external tariffs. Of 100 or so regional trade agreements reported to the WTO, by the year 2000 only one was approved (that between the Czech Republic and Slovakia). But the others, such as NAFTA, were not forbidden; WTO members simply agreed not to take action on them.

Anti-dumping duties have emerged as another way to protect trade in an emergency, supposedly when competitors engage in dumping, or selling below costs. In the late 1980s, the United States, the European Union, Australia, and Canada accounted for about four-fifths of all anti-dumping cases. By 1998, they accounted for barely one-third of the 225 cases opened in that year. Instead, the developing countries became leaders in anti-dumping initiatives, especially India (which also maintained almost permanent import surcharges to protect its balance of payments), Brazil, and Mexico. As other types of trade barriers decreased, anti-dumping suits rose in importance. Thus Argentina's steel industry, a showcase of restructuring, cut tariffs unilaterally to a "mere" zero to 24 percent. But when Brazilian steel started to flood the Argentine market in 1992, a tax on imports was "temporarily" increased by almost fourfold (Toulan and Guillen 1996).

In response to U.S. pressure, the Uruguay Round of negotiations was extended to trade in services, which includes foreign investment. The results of the Uruguay Round on trade-related investment measures (TRIMs), however, were "relatively modest" (Startup 1994, 189). They can retain trade-balancing stipulations and the 100 percent export requirement of export-processing zones, forms of export promotion. In 1995, for example, Brazil hammered out an agreement with the countries representing its major automobile assemblers. All consented to export cars whose value equaled the imports of parts and components that assemblers were bringing into Brazil. Countries that had notified the WTO of their local content or trade-balancing programs under a new 1998 TRIMs agreement include Argentina (automotive industry), Chile (automotive industry), India (pharmaceuticals and, in the case of dividend balancing, 22 consumer goods industries), Indonesia (selected products), Mexico (automotive industry), Malaysia (automotive industry), and Thailand (selected products) (United Nations Conference on Trade and Development 1998).

Thus safeguards of various sorts enable countries to buttress their balance of payments and sustain an industry under siege. Safeguards can also be used to protect an infant industry; eight years of protectionism are virtually guaranteed. The major risk is triggering unilateral trade sanctions under Section 301 of the U.S. Omnibus Trade Act, but not until an American industry is actually threatened by foreign competition are sanctions likely to be invoked (Low 1993).

Subsidies also receive relatively permissive treatment under WTO law. They fall into three categories. Some are prohibited (for exports and for domestic rather than imported inputs); others are actionable (they can be punished subject to proof of injury); and three are permissible (all heavily utilized in the North Atlantic). Permissible subsidies include those to promote R&D, regional development, and environmentalism. Any high-tech industry, therefore, can receive unbounded subsidies for the purpose of strengthening science and technology.

All in all, the liberal bark of the WTO appears to be worse than its bite. The neodevelopmental state can continue to subsidize new industries where necessary and to ensure that subsidies are result-oriented through the imposition of performance standards. Instead, the most coercive part of the new international economic order is informal. Coercion takes the form of political pressure by the North Atlantic on emerging economies to open their markets, most of all their financial markets, in light of the growing importance of financial services in the national incomes of North

Atlantic countries and the scale economies to which most financial services are now subject.

NATIONALISM AMID GLOBALISM

By 1990, all late-industrializing countries had become more global in orientation. Unilaterally, they had lowered their tariffs, as noted earlier. Voluntarily, they had become more courtly toward foreign investment, whether greenfield projects or cross-border mergers and acquisitions. Outward foreign investment by latecomers themselves had also increased, whether in manufacturing or distribution, whether regional in orientation (as in intra–Latin American investment) or international in scope (as in the outward foreign investment of Korea and Taiwan). Liberalization, when it occurred, largely left "the rest's" industries intact. Their much maligned import substitution sectors survived the test of freer markets.

Rather than deindustrialization, a more liberal global economy had divided "the rest" along lines of national ownership. China, India, Korea, and Taiwan—call them the "independents"—were pointed down a path of creating national leaders based on heavy investments in proprietary technologies and the construction of national innovation systems. Argentina and Mexico, by contrast, invested almost nothing in R&D (call them the "integrationists"). Instead, they had committed themselves to a long-term growth strategy based on close integration with North Atlantic companies, depending on spillovers from such foreign investors to satisfy their technology needs. Mexico's allegiance to NAFTA was emblematic of the integrationist approach. Brazil and Turkey fell somewhere in between these extremes, while Malaysia, Indonesia, and Thailand were still uncommitted to either strategy due to the relative immaturity of their industrial base.

The legal feasibility of an independent approach is suggested by Taiwan's buildup of science parks and Korea's G7 government-business national R&D projects ("G7" in recognition of Korea's aim to catch up with the seven most advanced industrial economies). To modernize science and technology, China combined science parks and national R&D projects and nurtured the rise of high-tech firms. The Beijing city government, for example, established a leading-edge R&D testing zone dubbed "Beijing's Silicon Valley"; it had exports in 1998 of $267 million (expected to have reached $1 billion by 2000). Lu writes, "In the enterprise zone, the government adopted institutional devices nested in the taxation process and investment process that redistributed resources to strategic sectors." Targeted industries were given tax breaks, special loans from state banks with below-market interest rates, and permission to exceed normal debt-equity ratio ceilings (Lu 1997, 234). On the other hand, the Chinese government also emphasized national R&D projects and the formation of "science and technology enterprises" that were neither state owned nor private. The State Planning Commission announced a policy to build approximately 100 national key laboratories (analogous to corporate central R&D laboratories) in selected fields of basic science in which Chinese capabilities already excelled. "Science and technology enterprises" were spun off by city, provincial, or national governments to commercialize the knowledge of public labs. Although these enterprises were nominally independent,

in granting [science and technology] enterprises a special legal status, the government obliged them to meet certain requirements (analogous to performance standards under a reciprocal control mechanism). These requirements included the percentage of technology personnel, the percentage of sales contributed by new products, the percentage of products exported, the allocation of retained earnings, etc. (Lu 1997, 235)

Thus, to a greater or lesser degree, the neodevelopmental state in China, as well as in India, Korea, and Taiwan, retained its condition-based form of subsidy allocation in the high-tech phase of industrial transformation.

Whether independent or integrationist, all latecomers defended liberalism in principle, with the possible exception of the Mahathir of Malaysia. Governments continued to intervene economically, but the prevailing discourse became free markets. The reasons for a disjunction between a continued buildup of national industries in practice and an intensified liberal rhetoric in principle are at once phenomenological and strategic.

As a phenomenon, globalism in the 1990s was predicated on foreign investment, direct (equity) and indirect (debt). Restructuring in late-comer countries increasingly became defined in the North Atlantic in these terms. Given international capital flows, company ownership supposedly did not matter for economic development. As a matter of fact, it probably did not matter in the case of highly advanced economies, where new foreign investment left average ownership more or less unchanged and merely altered ownership patterns at the margin. For newcomers, on the other hand, foreign investment could change the whole composition of a particular industry. Moreover, ownership vitally mattered for long-term growth. It mattered in terms of the formation of knowledge-based assets, the heart of modern capitalism, insofar as foreign firms did not, for the most part, undertake R&D locally. In the North Atlantic, most R&D activity, even by multinational firms, occurred at home: "far from being irrelevant, what happens in home countries is still very important in the creation of global technological advantage for even these most internationalised firms" (Patel and Vega 1999, 154).

The share of foreign firms in total R&D expenditure in Taiwan in 1995, for example, was estimated to be only 0.0009 percent (Republic of China 1996, 22). In Korea, it was roughly 0.1 percent in 1991 and 1997 (Korea Ministry of Science and Technology 1998). In Brazil, Chile, and Mexico, it was estimated to be nil, while in Argentina (in 1992) it approximated merely 2.0 percent (Alcorta and Peres 1998). In Malaysia, where multinationals dominated in the electronics sector, Malaysia's major export industry, they conducted "little or no long-term R&D into new materials, novel product designs, production technologies or advanced software" (although "most firms carried out substantial innovative activity related to near-term production process improvements") (Hobday 1999). In the Brazilian electronics industry, "what is significant is that all R&D efforts have come from state enterprises, institutions, and national firms, and only later from multinational corporations under policy pressure" (Sridharan 1996, 89). Even if multinationals invested in local learning in order to adapt the products they sold domestically to suit consumer tastes (as in Proctor & Gamble's customization of Pampers for hot, low-income climates), and even if they transferred advanced production skills, as in the Mexican automobile industry, research for entirely new products or processes at the world frontier was rare (Amsden forthcoming).

To acquire their own proprietary products and processes, latecomer countries had to rely on national firms to invest in their own R&D (broadly defined). As a vision, however, such nationalism was inimical to the ethos of globalism. Nationalism might also bring down the wrath of foreign firms and hence foreign governments. Private national companies themselves were of two minds about ownership. On the one hand, national ownership meant the appropriation of full entrepreneurial rents. On the other hand, takeover by foreign firms, real or potential, raised the value of nationally owned assets. Thus the alternative vision to integrationism, the buildup of national leaders and national skills, largely operated underground.

The advantage of operating underground is neglect by competitors, as just suggested; the benign neglect of the North Atlantic appears to have been critical in "the rest's" rise after World War II. The disadvantage of clandestine behavior is the absence of an explicit growth strategy to guide policymaking, to mobilize popular support, to justify operations, and to counterattack further external demands for policies that conflict with national interests. By the year 2000, therefore, the price of neglect has become steep and is on the rise.

Notes

1. "The rest" includes Argentina, Brazil, Chile, China, India, Indonesia, Korea, Malaysia, Mexico, Taiwan, Thailand, and Turkey. For the criteria used to select "the rest," mostly related to pre–World War II manufacturing experience, see Amsden forthcoming.

2. Article numbers refer to the rules of the GATT, since adopted by the WTO.

References

Alcorta, L. and W. Peres. 1998. Innovation Systems and Technological Specialization in Latin America and the Caribbean. *Research Policy* 26: 857-81.

Amsden, Alice H. Forthcoming. *The Rise of the Rest: Latecomers' Challenge to the West*. New York: Oxford University Press.

Chandler, Alfred D., Jr. 1990. *Scale and Scope: The Dynamics of Industrial Capitalism*. Cambridge, MA: Harvard University Press.

Deardorff, Alan V. 1994. Market Access. In *The New World Trading System: Readings*, ed. Organization for Economic Cooperation and Development. Paris: Organization for Economic Cooperation and Development.

Hobday, Michael. 1999. East vs. South East Asian Innovation Systems: Comparing OEM and TNC-Led Growth in Electronics. In *Technological Learning and Economic Development: The Experience of the Asian NIEs*, ed. Linsu Kim and Richard R. Nelson. New York: Oxford University Press.

Korea. Ministry of Science and Technology. 1998. *Science and Technology Annual*. Seoul: Ministry of Science and Technology.

Low, Patrick. 1993. *The GATT and U.S. Trade Policy*. New York: Twentieth Century Fund Press.

Lu, Q. 1997. Innovation and Organization: The Rise of New Science and Technology Enterprises in China. Ph.D. diss., Harvard University.

Mandeville, Bernard. [1714] 1924. *The Fable of the Bees: Or, Private Vicese, Publick Benefits*. London: Oxford University Press.

Organization for Economic Cooperation and Development, ed. 1996. *Trade Liberalization Policies in Mexico*. Paris: Organization for Economic Cooperation and Development.

Patel, P. and M. Vega. 1999. Patterns of Internationalisation of Corporate Technology: Location vs. Home Country Advantages. *Research Policy* 28: 145-55.

Raby, G. 1994. Introduction. In *The New World Trading System: Readings*, ed. Organization for Economic Cooperation and Development. Paris: Organization for Economic Cooperation and Development.

Republic of China. 1996. *Indicators of Science and Technology, Republic of China*. Taipei: Republic of China.

Schott, J. J. 1994. Safeguards. In *The New World Trading System: Readings*, ed. Organization for Economic Cooperation and Development. Paris: Organization for Economic Cooperation and Development.

Sridharan, E. 1996. *The Political Economy of Industrial Promotion: Indian, Brazilian, and Korean Electronics in Comparative Perspective, 1969-1994*. Westport, CT: Praeger.

Startup, J. 1994. An Agenda for International Investment. In *The New World Trading System: Readings*, ed. Organization for Economic Cooperation and Development. Paris: Organization for Economic Cooperation and Development.

Toulan, Omar and Mauro Guillen. 1996. *Internationalization: Lessons from Mendoza*. Cambridge and Mendoza: CIT/MIT.

United Nations Conference on Trade and Development. 1998. *Foreign Investment Report*. Geneva: United Nations Conference on Trade and Development.

ANNALS, *AAPSS*, **570**, July 2000

Coping with Globalization: A Suggested Policy Package for Small Countries

By FRANK B. RAMPERSAD

ABSTRACT: This article identifies the specific problems that small countries have to grapple with as a consequence of globalization. It argues that developing countries with limited population size have tended to give inadequate attention to the pressures that globalization places on their institutional structures, particularly with regard to finance. In discussing survival tactics for such nations, the article identifies three possible scenarios that might be adopted. It concludes that small states must play a much more active role than they have in the past in defending their interests in the emerging global economy.

The late Frank B. Rampersad was a senior civil servant in Trinidad and Tobago and in the Commonwealth Secretariat. He was also a prolific economist. His most recent publication was The New World Trade Order: Uruguay Round Agreements and Implications for CARICOM States *(1997).*

THE Commonwealth Secretariat has defined for the sake of their deliberations that any country of 1.5 million people is small. However, the definition of smallness, in the context of globalization, should be interpreted as a continuum, and countries with much larger populations could also be considered small.

Taken as a group, the economies of small countries grew at a slower pace than the high-income countries, particularly in the area of manufacturing, since low-income countries as commodity producers also suffered from declining barter terms of trade. This and the historical evidence indicate that, under the existing international economic regime, there is no basis for predicting a narrowing of the income gap that separates the rich countries from the poor.

The introductory note for the seminar on new initiatives to tackle the international financial turmoil, which the Inter-American Development Bank organized for Latin American countries in March 1999, stated that "international turmoil is wreaking havoc in all emerging markets. It threatens the social and economic progress achieved in the last decade and the political consensus for greater economic and financial progress, which underpins the progress" (Inter-American Development Bank 1999, 1).

This turmoil, along with sharply declining barter terms of trade for the developing countries and the inexorably widening disparities in income both between the rich and not rich countries and within the countries themselves, can ignite a process that can stoke a global fire of social conflict. Soros warns against the possibility of this taking place and the collapse of the global capitalist system (Soros 1998, chap. 6).

Such is the context in which the small developing countries must operate. This situation will continue until greater prudence and concern for human welfare assume the dominant position in the formulation of international economic policy and influence policy and action by the Bretton Woods institutions.

Developing countries as a group, and the small developing countries in particular, have in the past allowed themselves to be dictated to, with regard to the economic policy that they should pursue, by the large industrialized countries and the international financial community, especially the World Bank, the International Monetary Fund (IMF), the Inter-American Development Bank, and the Asian Development Bank. The first two of those institutions, in the words of Sachs (1998), have behaved with "stunning arrogance" toward the developing countries, and this is exemplified by the conditionalities that they place on borrowings from the developing world (4).

Such progress as these small countries have been able to achieve appears to have been almost fortuitous and automatic. It did not derive from their taking full control of their assets and liabilities and planning a definitive course of action for their development. This kind of apathy (or luxury) is no longer available to them; if they are to grapple with their own internal problems and derive benefit from the process of globalization, they must take greater control over their affairs or sink further into poverty.

Some of the specific problems with which countries, including small developing countries, have to grapple as a consequence of globalization include

— unstable exchange rates;
— extensive short-term debt by their private sectors;
— deteriorating terms of trade;
— rise of protectionism in some industrialized countries against manufactured goods in which developing countries have a comparative advantage, such as steel; and
— the raids of speculation against their currency.

Further, with the prospect of significant devaluation always before them, many individuals in developing countries, especially those that are small, seek safe havens for their funds by exporting national savings to the financial centers. Under globalization as dictated by the IMF, the national financial regulators cannot halt this outflow. This outflow is made worse by one of the fallouts of the movement of speculative funds, which is that the cost of borrowing to these small countries tends to increase as the speculators suck in much of the available savings, thus creating a growing gap between the need for long-term investment capital and its availability.

The package of problems and issues is formidable. Small developing countries are almost invariably unsuccessful in dealing with them

because of the requirement prescribed by the IMF (the policeman of globalization) that capital movements be granted uninhibited license to move funds from one country to another.

PRESSURES OF
GLOBALIZATION

In the face of this, and of the inadequacy of the regulatory institutional framework in most developing countries, it may appear perplexing that almost all developing countries adopted the components of the globalization process without significant protest. One exception appears to be India, which adopted a more measured approach to the removal of barriers, especially against capital imports and exports.

Carlos Diaz Alejandro (1995) had warned Latin America and the developing countries as a group that whereas the lowering of barriers to the transborder movement of goods and services was beneficial and should be encouraged (in that it could promote greater efficiency among national producers), complete freedom of movement of funds on capital could easily result in financial chaos. His advice was either not taken to heart or could not be acted upon. The adverse consequences have been serious, as the events in Southeast Asia, Argentina, and Brazil demonstrate.

The answer to the dilemma lies in the fact that powerful forces were aligned to push all developing countries in the direction of complete economic liberalization. Jeffrey Sachs encapsulated the forces arrayed against those who initially showed reluctance to liberalization when he stated that the underlying political basis for the process of globalization was that the United States, Europe, and Japan decided that they would define the parameters and requirements for cross-border trade in goods and services, especially in the area of telecommunication and financial services, and the IMF, through the conditionalities that it imposes, would ensure the installation of the necessary plumbing so that all countries would be brought in line with a new development paradigm (Sachs 1998, 1-4).

Small developing countries have tended to give inadequate attention to the pressures globalization would make on their institutional structures, especially in the area of finance, and to the institutional and human capability required to cope with the fallout of the globalization process. The result has been that they have become the flotsam and jetsam in the sea of economic change.

Besides, in the early 1990s, all developing countries, especially the small and the very poor ones, attached great importance to securing a multilateral agreement that would provide poor and small countries with improved access to the markets of the industrialized countries, particularly in textiles and garments, in which they have a comparative advantage. They therefore took the position that they should yield to the pressures from the industrialized countries in order to secure their agreement to reduce barriers against agricultural products and light manufacturers. The superior course of action for the small countries would have been to adopt a more measured approach to the dismantling of economic controls, in much the same way as India has done.

The Multilateral Trade Agreement, which countries signed in Marrakech in the mid-1990s (and which was a watershed event in the globalization process), is turning out to be less advantageous to the small countries than they thought it would be as new and unexpected forms of protection are emerging all the time. In addition, the environment is beginning to be cited by the industrialized countries as a reason to prevent the free movement of goods, especially wood and wood products, steel, and certain chemicals. Floating exchange rates introduced in the early 1970s also add new uncertainties to economic management in the small countries. In the meantime, the one superpower is bestriding the world, demanding adherence to the letter of the Uruguay Round Agreement (even where this would, as in the case of bananas, destroy the very foundation of the economies of small countries) while itself resorting to protectionism to such an extent that it has caused concern among some of its own senior economic managers.

The standard prescription of the World Bank for its borrowing members used to be (and, to some extent, still is) that they should adopt an IMF program, reduce public expenditure, and devalue the currency. Under certain circumstances, this prescription may work; however, it is equally likely to kill the patient as it transfers the burden of adjustments to the poor and makes the distribution of income more unequal.

SURVIVAL TACTICS

Small developing countries must now accept the need to take their own action to avoid economic malaise and social distress. But the action they take must include the introduction of a durable safety net if they are to avoid a breakdown of the social order. In every case, they have to test the measures that they contemplate against the yardstick that acceptable development cannot be anti-people but about people and for people. They have to take to heart the awareness that developing countries that have made provision for the poor and maintained some control over the movement of capital have fared much better economically than those that have not. The action that was taken by Chile in controlling the movement of funds, in promoting economic growth, and in giving attention to the needs of the poor provides useful guidance for small countries to follow.

Many analysts (and government officials) are convinced that the principal preoccupation of the Bretton Woods institutions has been to safeguard the integrity of the private commercial banks (Soros 1998, 121). This preoccupation has, on occasion, been extended to the point where the IMF "persuaded" its debtor country to take over the credit extended by the private international commercial banks—failing which the banks would have been wiped out, as happened in the case of the Baring Brothers financial institutions. This requirement by the IMF put further pressure on the people in debtor countries—witness the action taken by the IMF with respect to Korea, Thailand, and Indonesia.

A number of developing countries and nongovernmental organizations, including U.N. bodies such as the United Nations Development Programme, have also found that the prescriptions that the World Bank and the IMF impose are not adequately helpful to small countries. They are, therefore, actively searching for alternative systems that will be more beneficial to small countries in this era of globalization.

These bodies recognize, as do all analysts, that globalization will not go away. Out of these considerations, which have largely focused on reining in the international financial system, three scenarios seem to be occupying center stage. The small countries must choose which of these they will support.

THE FIRST SCENARIO

The first scenario has been the one put forward by Jeffrey Sachs (1998). He proposed the following:

1. A Group of Sixteen (G16) in the United Nations should be considered. It would include adequate representation from the G8 countries and the very large developing countries and also provide for representation from countries that are small.

2. The G16 would discuss and agree on the need for, and the elements to be included in, international monetary reform, especially the reformation of the Bretton Woods

institutions. Such discussions may also be examined from time to time, and member countries may agree on an approach to making additional distributions of special drawing rights, at least to the countries that need additional liquidity (this is a function now discharged by the Interim Committee). The G16 would also agree on a program of debt cancellation for the poor countries that are heavily in debt.

3. It would actively stimulate the search for ways to persuade donor countries to increase their international aid effort to reach the U.N.-agreed target of 0.7 percent of gross national product; much of this additional aid should flow to poor countries through regional agencies such as the Southern African Development Coordination Conference, the Association of Southeast Asian Nations, and, in Latin America, Mercosur, an arrangement that would bring peer pressure to bear on delinquent countries to ensure that aid is well utilized and that the conditions attaching to the aid package are adhered to.

4. The World Bank would become a development bank, focusing its attention on markets, market identification, and technology. Many of the lending functions that the World Bank now undertakes will be transferred to the regional development banks, which, because of their proximity to the borrowing countries, are likely to formulate their conditionalities so that violence will not be done to the overall development thrust of borrowing countries and borrowing regions (in the case of regional projects).

5. Individual developing countries will need to adopt a more self-reliant stance in guiding the development of their economies; in particular, these countries must undertake their own monitoring of their private sectors and banks and not rely solely on the international financial community for advice.

THE SECOND SCENARIO

The second scenario, which is now being discussed in Latin America and the Caribbean, would seek to arrive at an agreement between geographically proximate countries on the de facto pooling of their external reserves in order to withstand large movements of speculative capital of the kind that some countries in the region have experienced and that have made it extremely difficult to manage the exchange rate. So far, three possible areas have been mentioned in the literature. The first is a grouping of most of the Western Hemisphere countries; the U.S. dollar will be the currency of settlement for this area. The second is the Euro-African area, in which Europe, Africa, and such other countries as are willing to join will pool their resources to cope with speculative capital flows. The euro will be the common currency for this area. The third area is the Asian-Japanese, which would involve countries of Asia along with Japan. The yen will be the common currency.

This second scenario appears to have been under serious discussion only in Latin America so far. It has not yet addressed the question of the reform of the Bretton Woods system, nor has it yet focused attention on increasing international economic assistance.

One of the major unknowns in the proposal is the price that the country of the common currency will exact from the participants to be their de facto lender of last resort. What appears to be certain is that, at least in political and policy terms, there will be a significant price to pay.

THE THIRD SCENARIO

The third scenario seeks to correct deficiencies in existing international policy and international infrastructure for promoting economic and social development on the global scale.

The proposal is contained in the report of the international Commission on Global Governance (1995, 156-57). It proffers the establishment of an apex body in the United Nations—an Economic Security Council (ESC)—that would focus global attention on economic affairs and the human condition worldwide, but especially in small poor countries, in much the same way that the present Security Council operates in its dealings with conflicts between nations, and conflicts within countries, that are deemed by the Security Council to warrant its intervention.

The functions proposed for the ESC are essentially "to continuously assess the overall state of the world economy and the interaction between major policy areas." The functions would include the following:

— to provide a long-term strategic policy framework in order to promote stable, balanced, and sustainable development;
— to secure consistency between policy goals of the major international organizations particularly the main multilateral institutions (Bretton Woods institutions and the World Trade Organization), while recognizing their distinct roles; and
— to promote consensus building between governments on the evaluation of the international economic system while providing a global forum for some of the new forces in the world economy such as the regional organizations.

The ESC would also undertake the technical studies needed to garner for the U.N. system the income that now resides in the international commons—the air, sea, outerspace, and the rest of the natural environment—and other sources of income that have periodically surfaced, for example, the Tobin tax.

The ESC would consist of some 25 members; it would have very little of its own bureaucracy and would meet at least once a year. It would draw its membership on a constituency basis from the G8, the regional commis-

sions, India, and China, with due recognition being given to small countries. No group would exercise a veto
power.

IMPLICATIONS OF
SURVIVAL TACTICS FOR
DEVELOPING COUNTRIES

The proposal by Sachs (the first
scenario) is very attractive for small
countries. It addresses some of the
principal economic problems that
small countries face in this area of
globalization and calls for little
structural change to the existing
U.N. edifice. Its basic elements therefore are not likely to run up against
the obstacles that the G8 countries
have traditionally raised to prevent
reform of the U.N. system, which was
established at the San Francisco conference more than fifty years ago.

However, as proposed, the G16
will not be an apex institution in the
U.N. system but merely a special
grouping of countries. Discussions
relating to the human condition are
therefore likely to be filtered as to
substance as they move up the decision-making chain, ending with very
little qualitative change. This was
the experience of the New International Economic Order and the
Cancún summit during the first half
of the 1970s.

The proposal does, however, cover
all the principal issues involved in
the globalization process, with the
exception of processes to mobilize the
additional resources required to
finance recovery from natural disas-
ters and to mount meaningful efforts

in addressing some of the world's ills,
such as famine, AIDS, desertification, river blindness, and loss of
biodiversity (the Caribbean is particularly vulnerable to hurricanes and
earthquakes, which, because of the
small size of these countries, destroy
much of the economic base of affected
countries). The reference to international economic assistance goes only
part of the way to be traversed.

With regard to the second scenario, the intention is to establish
much larger pools of foreign
exchange to deal with the issue of
speculative currency movements and
the associated instability in
exchange rates. The proposal does
not deal with the international decision-making machinery, nor does it
address frontally the serious weakness in the structure and policies of
international financial institutions,
notably, the IMF and the World
Bank.

Perhaps the area in the second
scenario that will cause the most difficulty among the small developing
countries, most of which have only
recently emerged from colonialism,
is the fact that the proposal smacks of
the introduction of imperialism in
new clothes. The experience of the
recent past in countries that are still
struggling to secure their political
independence and the traditional
jealousies that still affect relations
between states in Asia make it
unlikely that the proposal will find
easy acceptability. There is also
likely to be difficulty over the political and financial price that borrowing participants will have to pay.

With regard to the third scenario, it is useful to recall that the developing countries have been treated with "stunning arrogance" by the Bretton Woods institutions (Sachs 1998, 4). The establishment of a new apex body within the United Nations that can, as of right, receive reports from the institutions and debate them at high political levels ensures that the special problems that small countries experience will at least be given a hearing by the world body.

The establishment of the ESC as an apex body within the U.N. system will also give the international community a powerful tool with which to formulate action that would bring significant benefit to the small countries. The focus of such attention should be the improvement in the quality of the human condition in the poor countries, and priority attention should be given to reducing the proportion of the population falling below the poverty line.

In order to be an effective agent in its fight against poverty and disease, however, the United Nations should increase directly the flow of resources to its specialized agencies to enable them to take and guide action in improving the human and physical capital in poor countries, thus improving the opportunity available to them to emerge from the conditions that now trap them in their present state.

This is a strong argument in favor of an increase in international economic assistance, and Sachs and others are on firm ground in attaching high priority to encouraging donor countries to advance rapidly toward the U.N. target for international aid of 0.7 percent of gross national product. However, much more than urging is required. Donor countries are claiming that they are suffering from "aid fatigue." Therefore the probability of an early reversal of the trend of declining international aid budgets, and a shift in such budgets to infrastructure projects in individual or groups of poor countries, does not appear to be a durable expectation in the foreseeable future. Besides, small countries must adopt or support systems that would reduce their mendicant role and seek to replace alms by payment for services rendered.

This establishes an important task for the ESC, namely, to embark upon early studies on the modalities of mobilizing the income that remains to be tapped in the international commons, for the introduction of the Tobin tax, and for the imposition of a levy on sales of arms as a surrogate for the peace dividend. A listing of these potential sources of revenues for the United Nations, which would be collected by the Trusteeship Council working under an enlarged mandate—which, in fact, would have beneficial spin-offs in terms of environmental enhancement—is recorded in a 1995 report issued by the Commission on Global Governance.

The resources would enable the United Nations and its agencies to take sustained action against problems that require the collective action of more than one country and that under prevailing circumstances now fester and become worse every year. They would also permit action against problems such as desertification, river blindness, AIDS, other diseases such as malaria, and reduction in biodiversity.

The magnitude of the task involved in devising feasible programs for mobilizing these sources of international funds and the prioritizing of their use justify the existence of the ESC. Small countries will naturally be among the principal beneficiaries, and the programs to which the resources might be put would be a valuable counterpoise to the difficulties inherent in the globalization process. Indeed, the ESC provides perhaps the only vehicle that the small countries can use in order to influence for their benefit the shape and form of international economic action.

The proposal must, however, overcome two major obstacles. First, even at the best of times, the industrialized countries show great unwillingness to give up any part of the total control that they now exercise over the United Nations and other international bodies. Second, it would be difficult to secure international agreement in a short period to establish the ESC and enable the U.N. system to tap into the potential sources of revenues that exist in the international commons.

However, small developing countries have faced these problems in the past, for example, in the Law of the Sea negotiations. It is difficult to see what alternatives they have except working through the U.N. system.

Small developing countries must also press their case more vigorously than they have done in the past for a special regime to be applied to them in international trade and finance. The U.S. argument of "no free riders" is nonsense when it is made to apply to these countries, which have limited opportunity for diversification of their production base and encounter severe obstacles in seeking access through migration to the industrialized countries, where employment opportunities exist, and the resulting extreme volatility in their incomes.

In trade, small countries should be given much longer periods to adjust their tariff levels. In finance, they should not be brought under the graduation rules that the multilateral lending agencies apply.

In this group of small countries, small island economies (42 of the 49 small countries identified by the Joint Commonwealth Secretariat/ World Bank Task Force on Small States [1999] are islands) face particularly intractable problems. They have to cope with long distances from their markets and with the full list of natural hazards—hurricanes, cyclones, sea-level rises, volcanoes, earthquakes, and tidal waves. Only the most unreasonable among the industrialized countries would fail to recognize this special category of countries.

In the final analysis, globalization is here to stay; it will not go away. The task is to introduce changes that will optimize the quantum and the distribution of the benefit and minimize the cost. There is no other way. It used to be said that when the U.S. economy sneezed, Europe caught a cold, and the Third World would go down with pneumonia. The events in Southeast Asia and Mexico and their impact on the economies of North America and Europe seem to harbinger a change in the transmission mechanism in that these large countries are now beginning to feel the negative impact of the collapse of countries at the periphery. All countries therefore—those that are rich and those that are poor, those that are large and those that are small—have an interest in strengthening global economic management and putting an end to the growing gap in incomes that separates the rich from the poor countries. Small countries can no longer wait for the signal of readiness for change from the large rich countries, however. They must prepare to bite the bullet now.

References

Commission on Global Governance. 1995. *Our Global Neighbourhood*. Available at http://www.cgg.ch/contents.htm.

Diaz Alejandro, Carlos. 1995. Transborder Barriers. *IDB America*, July.

Inter-American Development Bank. 1999. Introduction to the Seminar "New Initiatives to Tackle International Financial Turmoil." Annual meeting of the Inter-American Development Bank, 14 Mar., Paris, France.

Joint Commonwealth Secretariat/World Bank Task Force on Small States. 1999. *Small States: A Composite Vulnerability Index*. Available at http://www.worldbank.org/lac/smstates/vulindex.com.

Sachs, Jeffrey. 1998. Making It Work. *Economist*, 12 Sept. Available at http://www.economist.com.

Soros, George. 1998. *The Crisis of Global Capitalism: Open Society Endangered*. New York: Public Affairs.

Globalization and Justice

By JON MANDLE

ABSTRACT: In an era of globalization, basic institutional structures that shape our daily interactions transcend national boundaries. According to the institutional approach to social justice favored by John Rawls, we have a special obligation to ensure that the basic terms of these interactions are just. Two recent proposals would help accomplish this: a global resource dividend and a Tobin tax. Both of these proposals work within markets. Some have objected that globalization will lead to the homogenization of previously diverse cultures. However, although globalization will increase the pace of cultural and social change, the path of these developments is unpredictable.

Jon Mandle is an assistant professor of philosophy at the University at Albany–State University of New York. He is the author of What's Left of Liberalism? An Interpretation and Defense of Justice as Fairness *(2000). His articles have appeared in the* Canadian Journal of Philosophy, Social Theory and Practice, *the* Journal of the History of Philosophy, Socialist Review, *and* Challenge, *among others.*

S INCE the publication of John Rawls's *A Theory of Justice* in 1971, political philosophers have enthusiastically embraced the normative investigation of justice. Until the 1990s, however, most political philosophers, with a few notable exceptions, confined their studies to issues of domestic justice. Rawls himself develops principles for the evaluation of the institutions of "the basic structure of society," and therefore in *A Theory of Justice*, he does not consider "except in passing the justice of the law of nations and of relations between states" (7-8).[1] Specifically, Rawls makes the idealizing assumption that the society for which he is devising principles of justice is "more or less self-sufficient" (4). It has been only in the last decade or so that political philosophers have become increasingly concerned with issues of nationalism and international justice.

For some critics, raising the question of international relations is already assuming too much, namely, the continued existence of nation-states in something like their present form. They argue that morality requires that we work toward a single global state (see Nielsen 1988). Since Kant, however, most cosmopolitans have attempted to articulate a conception of justice that is compatible with the existence of a plurality of states (Kant 1983). Martha Nussbaum, for example, has argued recently that "the worthy moral ideals of justice and equality" are best served by a cosmopolitanism in which we "give our first allegiance to no mere form of government, no temporal power, but to the moral community made up by the humanity of all human beings" (Nussbaum 1996a, 7). It is crucial to her argument, however, that this ideal does not require that we "give up our special affections and identifications" (9). Indeed, she claims, "None of the major thinkers in the cosmopolitan tradition denied that we can and should give special attention to our own families and to our own ties of religions and national belonging" (Nussbaum 1996b, 135). But how can a cosmopolitan who believes in some form of the universality of morality also believe that any special concern is permitted for oneself, one's family, or one's nation?

Liberal theories of justice, such as that of Rawls, suggest one answer (see Mandle 2000). These theories start from the assumption that there is a wide diversity of reasonable conceptions of the good life—a wide diversity of religions, cultures, worldviews. When individuals hold conflicting, yet reasonable conceptions of the good, they are likely to disagree concerning which ends are worth pursuing and how they should be pursued. The principles of justice are standards to be used in evaluating the institutional mechanisms that will resolve these conflicts fairly. Just individuals will be motivated to uphold and follow fair mechanisms of adjudication even when abandoning them might allow them better to pursue their more particular goals. Liberal theories of justice, therefore, recognize a certain complexity in the structure of our ends. They force us to distinguish between the goal of maintaining fair background conditions, on the one hand, and the pursuit of specific ends within those structures, on the other. They postulate, that is, a split between the right and the good, and they aim to provide an account only of what is right—as defined by the principles of justice. This does not mean, however, that they denigrate the importance of the good. Rather, recognizing the diversity of reasonable conceptions of the good, liberal theories of justice aim to allow people to affirm the way of life they find most compelling. To be sure, any conception of justice will rule out certain conceptions of the good as impermissible. But it is crucial to the liberal approach that these principles not limit conceptions of the good too narrowly.

The choice of an institutional scheme often has predictable moral consequences at a macro level, even if the specific details cannot be anticipated.[2] Typically, however, no single individual is able to bring about the implementation of a full institutional scheme. It might seem, then, that an emphasis on institutional justice would tend to absolve individuals of responsibility for the predictable consequences of the selection of one institutional scheme rather than another. On the contrary, however, this approach shows how people can be collectively responsible for an unjust institution even if within those institutions they do not act in objectionable ways. It is true that most of our decisions and actions take place against a relatively stable background system of institutions. We are rarely in a position as individuals to transform basic social institutions. Yet, as Rawls (1971) points out, "the social system is not an

unchangeable order beyond human control but a pattern of human action" (102). Social institutions are sustained, transformed, or abolished by the actions and attitudes of people collectively.

Although it is clearly important, institutional justice is not the only component of morality. There are noninstitutional duties that we owe to one another simply by virtue of our common humanity. Thus Rawls (1971) observes that there are natural duties to refrain from torture and murder and a duty to help others when they are "in need or jeopardy, provided that one can do so without excessive risk or loss to oneself" (114). These duties apply to us regardless of our institutional relationships and do not depend on our having acted to bring these duties upon ourselves by making a contract or promise, for example.

To illustrate this, consider the example of the deprivation associated with poverty in poor countries. In 1998, the United Nations reported that "around 1.3 billion people [in developing countries] live on less than $1 a day" (88). This extreme poverty has predictable results. Thomas Pogge reports, for example, that "some 3 million children annually die of simple diarrhea because their parents cannot obtain a 15-cent oral rehydration pack" (1998a, 484, n. 30) and that "some 20 million . . . die each year of starvation or easily curable diseases" (1998b, 501). The extent of the responsibility of those of us who are relatively wealthy to avert these preventable calamities is a matter of controversy. Some have argued that the natural duty of mutual aid is strong enough to justify a duty to provide assistance to avert these moral catastrophes, while others reply that we may properly exclude from moral concern those who are not part of our political communities (cf. Singer 1972 and Rorty 1996). But most people agree that whatever our level of responsibility for averting disasters, we have a greater responsibility for not bringing them about ourselves: we have a duty to prevent others from being tortured, but we have a stronger duty not to engage in torture ourselves; we have a duty to help people who are starving, but we have a stronger duty not to bring about their starvation. If we have a strong duty not to impose torture or starvation on others, it follows that we have a strong duty to ensure that the institutions for which we are collectively responsible do not bring about torture or starvation. The institutional approach to justice shows how we have a strong duty not to impose unjust institutions on others.[3]

As shown earlier, Rawls assumes that the institutions to which the principles of justice are applied are within a single society. But globalization means that this assumption is becoming less and less plausible. Just as we have a requirement to ensure that the background institutions within which we interact with our fellow citizens are fair, so, too, we must not impose unjust background institutions on people in foreign countries. This extends beyond the natural duty to assist others in need. And as we have seen, the current system results in the extreme impoverishment and preventable deaths of many millions of people. Certainly, other systems might be worse, but if we can identify arrangements that would be likely to do better, we have a strong moral obligation to help bring them about.

In our current global institutional scheme, land is divided up more or less exhaustively among countries. Within its territory, each country has more or less exclusive control of the land and resources. Each sets up its own rules and decides what resources are to be held in common, the type and level of taxation, which environmental regulations to enforce, whether squatters' rights will be recognized, and innumerable other matters. This entire system of territorial sovereignty is itself a social arrangement that depends on our recognition of the authoritative decisions of each country over its land. We can imagine many alternative arrangements—for example, one in which all of the land and resources of the world are commonly held. When someone claims an exclusive property right, we might reply with Rousseau, "You are lost if you forget that the fruits are everyone's and the Earth no one's" (Rousseau 1986, 170, pt. II, par. 1). In fact, a standard project for Enlightenment philosophers was to assume that collective possession of the earth was the normative baseline, so to speak, and to attempt to show how exclusive property claims could possibly be justified from that basis (see Locke 1980, chap. 5; Kant 1996, chap. 2, sec. 1).

Property rights are held against other people, not against things. Among the many consequences of our current scheme is the fact that it prevents people who are starving (or their representatives) from taking the resources that would save their lives. The crucial point is that the existence of our current scheme of international property rights is a system for which we are collectively responsible. That is, it is not simply the case that we are letting many millions of people starve; rather, our enforcement of this particular institutional scheme predictably leads to their deaths. If we have a strong duty not to impose starvation on people, we have a strong duty to do what we can to change the institutional structures that lead to this result.

Of course, this analysis depends on the possibility of an institutional scheme that does not lead to these results. Against a scheme that completely eliminates private property, consider two familiar arguments in favor of some form of private property and market mechanisms. First, there is good reason to believe that reliance on markets is often more efficient than feasible alternatives. Second, markets allow for the decentralization of economic power. Participants in markets need only agree on the mechanisms of the transaction, so they can pursue a diversity of goals without requiring that others share their ends. Instead of making a single, binding political decision, markets allow multiple decisions in accordance with what people are able and willing to pay. Markets relieve individuals and groups of the burden of reaching broad consensus on values and the ends to which resources are to be devoted.

Certainly, there are many reasons that market relations should not characterize all of our interactions. As Rawls (1971) observes, "Since the market is not suited to answer the claims of need, these should be met by a separate arrangement" (277). Furthermore, for most people, it is important that they interact with some people on the basis of deeply held, shared values. But in an age of globalization, people will more and more interact with those who do not share their conception of the good. Markets facilitate such interactions without undermining the diversity of ends that individuals and groups may pursue. To be sure, the goals of efficiency and the decentralization of economic power do not exhaust the demands of justice. Still, other things being equal, if one system is more efficient and if, by decentralizing economic decisions, it allows a greater diversity of ends to be satisfied, these are powerful arguments in its favor. These considerations in favor of markets are often compelling, but the advantages they identify are not automatic or inevitable. Markets must be kept competitive through the regulation of monopolies, and property must be widely dispersed if individuals are to be able to exert decentralized, market power.

These considerations apply in both the domestic and international contexts. Most economists agree that international markets in goods and services lead to greater efficiency than various forms of protectionism do. International trade pressures countries to specialize in those areas in which they have a comparative advantage over others. This leads to greater efficiency in production. Trade, then, is a non-zero-sum game that works to increase aggregate wealth. Despite the appalling poverty cited earlier, there is little doubt that economic development, encouraged by the process of globalization, has succeeded in relieving poverty to a degree unprecedented in human history. The same 1998 United Nations report cited previously also informs us,

A child born today in a developing country can expect to live 16 years longer than a child born 35 years ago. Developing countries have covered as much distance in human development during the past 30 years as the industrial world managed over more than a century. . . . Their infant mortality rate has been more than halved since 1960. . . . Combined primary and secondary school enrol[l]ment has more than doubled. (19)

Since it leads to an increase in aggregate wealth, free trade is often defended in frankly utilitarian terms. But an increase in the wealth of a society is not necessarily shared by all of its members. In particular, when an aggregate increase in wealth results from specialization and modernization in production, there will usually be both winners and losers. Justice requires that society take steps to ensure that those disadvantaged in the short term by these changes are able to participate fully in the new economic conditions. This requires a significant social commitment to training and education, as well as a social safety net. If a society is unwilling to make such a commitment, justice suffers since the gains for some come at the expense of others. Fortunately, when such changes lead to an aggregate gain in wealth, the society will be in a better position to undertake these commitments. Whether it has the political will to do so, of course, is another matter. As with the domestic case, international markets require institutional backgrounds that must be assessed from the point of view of justice. A defense of globalization is not necessarily a defense of laissez-faire policies. As James Tobin (1998) has written recently, "Effective internationalization is not unmitigated laissez faire" (15).

TWO PROPOSALS

I now want briefly to discuss two proposals that are intended to make the international order more just by stabilizing the global economy over the long run and providing the means by which dire poverty might be alleviated more immediately. The first is what Thomas Pogge (1998b) calls a "global resource dividend" (GRD). Instead of granting countries virtually unlimited, libertarian property rights over their resources or establishing collective ownership, Pogge suggests something closer to the idea of preferred stock. This would reflect our collective stake in the earth's resources. Many variations are possible, but the basic idea is that each country would continue to choose whether or not to extract natural resources found in its territory, but if it does so, it will be required to pay a 1 percent dividend on their value:

Under my proposal, the Saudis, for example, would continue fully to control their crude oil reserves. They would not be required to pump oil or to allow others to do so. But if they did choose to do so, they would be required to pay a linear dividend on any crude oil extracted, whether for their own use or for sale abroad. (Pogge 1998b, 511)

A GRD would be an important source of revenue to help those in the most dire need. Pogge (1998b) estimates that

a 1 percent GRD would currently raise about $300 billion annually. This is equivalent to roughly $250 per person in the poorest quintile, vastly more than their current average annual income. Such an amount, if well targeted and effectively spent, would make a phenomenal difference to them even within a few years. (512)

Countries that extract natural resources would be unlikely to absorb the full cost of a GRD. Rather, they would pass on a considerable part of their cost to the consumers of their resources in the form of higher prices. Pogge estimates that a $2.00 per barrel GRD on crude oil extraction alone (approximately $0.0475 per gallon) would generate approximately $50 billion annually (512).[4] Depending on the elasticity of demand for petroleum, there would be a decrease in the consumption. (This is why producers would still have to bear some of the cost of the GRD.) We very well might have independent grounds to support such a result since it would "encourage conservation and environmental protection for the sake of our own and future generations" (Pogge 1998b, 513). Consumers of petroleum—both indi-

viduals and firms—would have incentives to substitute more renewable and less polluting alternative forms of energy.

It is very difficult to anticipate the full economic consequences of a GRD. On the one hand, it would raise production costs and therefore would tend to contribute to inflation. Furthermore, increased production costs could squeeze profits and lead to stagnation in economic activity, perhaps even to a recession. These consequences would be especially harmful to the poor, as unemployment would increase along with inflation. On the other hand, as Pogge (1998b) points out, "the funds raised through the GRD scheme do not, after all, disappear: They are spent by, and for the benefit of, the global poor and thereby generate effective market demand that spurs economic activity" (533, n. 30). Indeed, one might argue that the GRD would actually increase economic activity since it would transfer wealth from the rich to the poor, who have a higher propensity to consume. This is especially true of the very poor, who would spend virtually all of their additional income on basic necessities such as food and medicine. Such a transfer of wealth, therefore, would likely result in a net increase in demand, perhaps offsetting the change in the aggregate supply function. The combined results of these changes are extremely difficult to anticipate. Therefore, there is inevitably some uncertainty in the implementation of such a program. Still, it is worth recalling that in 1993, when the United States raised the federal tax on gasoline by $0.043 per gallon to $0.183 per gallon, the change was barely felt in the economy.

Leaving the GRD, let us consider now a second proposal. Currently, more than $1.3 trillion changes hands daily in foreign currency markets (Tobin 1996, xvi). (This is not to be confused with direct foreign investment, when a company invests resources for production in a foreign country.) According to an analyst from the Federal Reserve Bank of San Francisco, "It is estimated that 40% of all [such currency] transactions involve round trips of fewer than three days" (Kasa 1999). There is evidence that "80% of foreign exchange transactions involve round trips of seven days or less" (Tobin 1996, xii). It is widely believed that these short-term currency transactions exacerbated the Asian financial crisis in 1997. For almost 30 years, James Tobin has argued for a small tax on such currency transactions. The economic results of a Tobin tax seem more predictable than a GRD. Such a tax would have three important consequences. First, because it would be levied on each transaction, it would be felt most heavily by short-term speculators. For Tobin (1996), "the essential property of the transactions tax—the beauty part—[is] that this simple, one-parameter tax would automatically penalize short-horizon round trips, while negligibly affecting the incentives for commodity trade and long-term capital investments" (xi). Thus, while allowing currencies to float, the tax would reduce short-term volatility.

Second, Tobin's original reason for proposing the tax was as a means to allow countries to retain some degree of macroeconomic control over their own economies:

To preserve a local currency with residual monetary sovereignty, some friction in international financial institutions and markets needs to be retained. . . . The new global financial system should be able to contribute to development without rendering central banks impotent or whole currencies obsolete. . . . Flows of capital to developing countries should preferably take the form of fixed direct investment or equity. (Tobin 1998, 7)

The idea is that central banks will better be able to respond to local economic conditions and needs.

Finally, like the GRD, a Tobin tax would generate considerable revenue that could be used to relieve the most extreme poverty and encourage development. Even if it were substantially successful in reducing short-term currency speculation, it would still be likely to generate large sums, comparable in size to that generated by a GRD. Estimates vary greatly, but one fairly conservative assessment, figuring substantial exceptions, evasions, and a 40 percent reduction in currency transactions, projects that a 0.1 percent Tobin tax would generate $54 billion annually.[5] Although neither a Tobin tax nor a GRD currently has extensive support, it is significant that on 23 March 1999, the Canadian Parliament passed a (largely symbolic) resolution supporting such a tax.

It is important to note that both the Tobin tax and the GRD would work through, rather than replace, markets. A Tobin tax does not peg currency prices at fixed levels; a GRD allows countries to determine the extent of their resource extraction. Both systems specify property rights in such a way that market institutions would be geared to help those who would otherwise be left behind. Clearly, then, both of these arrangements aim not to arrest globalization but to ensure that it is more just and that its benefits are more widely shared than they would be under a laissez-faire regime.

CULTURE

Both Pogge and Tobin fundamentally accept global economic integration and look for ways to make it more just. Both of their proposals would achieve increased levels of well-being for the least advantaged through institutions that rely on market mechanisms. For some critics, however, globalization and its reliance on markets is precisely the problem. The real threat of globalization, these critics claim, is of a homogenized, shallow, inauthentic culture. For Benjamin Barber (1995), for example, "small stories of local tragedy and regional genocide" are not as threatening, at least in the long run, as globalization's "homogenization [that] is likely to establish a macropeace that favors the triumph of commerce and its markets" (19-20). Barber's suggestion that homogenization is a greater threat than "regional genocide" is no aberration. In reply to Thomas Friedman's argument (1999) that globalization will make war less likely, Barber does not exactly reject Friedman's claim. Rather, he denigrates

the importance of peace if it is accompanied by what he takes to be consumer culture:

But peace is not democracy. McWorld's denizens are consumers and clients whose freedom consists of the right to buy in markets they cannot control and whose identity is imposed on them by a consumerism they scarcely notice. Palestinians and Zulus and North Ireland Catholics will be freer to do business in and outside of their stabilized countries, but they will not necessarily be any freer. (223)

There is no doubt that the introduction of market mechanisms is often a powerful force that changes traditional cultures and ways of life. Furthermore, it is clear that not all changes brought about through markets are good. But for several reasons, it is often a distortion to complain about the homogenizing tendency of globalization.[6] First of all, some forms of homogenization are to be welcomed. For example, fewer and fewer countries around the world engage in official torture. Indeed, although the United States continues to buck the trend, fewer and fewer countries engage in capital punishment. Nobody should lament the end of unjust practices even though they bring previously divergent ways of life closer together.

Second, while there is little doubt that globalization leads to important cultural changes, the changes are extremely complex and not well understood. One area in which critics fear that globalization will lead to homogenization is the loss of traditional languages and dialects. International business, it is often asserted, is conducted in English. This may be the case, but there are important countertendencies. For example, in the United States, between 1980 and 1990, the percentage of people who spoke English at home fell from approximately 89 percent to approximately 86 percent (calculated from U.S. Bureau of the Census 1980, 1-68, tab. 99; 1998, 56, tab. 59). Furthermore, contrary to popular belief, in the United States, regional dialects seem to be diverging from one another. Perhaps the leading researcher in the field is the linguist William Labov (1996), who writes,

Sociolinguistic research on linguistic change in progress has found rapid development of sound changes in most urbanized areas of North America, leading to increased dialect diversity. It appears that the dialects of New York, Philadelphia, Detroit, Chicago, Saint Louis, Dallas and Los Angeles are now more different from each other than they were 50 or 100 years ago.

Some cultural changes that critics describe as increases in homogeneity are often the exact opposite. The spread of information and the reduction in transportation costs has led to changes in cuisine in many parts of the world, including the United States, where it is a widely observed fact that salsa sales now exceed sales of ketchup (see Hannon 1997). In parts of Britain far beyond the Indian community, apparently, curry has recently become something of a staple. Critics lament the decline of regionally and ethnically specific cuisine—all cities now look and taste the same, they claim. One no longer

has to travel to New Orleans for gumbo, San Francisco for sourdough bread, Philadelphia for cheese steaks, or Seattle for gourmet coffee. But this is because in many areas there is a wider range of foods available than ever before. This is not homogenization but its precise opposite. Almost by definition, globalization means that products, production techniques, and cultural practices are less restricted to particular regions, either domestically or internationally. It means that not only wealthy tourists are able to experience cultural diversity. Call this the democratization of diversity.

The spread of American fast-food restaurants is often cited as the key evidence of the homogenization and Americanization of culture. There can be little doubt of their immense popularity throughout the world.[7] Critics seem to suggest that this is due to advertising alone and that corporations continuously dupe unsophisticated and inexperienced consumers into seeking glamour and excitement through fast food. No doubt, part of the reason for their success is symbolic. In much of the world, fast food symbolizes what is modern, glamorous, and American.[8] This is certainly the image that fast-food corporations project with their advertising. But symbols and meanings can vary in unpredictable ways. Friedman (1999, 143) cites the case of an Indonesian man who took his son to McDonald's once a week as a political protest against Suharto. Over time, the excitement of the new fades, so excitement can hardly explain the immense staying power of fast-food restaurants. Few in the

United States would claim that fast food is glamorous, yet it is immensely popular here, too. My guess is that fast food will have staying power in the rest of the world for reasons similar to why it remains popular in the United States: quite simply, it is fast, consistent, and relatively inexpensive. There are many reasons that these considerations might make fast food appealing, but one stands out. As women enter the workforce in greater numbers throughout the world, they do not have the time to spend preparing meals that they had in previous generations. No doubt there are many other reasons as well. The point is that the popularity of fast food is very strongly linked to deeper cultural changes. The assumption that it is inauthentic or that it is and must remain alien depends on an illusory picture of culture in which there are no dynamics of change.

The problem with much of the cultural criticism of globalization is that it treats culture as a museum piece to be preserved for the inspection and entertainment of tourists.[9] These critics forget that there are real people whose lives are structured by their culture and who influence and transform their cultural practices as they cope with new situations and dilemmas. Critics of globalization often embrace a naive conservatism in which creative and dynamic elements of culture must be suppressed in the name of preserving traditional cultures and cultural diversity. It is sometimes said that globalization denies people their history. But Jeremy Waldron (1992) points out

that exactly the opposite may often be the case. A crucial element of cultures is how they adapt to new circumstances. To deny a culture the ability to incorporate new elements and reinterpret old elements in response to new pressures and opportunities is to deny it "what many would regard as its most fascinating feature: its ability to generate a history" (788).

Of course, when people make their own history—when they adapt their culture to new circumstances and incorporate elements from other cultures—they will sometimes do this poorly and sometimes well. I have not here defended or criticized any particular cultural developments brought about by globalization. At this level of abstraction, little can be said about when such changes are on the whole progressive and when they are mistaken. Rather, such evaluations must be made only through a careful examination of the particulars of a specific case.

Furthermore, as cultures change, even in generally positive ways, there is inevitably loss as older forms are abandoned or transformed. Almost all cases of cultural change will be controversial. Some people will embrace the new, while others will cling to the familiar. For some, a more cosmopolitan life in which traditional customs are gradually dropped and formerly foreign practices are incorporated into a new hybrid is a rewarding, authentic, creative life that allows them to escape traditionally confining roles. For others, precisely because it involves the abandonment or transformation of traditional practices, such a life must be shallow, inauthentic, and unrewarding. We cannot hope to resolve such conflicts for all people, in all circumstances, to everyone's satisfaction. What we can do, however, is to try to spell out background institutions in which people holding conflicting conceptions of the good life can interact with one another fairly.

Globalization means that more and more we will interact with people from different cultures, who are at home with distinct practices. Although this increased interaction will cause cultural practices to change and to be less tightly confined to a particular geographic location, they will not fuse into a single uniform global way of life. Precisely because of this, it will become all the more important to ensure that we have institutions in place that allow for fair interactions between people who embrace different and conflicting ways of life. Although economic development, facilitated by globalization, has reduced poverty more rapidly in the past century than at any other time in human history, many millions of people are forced to live in extreme poverty, which prevents them from participating in a meaningful way in any cultural practices. Since there are feasible institutional arrangements in which these numbers would be dramatically reduced, we have a strong obligation to try to bring them about. It is for this reason that Pogge's and Tobin's proposals should be seriously considered. As globalization ties the world more closely together, we must ensure that the institutions that form the background to our interactions are just. Only then will people have a fair opportunity to shape their own lives and history.

Notes

1. More recently, Rawls has attempted to extend his theory to international relations (see Rawls 1993, 1999 [the latter had not been published when the present article was written]).

2. Cf. Thomas Pogge's discussion (1989, 30-31) of the macroexplanation of homicide rates (in which institutional schemes may be important) and the microexplanation of specific homicides (in which individual psychological states are crucial).

3. Although this approach is suggested by the work of Rawls, Pogge (1998a, 478-96) argues that Rawls's characterization of the natural duty of justice is too weak.

4. Actually, this would be closer to a 10 percent GRD than Pogge's stated 1 percent GRD. It is worth remembering, however, that the GRD need be imposed not only on oil but also on other natural resources or on pollution.

5. See Schmidt 1995. This is close to the estimate of Hans D'Orville and Dragoljub Najman, cited in Frankel 1996, 60. Frankel points out, however, that these estimates are usually based on brokered transactions alone, which account for only about one-third of all currency transactions.

6. Of course, some forms of homogenization have little to do with globalization as such, although they are often confused with it. In the United States, television and radio have become less and less diverse as large conglomerates have bought up more and more stations. But this is the result of a deliberate political decision on the part of the Federal Communications Commission to relax its regulation of the public broadcast spectrum.

7. Barber (1995, 18) reports that in 1992 McDonald's and Kentucky Fried Chicken were the top two restaurants in Japan in terms of customers served.

8. Thomas Friedman (1999, 235) reports an interview with the owner of the Kentucky Fried Chicken franchises in Malaysia: " 'Tell me something,' I asked. 'What is the great appeal of Kentucky Fried Chicken to Malaysians?' Not only did they like the taste, he said,

but they liked even more what it symbolized: modernity, Americanization, being hip."

9. Even someone as generally supportive of globalization as Thomas Friedman falls into this trap. See Friedman 1999, 220-22, but cf. 234-35.

References

Barber, Benjamin. 1995. *Jihad vs. McWorld*. New York: Times Books.

Frankel, Jeffrey. 1996. How Well Do Foreign Exchange Markets Work? In *The Tobin Tax*, ed. Mahbub ul Haq, Inge Kaul, and Isabelle Grunberg. New York: Oxford University Press.

Friedman, Thomas. 1999. *The Lexus and the Olive Tree*. New York: Farrar, Straus & Giroux.

Hannon, Kerry. 1997. Let Them Eat Ahi Jerky. *U.S. News and World Report*, 7 July. Available at http://www.usnews.com/usnews/issue/970707/7trad.htm.

Kant, Immanuel. 1983. To Perpetual Peace: A Philosophical Sketch. In *Perpetual Peace and Other Essays*, ed. Ted Humphrey. Indianapolis: Hackett.

———. 1996. The Doctrine of Right. In *The Metaphysics of Morals*, ed. Mary Gregor. New York: Cambridge University Press.

Kasa, Kenneth. 1999. Time for a Tobin Tax? In *The Federal Reserve Bank of San Francisco Economic Letter*, 9 Apr. Available at http://www.sf.frb.org/econrsrch/wklyltr/wklyltr99/el99-12.html.

Labov, William. 1996. The Organization of Dialect Diversity in North America. Paper presented at the Fourth International Conference on Spoken Language Processing. Available at http://www.ling.upenn.edu/phono_atlas/ICSLP4.html.

Locke, John. 1980. *Second Treatise of Government*, ed. C. B. Macpherson. Indianapolis: Hackett.

Mandle, Jon. 2000. *What's Left of Liberalism? An Interpretation and Defense of Justice as Fairness*. Lanham, MD: Lexington Books.

Nielsen, Kai. 1988. World Government, Security, and Global Justice. In *Problems of International Justice*, ed. Steven Luper-Foy. Boulder, CO: Westview.

Nussbaum, Martha. 1996a. Patriotism and Cosmopolitanism. In *For Love of Country*, ed. Joshua Cohen. Boston: Beacon Press.

———. 1996b. Reply. In *For Love of Country*, ed. Joshua Cohen. Boston: Beacon Press.

Pogge, Thomas. 1989. *Realizing Rawls*. Ithaca, NY: Cornell University Press.

———. 1998a. The Bounds of Nationalism. In *Rethinking Nationalism*, ed. Jocelyne Couture, Kai Nielsen, and Michel Seymour. Calgary: University of Calgary Press.

———. 1998b. A Global Resource Dividend. In *Ethics of Consumption*, ed. David Crocker and Toby Linden. Lanham, MD: Rowman & Littlefield.

Rawls, John. 1971. *A Theory of Justice*. Cambridge, MA: Harvard University Press.

———. 1993. The Law of Peoples. In *On Human Rights: The Oxford Amnesty Lectures, 1993*, ed. Stephen Shute and Susan Hurley. New York: Basic Books.

———. 1999. *The Law of Peoples*. Cambridge, MA: Harvard University Press.

Rorty, Richard. 1996. Who Are We? Moral Universalism and Economic Triage. *Diogenes* 44(Spring): 5-15.

Rousseau, Jean-Jacques. 1986. Discourse on the Origin and the Foundations of Inequality Among Men. In *The First and Second Discourses*, ed. Victor Gourevitch. New York: Harper & Row.

Schmidt, Rodney. 1995. *Feasibility of the Tobin Tax.* Available at http://www.igc.apc.org/globalpolicy/finance/alternat/schmidt2.htm.

Singer, Peter. 1972. Famine, Affluence, and Morality. *Philosophy and Public Affairs* 1(Spring): 229-43.

Tobin, James. 1996. Prologue. In *The Tobin Tax,* ed. Mahbub ul Haq, Inge Kaul, and Isabelle Grunberg. New York: Oxford University Press.

————. 1998. Financial Globalization: Can National Currencies Survive? Keynote address to the Annual World Bank Conference on Development Economics. Available at http://www.worldbank.org/html/rad/abcde/tobin.pdf.

United Nations. 1998. *United Nations Human Development Report: 1998.* New York: Oxford University Press.

Waldron, Jeremy. 1992. Minority Cultures and the Cosmopolitan Alternative. *University of Michigan Journal of Law Reform* 25(Spring and Summer): 751-93.

U.S. Bureau of the Census. 1980. *Census of Population, General Social and Economic Characteristics.* Washington, DC: Government Printing Office.

————. 1998. *Statistical Abstract of the United States: 1998.* Washington, DC: Government Printing Office.

Globalization's Cultural Consequences

By ROBERT HOLTON

ABSTRACT: Globalization has been associated with a range of cultural consequences. These can be analyzed in terms of three major theses, namely, homogenization, polarization, and hybridization. The homogenization thesis proclaims that global culture is becoming standardized around a Western or American pattern. While some evidence supports this view, the presence of cultural alternatives and resistance to Western norms suggests that polarization provides a more convincing picture of global cultural development. Global interconnection and interdependence do not necessarily mean cultural conformity. Culture, it seems, is harder to standardize than economic organization and technology. Yet the idea of polarization has its limits, too. The hybridization thesis argues that cultures borrow and incorporate elements from each other, creating hybrid, or syncretic, forms. Evidence to support this view comes mainly from popular music and religious life. The cultural consequences of globalization are therefore diverse and complex.

Robert Holton is professor of sociology at Flinders University of South Australia. He is author of a number of books on social theory, historical sociology, and immigration. His most recent publication is Globalization and the Nation-State *(1998). In 1995, he was elected to a fellowship of the Academy of the Social Sciences in Australia.*

WE clearly live in an epoch of rapid social change, where capital, technology, people, ideas, and information move relentlessly across the inherited map of political borders and cultural boundaries. Cross-border processes such as inter-regional trade, population migration, technological diffusion, religious conversion, and military conquest are not new (McNeill 1986). Globalization as it stands in the year 2000 has clearly built upon previous upswings of cross-border activity and internationalism, including the much-cited phase of global expansion that culminated in 1913. The distinctiveness of contemporary global change is nonetheless connected with new forms of integration and interdependence between the various parts of the globe. Integration and interdependence now have an intensified spatial and temporal dimension to them, something lacking in the pre-1913 developments. This may be referred to usefully as the compression of space and time (Harvey 1989). Information technology has meant not only the obliteration of the tyranny of distance but also the creation of a global virtual reality, in which time presents no fundamental barrier to social exchange.

The present epoch may justly be termed the age of globalization. And yet there is much about the dynamics of and limits to globalization that remains unclear. This is especially true of the relationship of globalization to cultural life, which is my theme in this article. Concerning this relationship, most attention has been given to the question of the consequences of globalization for culture, and rather less to the issue of cultural causes of globalization. Closer scrutiny of debates about consequences reveals an unresolved argument between three basic positions: the homogenization thesis, in which globalization leads to cultural convergence; the polarization thesis, which posits cultural wars between Western globalization and its opponents; and, finally, the hybridization, or syncretism, thesis, in which globalization encourages a blending of the diverse set of cultural repertoires made available through cross-border exchange. The debate between these positions, as it currently stands, is long on speculative advocacy and short on empirical depth or substantiation.

In sorting out this debate, it is well to recall Raymond Williams's comment that "culture" is one of the two or three most complicated words in the English language (1976, 87). The connotations that "culture" means high culture or that its scope is concerned with beliefs and values rather than practical activities and dispositions remain largely intact. This situation has helped to give culture something of a Cinderella status in the social sciences. Economics and political science tend to treat it as a fuzzy residual to be invoked when other types of rational or interest-based explanation or analysis have failed, while sociology has only recently moved beyond its earlier reliance on anthropology in conceptualizing and theorizing culture more adequately.

Clifford Geertz's much-cited definition of culture assists in broadening inquiry beyond the belief-based focus into popular and practical activities. Here culture is defined as "an historically transmitted pattern of meanings embodied in symbolic forms by means of which men [sic] communicate, perpetuate, and develop their knowledge about and attitudes toward life" (1973, 89). There is room here for Coca-Cola as much as Chopin, for practical knowledge as much as religious symbolism. So far so good. But how relevant is such an emphasis on the historical durability of culture in an epoch of rapid social change? Does the order-creating function of culture persist under the impact of globalization? If so, does culture remain organized around nations or around some larger regional or even global cosmopolitanism? If not, are we faced with Marx's prognosis whereby "all that is solid melts into air," or some kind of Balkanization of cultural identity and identity politics?

THE HOMOGENIZATION THESIS

The most widely held belief about globalization and culture is probably that of convergence toward a common set of cultural traits and practices. Anecdotal commentary suggests that one shopping mall or hotel looks very much the same whether it be in Singapore, St. Louis, or São Paulo. Phrases such as the "Coca-Colonization" or "McDonaldization" of the world reflect a belief that global culture follows the global economy. Homogenization is then equivalent to Westernization or even Americanization. The mechanisms of change, in this view, are associated with the worldwide spread of a market economy and the global strategies of multinational companies. Consumer capitalism of this type has been built upon a standardized brand image, mass advertising, and the high status given by many Third World populations to Western products and services. The creation of the global consumer has been based not merely on the utilitarian convenience of global products but also on the sale of dreams of affluence, personal success, and erotic gratification evoked through advertising and the culture industry of Hollywood. When movies such as the *Terminator* series or *Titanic* gross millions around the globe, the fear is that patterns of American or Western sensibility are transferred, too, along with the other cultural baggage.

This picture of homogeneity, evident from the 1950s onward, has been further enhanced with the recent development of information technology and global communications. Microsoft, Motorola, Yahoo!, and Amazon.com have now joined and possibly surpassed the status of Coca-Cola and McDonald's as cultural icons. Top-down fast-food and soft-drink marketing is rapidly being supplanted by a more interactive Internet culture, at least among the more affluent populations of the world. This indicates both that global consumer culture is itself changing very rapidly and that patterns of homogeneity, insofar as they exist, are far from static and secure. What remains unclear is the extent to which global usage of new communications technologies such as the Internet involves any more than a convergence of technical means of information exchange. With the vast diversity of Web-site surfers able to consume anything from neo-Nazi anti-Semitism and pornography through Puritan sermons, commentaries on the Koran, and Zapatista political programs, to mundane forms of e-commerce and corporate public image-building material, it is not at all clear that usage of the Internet necessarily has any particular cultural consequence, let alone absorption into global consumer culture.

Another dimension of the issue of homogeneity is the integration of elites from around the world in the educational, economic, and political life of Western societies. The experience of a Western education, whether at Harvard, Oxford, the Sorbonne, or the University of Sydney, not only diffuses Western forms of knowledge but also helps to create interpersonal networks of value in the functioning of international organizations like the United Nations, the World Bank, and the United Nations Educational, Scientific, and Cultural Organization (UNESCO), as well as global corporations. In this sense, the development of a global culture is driven not only by mass-marketing strategies but also through the emergence and interests of a cross-national global elite. What is far less clear is whether this involves convergence around some kind of extranational commitment to cosmopolitanism or whether the fault lines of national and perhaps regional allegiance and ideology remain more significant. The global economy and polity may not, in fact, require complete cultural

homogeneity among elites at the level of belief and identity in order to function effectively.

The homogenization thesis, provided it is regarded in a dynamic way, has much to be said for it, but it is liable to a range of criticisms and limitations. First, the strong association of cultural globalization with Americanization is overstated. This is partly because other Western nations, such as the United Kingdom and France, retain a special cultural relationship with their former recent colonies, affecting patterns of migration, sport, food, and religious practice, as well as many public cultural assumptions built into law and politics. Baseball is not the mass sport of choice in cricket-mad India. Even the Coca-Cola consumed in the former French Congo is not the bottled form produced locally under U.S. license, but the cans imported from Europe, to which the French-speaking Congolese look for cultural status (Friedman 1994). Paris is the cultural magnet, not New York or California.

Limits to Americanization are also set by forms of cultural resistance in Europe and Japan as well as non-Westernized populations. The political effectiveness of this resistance may well have been reduced, as Schiller (1976) points out, by consistent U.S. opposition to attempts by other governments and UNESCO to comprehensively regulate the information media. Only very limited forms of protection of national culture industries through local content regulations or public subsidies to film companies have emerged, as in countries such as France or Australia. These have certainly not rolled back Hollywood or Disney, but their net effect has been a positive one in terms of the preservation or promotion of national cultural output. The French cultural influence, meanwhile, is also evident in a diffuse way in many of the social and cultural interventions of UNESCO. These promote social development through proactive public policy rather than social policy initiatives driven by the agendas of economic rationalism.

In a more general sense, Arjun Appadurai (1990, 170) has made the point that cultural threats in many countries are often perceived in terms other than Americanization. Thus "for the people of Irian Jaya, Indonesianization may be more worrisome than Americanization, as Japanization may be for Koreans, Indianization for Sri Lankans, Vietnamization for Cambodians," and so forth. Cultural power is, in other words, multicentered rather than organized within a unitary core-periphery relations system centered on the United States. It may emanate as much from the Vatican, Mecca, or Bombay as from Manhattan or Sunset Boulevard.

Finally, America is not necessarily the dominant force in a number of the leading sectors of multinational corporate activity. If we look beyond Coca-Cola, McDonald's, and Microsoft, for example, European corporations such as Benetton, in apparel; Nokia and Ericsson, in mobile phones; and Bertellsman, in the media, all have a major global presence and offer many contrasting cultural images to those associated with the Americanization thesis. Benetton, for example, projects a multicultural image around the idea of "the united colours of Benetton." Allied with this is the abandonment of product standardization and the development of marketing, design, and production strategies that are alive to variations in consumer demand in different markets. Here the idea of glocalization, originally developed in Japan as a label for locally sensitive niche marketing (Robertson 1995), has been used to suggest that the global and the local may be mutually reinforcing rather than necessarily in conflict. The term "glocal" applies, as the Swedish telecommunications equipment firm Ericsson (1998) puts it, where "the market, customers, and products" are "global in many contexts, but local in design and content" (6).

The discussion so far does not challenge the idea of global economic convergence to a market-based liberal capitalist economy. It also does not contradict evidence of certain kinds of homogenization in popular and elite culture. But it does erode any simplistic sense of economic globalization leading inexorably toward cultural Americanization or of cultural modernization looking identical in any given location. This is not simply because Western attempts to create homogeneity have come up against limits but also because various parts of the globe have differing cultural histories and dissimilar patterns of intercultural engagement with other parts of the globe. Here the historical terms of engagement with the West may range from direct colonization and enslavement as in the Afro-Caribbean world, through different types of economic, cultural, and linguistic domination, to the relative political and cultural autonomy of Japan. British imperial rule in India involved the Anglicized education of a historically literate middle class, whereas in most parts of British Africa, advanced educational provision was reserved for the few able to finance accreditation through a British university. Parts of India (notably Bangalore) now function as important centers of information technology design and production, whereas the continent of Africa, with a few exceptions like South Africa, remains poorly integrated into the global information society. The cultural reception and consequences of contemporary processes of globalization are refracted through these complex and diverse historical legacies. Even though the tyranny of geographic separation may have been obliterated, it is far from clear that globalization can obliterate the impact of the past on the present.

THE POLARIZATION THESIS

The limits to cultural homogenization in the contemporary world have often been recast as evidence of polarization. In an epoch characterized by nationalism more than cosmopolitanism, by ethnic cleansing and rancorous identity politics as much as cross-cultural cooperation, and by global insecurities associated with civilizational conflict rather than urbanity and international tolerance, this alternative has much to be said for it. Technological changes in the globalization of information can as easily be used for purposes of hate and the defense of ethno-nationalism and racial hatred as for intercultural dialogue and the sharing of experience. They have been used by ethnic diasporas in recent years in a manner that Benedict Anderson (1994, 326) calls "long-distance nationalism" and therefore have no necessary connection with cultural globalization as a transnational identity. Culture, it seems, is harder to globalize than politics or economic activity.

Analysts as diverse as Samuel Huntington, Edward Said, and Benjamin Barber have had an enormous impact on thinking of the globe in a dichotomous manner, integrated by conflict or hate rather than peace or love. Said's influential work on orientalism (1978) looks at the ways in which cultural dichotomies have been constructed between Western and non-Western ways of life. He argues that Western cultural imperialism operates through discourses of power, whereby the non-Western world is constructed as the Other, that is, as fundamentally different in nature from the West. The prime example is the construction of the Middle Eastern Islamic world as Oriental by many generations of Western colonialists, explorers, academics, novelists, and painters. Whereas the Orient is typically seen as stagnant and unchanging, or erotic, or authoritarian, the West is constructed as dynamic and innovatory, rational and tolerant. The point here is not that these dichotomies lack elements of truth, rather that truth is subordinated to the desire for power and domination. The net effect is to marginalize and discount the experience of the Other. It can be argued that contemporary Western stereotypes of Islamists and Arabs as inherently violent terrorists and uncompromising fundamentalists perpetuate this kind of thinking.

Said has been criticized for neglecting the wide variety of views held by orientalist scholars and travelers, including those Westerners who in a sense became Easternized through intercultural contact. There is merit in this line of argument. The idea of a world fractured by powerful cultural dichotomies in the ways different peoples think of each other nonetheless remains important. Said himself has come, over time, to place greater emphasis on parallel dichotomies whereby the West is seen as the Other by non-Western peoples, whether Islamic or African. Occidentalism in this way mirrors orientalism or Afrocentrism. Where the West is seen as immoral and pathologically individualist, the East or Africa is seen as respectful of moral order and supportive of community. In this way, global culture is presented in terms of a conflict between two contrasting cultural stereotypes. Said himself balks at this vision, rejecting Afrocentric or Islamocentric worldviews even while sympathetic to the West's cultural subordinates.

The idea of global cultural polarization continues, nonetheless, to have a widespread currency. It may be found for example in Samuel Huntington's argument (1996) about civilizational conflict between the West and an emergent Islamic-Confucian axis. With the end of the geopolitical Cold War, global conflict will, in his view, see culture wars, leading perhaps to a "global civilizational war." The civilizational fault line fracturing global culture is associated with conflicts over matters such as human rights or the choice of venue for the Olympic Games. In the global politics of culture, Western nations tend to line up on one side of the issue, in favor of human rights and of a Western site for the games, while non-Westerners tend to line up on the other. These conflicts arise in part through the historical tendency of humans through history to think in dichotomies, as noted by Said, but they also reflect more recent social trends. Economic development, according to Huntington, has made East Asia more assertive, while the Islamic resurgence has emerged as a renewed source of identity, meaning, stability, and hope in response to Western dominance and the uprooting of Islamic populations through rapid rural-urban migration.

Benjamin Barber (1995) characterizes global cultural polarization in terms of conflict between McWorld and jihad. These powerful metaphors stand for global consumer capitalism, on the one side, and the fundamentalist struggle for justice for the downtrodden, on the other. Where McWorld means a combination of fast food (McDonald's), fast music (MTV), and fast computers (Apple Mac), jihad (the Arabic word for just or holy war) stands for the forces of cultural fundamentalism and tribalism. McWorld promises to tie us together through the soulless consumption of commodified cultural production, while jihad promises moral liberation from mammon through communitarian political mobilization in pursuit of justice.

The polarization approach to global culture tells two powerful and interconnected stories about the contemporary world. Many commentators are convinced by the simplicity of the approach. A good deal of evidence is consistent with it, while many interesting issues arise when we think in terms of polarization rather than homogenization. One issue is that Western globalization has limits, engendered through cultural resistance. It does not carry all before it. A second underexplored issue concerns the nature of this resistance. Is it mainly a kind of antiglobalism that serves to fragment global culture into warring tribes, as suggested in much of Barber's work? Or is the emergent Islamic-Confucian axis that Huntington sees challenging Western liberal democracy an alternative kind of globalization? And where in all of this do we place movements that are more than national but less than global in scope, such as pan-Islamism or Afrocentrism?

The mechanisms that drive such developments include the globalizing tendencies of world religions, such as Islam. Monotheism, in this context, encourages the development of imagined communities, that is, links between geographically separated sets of believers, believers who will never meet each other. One might see this as a kind of spiritual globalization with a particular appeal to those who feel excluded from or morally challenged by economic globalization. Another important mechanism encouraging resistance to economic globalization involves mass migrations of people, whether through choice, enslavement, or as refugees. This tends to create global diasporic communities among those who share a religious, ethnic, or linguistic heritage but live in different places or continents. Rastafarianism, for example, with its belief in the divinity of Black King Haile Selaissie of Ethiopia and the moral corruption of the West as the new Babylon, originated in the former slave populations of the Afro-Caribbean, notably Jamaica. But it now has a presence in Western capitals such as London and New York, where Caribbean populations have migrated and where Rastafarian culture has been disseminated through records, tapes, and compact disks. Unlike the Islam example, however, this current is less globalized in its scope, even though some outreach has been made to white youths through a reversal of the Westernization process.

Against the objection that unity between Confucian, Islamist, and Afro-American is at best episodic and politically directed, rather than organic and cultural, it is worth considering whether Western unity between the English-speaking world and the French, German, and Spanish worlds is any stronger. For Huntington, the West was the West even before it was modern. Yet, if this is so, it becomes rather more difficult to identify the West with those liberal traditions that only really emerged in the modern period. If the historical unity of Christendom against the infidel has long since past, consistent commitment to liberalism during the twentieth century has proven far stronger in English-speaking parts of the West than many others. If the question, What is it that Europeans have in common? is not easy to answer (Delanty 1995), then the core of Western civilization would appear even harder to determine. The historical integrity of ideas of the West is therefore largely mythical in function.

The polarization thesis tells a vivid, morally loaded story, easy to translate into one or another version of the struggle between good and bad, sacred and profane, depending on the location of the storyteller in time and space. The problem is that the story is too simplistic and also perhaps too pessimistic inasmuch as it assumes, with Huntington (1996, 130), that "it is human to hate." The consequence of this proposition is that bounded definitions of identity prevail whereby we define ourselves more in terms of who we are not and less in terms of who we are. In a world of resurgent ethnonationalism and identity politics, this view of human nature has considerable empirical backing. The problem with it lies less in terms of plausibility and more in terms of what it leaves out. One fundamental omission is the presence of multiple cross-cutting identities and hybrid, or syncretic, cultural forms.

THE HYBRIDIZATION THESIS

Consider the following example outlined by cultural anthropologist Ulf Hannerz (1992):

Each year the countries of Europe meet in a televised song contest . . . watched by hundreds of millions of people. There is first a national contest in each country to choose its own entry for the international competition. A few years ago a controversy erupted in Sweden after this national contest. It was quite acceptable that the . . . first runner up was performed by a lady from Finland, and the second runner up by an Afro-American lady. . . . Both were thought of as representing the new heterogeneity of Swedish society. . . . What was controversial was the winning tune, the refrain of which was "Four Buggs and a Coca-Cola": Bugg . . . was brand name for chewing gum. . . . Of the two Coca-Cola was much more controversial, as it was widely understood as a symbol of cultural imperialism. . . . what drew far less attention was that the winning tune was a Calypso. (1992)

This anecdote draws attention to a third thread woven into the complex fabric of globalization, that of hybridization, or syncretization. It centers on intercultural exchange and the incorporation of cultural elements from a variety of sources within particular cultural practices. Just as biological hybrids combine genetic material from different sources, so hybrid social practices combine cultural elements from a range of sources. Even if we accept the significance of homogenization and polarization, these two prominent threads in no way exhaust the complex multidimensional elements that make up global culture. Hannerz borrows the religious concept of ecumene, defined as "a region of persistent cultural interaction and exchange," in speaking of this neglected aspect of global culture.

Movement between cultures, engendered through mechanisms such as migration, cross-border employment, and colonization, is probably a necessary though not sufficient condition for interculturalism. Furthermore, movement does not always lead in this direction. Political exiles typically dream of return to the homeland one day rather than broadening their engagement with their country of exile. Travel may narrow rather than broaden the mind if it is suffused with preconceptions and prejudice. The migration of culturally diverse populations may sustain outward-looking intercultural exchange, but it may equally be conducted through the bounded solidarities of hatred.

What may be more significant in generating intercultural exchange rather than hate is not so much migration itself as intermarriage between people of different cultural backgrounds. This was a major theme in Israel Zangwill's celebrated play *The Melting Pot* (1914), written just before World War I. More recent work by Hebdige (1987) cites the following verbatim comments from a "white" respondent in the English migrant city of Birmingham.

There's no such thing as England any more . . . welcome to India, brothers! This is the Caribbean! . . . Nigeria! . . . There is no England, man. . . . Balsall Heath is the centre of the melting pot, 'cos all I ever see when I go out is half-Arab, half-Pakistani, half-Jamaican, half-Scottish. . . . I know 'cos I am [half-Scots, half-Irish]. . . . who am I? . . . where do I belong? . . . I'm just a broad person. The earth is mine. (158-59)

Opportunities for cultural exchange may, however, open up not only through the micro-interactions of intermarriage but even where less auspicious forms of cultural contact bring those of different cultural backgrounds into contact with each other. Colonial occupation and imperial domination represent one example. In the classical world, the ancient Roman conquest of the Mediterranean Greek world resulted in Roman absorption of much of the Greek cultural legacy. The cultural impact of India on the British empire was less powerful, yet intercultural exchange in areas of religion, culture, and politics did occur, generating syncretic forms of cultural life. These include the theosophy movement, which Easternized the spiritual life of many Westerners, or the integration of Western models of liberal democracy and self-government into Indian debates on national independence and cultural freedom.

The idea of cultural hybridization, or syncretization, has been most successfully applied to a range of phenomena, such as music (including jazz and world music), contemporary art and literature, and religious and spiritual life. But it is hard to assess its scale and scope. One reason for this is the rather blurry conceptual status of this cultural orientation. When the Birmingham respondent saw himself as a "broad person" claiming the earth as his, this seems to combine a sense of hybridity, generated by cultural fusion, with a sense of being cosmopolitan. Hybridity may nonetheless be more ambivalent in its effects than this case suggests. It can as easily lead to a hyphenated identity such as African American or "half-Scots, half-Irish" as to a sense of cultural membership in the world as such.

Cosmopolitanism has received some attention in the history of ideas but rather less in the social history of global culture. For Hannerz, its defining features include an orientation toward a plurality of cultural centers, preparedness to engage with others, and competence to function across cultural divides. This approach is useful in reminding us that culture is not simply a question of attitudes and values but also a quintessentially practical matter concerned with action as much as thought. While localism is largely reactive in nature, erecting boundaries against the outside and usually against change as well, cosmopolitanism is largely proactive in the sense of seeking out and incorporating new cultural experiences into personal repertoires.

International diplomats, bureaucrats, globally mobile academics, journalists, and businesspeople have all been touted as occupational groupings increasingly implicated in more than one cultural setting. To this rather top-down list might be added more bottom-up categories such as migrant workers, sailors, aid workers, musicians, artists, pilgrims, and sports people. One difficulty, though, remains the problem of deciding how far transnational experiences and occupational networks translate into transcontextual forms of cosmopolitanism. Do politicians or bureaucrats drawn from a range of countries to work in the United Nations or the World Bank develop new forms of identity and orientation to the world as such, or are their activities still heavily loaded with national or regional norms and therefore international rather than transnational in scope? Is cosmopolitanism perhaps stronger among aid workers from nongovernmental bodies such as the International Committee of the Red Cross or Médecins sans Frontières, whose primary purpose is humanitarian? There are as yet few hard answers to such questions.

Genuine cosmopolitanism may turn out to be comparatively rare. The failure of the world language Esperanto certainly points to this conclusion. This should not however obscure the importance of global syncretism, or hybridism, meaning cultural forms that are somehow transcontextual but less than cosmopolitan in scope. The major conceptual advance that this hybridization approach represents is the idea that what are called cultures have become so intermixed that there is no longer any pure or authentic culture distinct from others. Globalization, in the sense of population migration and mixture, has been around for centuries, if not millennia, progressively extending its hybridizing thrust. Just as the idea of biological race is a spurious basis for social and cultural distinction, so the idea of distinct cultures defined by purely endogenous characteristics is equally spurious from an analytical point of view. Cultural actors may not recognize, or want to recognize, the significance of exogenous elements in their cultural repertoire, since it is more reassuring to indigenize that which has been borrowed.

CONCLUSION

There are no easy answers to questions to do with the cultural consequences of globalization. This is because of the failure of grand theories to adequately explain the diversity and complexity of global cultural development. Homogenization is an important but far from dominant trend. The polarization thesis deals with the first level of complexity, that of countertrends, but at the expense of ruling out interculturalism and hybridization. The syncretization perspective is a corrective to the other two approaches, because it is able to include a second level of complexity, that of interaction.

We are clearly faced with the paradox that while global economic, technological, and political change exhibits high levels of convergence around market-driven capitalism, electronic technology, and liberal-democratic politics, culture is characterized by high levels of divergence. This snapshot observation made at the turn of the new millennium may be erroneous if it proves to be the case that one element of the picture becomes dominant. For Barber, the prognosis is that McWorld may triumph over jihad, in which case polarization would give way to homogenization. It is doubtful, however, that the picture

of global cultural syncretism could be easily undermined since it is a principle of such long-standing historical significance.

Globalization, as it has evolved over the last 5000 years (Holton 1998, chap. 2), has always depended on intercultural borrowing and exchange. Global diffusion, as Philip Curtin (1984) points out, has always been a major source of innovation in human history since "no human group could invent by itself more than a small part of its cultural and technical heritage" (1). The further paradox is that this diffusionist truth is rarely culturally acceptable, such that what is borrowed is typically indigenized or customized. This applies equally to the Indo-European linguistic heritage that gave us contemporary versions of English and to the Californian innovations that gave us the Internet. This circumstance gives history the quality of a dialectic between cosmopolitanism and localism, a process that powerful groups at any given time seek to dominate, but with only short- to medium-term success.

References

Anderson, Benedict. 1994. Exodus. *Critical Inquiry* 20: 314-27.

Appadurai, Arjun. 1990. Disjuncture and Difference in the Global Cultural Economy. In *Global Culture*, ed. M. Featherstone. Thousand Oaks, CA: Sage.

Barber, Benjamin. 1995. *Jihad vs. McWorld*. New York: Ballantine Books.

Curtin, Philip. 1984. *Cross-Cultural Trade in World History*. New York: Cambridge University Press.

Delanty, Gerard. 1995. *Inventing Europe: Idea, Identity, Reality*. London: Macmillan.

Ericsson. 1998. *Annual Report*. Available at http://www.ericsson.com/annual_report/1998/eng/apdf.shtml.

Friedman, Jonathan. 1994. *Cultural Identity and Global Process*. Thousand Oaks, CA: Sage.

Geertz, Clifford. 1973. Religion as a Cultural System. In *The Interpretation of Cultures*. New York: Basic Books.

Hannerz, Ulf. 1992. *Cultural Complexity*. New York: Columbia University Press.

Harvey, David. 1989. *The Condition of Postmodernity*. Oxford: Blackwell.

Hebdige, Dick. 1987. *Cut n' Mix: Culture, Identity, and Caribbean Music*. London: Methuen.

Holton, Robert. 1998. *Globalization and the Nation-State*. London: Macmillan.

Huntington, Samuel. 1996. *The Clash of Civilisations and the Remaking of World Order*. New York: Simon & Schuster.

McNeill, William. 1986. *Polyethnicity and National Unity in World History*. Chicago: University of Chicago Press.

Robertson, Roland. 1995. Glocalization, Time-Space, and Homogeneity-Heterogeneity. In *Global Modernities*, ed. M. Featherstone, S. Lash, and R. Robertson. Thousand Oaks, CA: Sage.

Said, Edward. 1978. *Orientalism*. New York: Penguin.

Schiller, Herbert. 1976. *Communication and Cultural Domination*. New York: International Arts and Sciences.

Williams, Raymond. 1976. *Keywords*. London: Flamingo.

Zangwill, Israel. 1914. *The Melting Pot*. London: Heinemann.

ANNALS, *AAPSS*, **570**, July 2000

Corporate Governance and Globalization

By MARY O'SULLIVAN

ABSTRACT: There is growing interest in pressures on national systems of corporate governance to converge that are allegedly being generated by the process of globalization, especially the global integration of financial markets. Advocates of the merits of globalization contend that the trend will lead to a more efficient allocation of capital. Drawing on the cases of the United States and Germany, the author argues that considerable change has indeed occurred recently in national governance systems. These changes cannot be understood, however, as the outcome of a market-driven, efficiency-enhancing process. Rather, realignments in corporate governance reflect the growing economic and political power of those who have accumulated financial assets, a trend that is highly dependent on the extent of population aging and the social arrangements for pension provision in domestic economies.

Mary O'Sullivan is an assistant professor of strategy and management at INSEAD. She has been a visiting scholar at the University of Tokyo and is a research associate at the STEP Group in Oslo and the Levy Institute in New York. Her new book is Contests for Corporate Control: Corporate Governance and Economic Performance in the United States and Germany. *She is currently codirecting "Corporate Governance, Innovation, and Economic Performance," a project funded by the European Commission.*

THE question of how corporations should be governed to enhance corporate and economic performance has been widely discussed in the past two decades in the United States and Britain. Until recently, the subject of corporate governance has attracted much less attention on the European continent, in Asia, and in other parts of the world. By the late 1990s, however, corporate governance had become a major, and highly contentious, issue in all of the advanced economies and, increasingly, in developing countries as well. International organizations have devoted growing attention to corporate governance as a topic of global concern.

Corporate governance is concerned with the institutions that influence how business corporations allocate resources and returns (O'Sullivan 2000). Contemporary debates about corporate governance largely stem from the recognition of the centrality of corporate enterprises in allocating resources in the economy. In most economies, corporate enterprises play a critical role in shaping economic outcomes through the decisions that they make about investments, employment, trade, and income distribution.

Much of the contemporary debate on corporate governance has focused on the merits of different national systems for generating favorable outcomes for corporations themselves and for the regional and national economies in which they are based. In the 1980s, for example, there was considerable interest in the apparent strengths of the German and Japanese systems of corporate governance, as compared with their U.S.

counterpart, for generating economic performance and social cohesion. However, in the 1990s and especially in the mid- to late 1990s, proponents of the alleged virtues of the U.S. model of corporate governance largely drowned out other voices.

Lately, in discussions of corporate governance, increased attention has been focused on pressures on national systems of corporate governance to converge that are allegedly being generated by the process of globalization, commonly understood as the development of commodity markets to permit the free flow of economic resources from one use to another across national economic borders. In discussions of corporate governance and globalization, particular attention has been paid to the effects on national systems of corporate governance of the global integration of financial markets.

Advocates of the merits of globalization contend that the freeing up of capital flows will lead to the more efficient allocation of capital by improving savers' access to investment opportunities and companies' access to financing. If nations are to take advantage of these opportunities, however, they must observe, as the Organization for Economic Cooperation and Development (OECD) put it, "basic principles of good corporate governance" (OECD 1999, 3). As to what constitutes "good" corporate governance, there is little dispute among "globalists": it is the Anglo-American model of corporate governance that generates pressures on corporate enterprises to maximize shareholder value as their primary objective.

That globalization is and should occur in the realm of corporate governance is one element of a more general argument that holds that the convergence of national economic systems toward a market-oriented ideal is both inevitable and desirable. That perspective is, in turn, based on a theory of the market economy, neoclassical theory, in which the perfection of capital, labor, and product markets is supposed to lead to optimal economic outcomes. For superior economic performance, nothing should inhibit the free flow of economic resources from one use to another, and any impediment to that flow is deemed a market imperfection. From this point of view, to the extent that economies will converge toward the American and British economic systems, that convergence will occur only because these systems are closer than those of most other countries to the market ideal.

In this article, I argue that the systems of corporate governance prevalent in the leading industrial economies in the postwar period have evolved substantially in recent years. Moreover, there has been a buildup of tension in these systems that is likely to lead to further change in the foreseeable future. In my discussion, I focus on the cases of the United States and Germany. There are important similarities in the sources and impacts of recent changes in the U.S. and German systems of corporate governance.[1] Of particular significance has been the postwar accumulation of financial assets by certain groups in the population and the growth of intergenerational dependence. Notwithstanding these common elements, their relative importance, the manner in which they have interacted with the national system of corporate governance, and the responses to these pressures differ considerably across countries because of variations in national institutions, especially in financial and pension systems. The analysis of the United States and Germany thus underlines the importance of studying the transformation of national politics and economics for understanding the recent evolution of corporate governance in these countries.

To emphasize the importance of domestic developments is not, however, to suggest that we ignore the international sphere in analyses of corporate governance. National developments have important international repercussions that, in turn, have further implications for national systems. There is, therefore, a need to complement studies of evolution within national systems with analyses of the interaction between internal realignment of domestic systems of governance and international developments.

Notwithstanding its popularity, the globalization perspective sheds little light on these developments. Its deficiencies stem largely from the fact that the theory in which it is rooted has difficulty dealing with the historical reality of the relationship between financial systems and economic development. Particularly problematic, as I shall argue, is the central role assigned to financial markets, especially the stock market, in channeling resources from savers to investors in capitalist economies.

RECENT EVOLUTION OF NATIONAL SYSTEMS OF CORPORATE GOVERNANCE

The alignment of the interests of strategic managers of U.S. public corporations with the demands of the stock market is now typically regarded as a defining feature of the market-oriented U.S. system of corporate governance. In historical perspective, however, shareholder influence on the allocation of U.S. corporate resources stands out as a recent phenomenon. For most of this century, salaried managers have exercised control over resource allocation by U.S. corporate enterprises. Shareholders were widely dispersed and had little, if any, direct influence on corporate actions. In the last quarter of a century, the degree to which the U.S. system of corporate governance has changed has been nothing short of dramatic.

In Germany in recent decades, the institutional foundation of the postwar system of corporate governance has proven to be more enduring than in the United States. None of the elements that characterized that system—extensive intercompany shareholding, close bank-industry relations, and codetermination—have broken down. Nevertheless, considerable pressures for change have built up in the system that may well bring about its transformation in the foreseeable future. Of particular importance are the recent changes that have affected perhaps the most distinctive characteristic of German capitalism, the close relations between major German companies and financial enterprises.

United States

The arguments in support of governing corporations' creating shareholder value came into their own in the United States in the 1980s. Until that time, the leading corporations in the United States tended to retain both the money that they earned and the people whom they employed. Retentions in the forms of earnings and capital consumption allowances provided the financial foundations for corporate growth, while the building of managerial organizations to develop and utilize productive resources enabled investments in plant, equipment, and personnel to succeed. Since around 1980, however, most major U.S. corporations have been engaged in a process of restructuring their labor forces in ways that have eroded the quantity of jobs that offer stable employment and good pay in the U.S. corporate economy. While U.S. corporate managers became focused on downsizing their labor forces in the 1980s and 1990s, they also became focused on distributing corporate revenues in ways that supported the price of their companies' stocks (O'Sullivan 2000, chap. 6).

Of central importance in encouraging the recent shift in the U.S. governance system was a transformation of the structure of financial institutions and their interaction with the real sector of the U.S. economy that began in the late 1960s and early 1970s. While the causes of this structural transformation are complex and various, the growing financial wealth of U.S. households and the changes in the way that they allocated that wealth among different financial instruments are critical elements of the story. An analysis of household financial assets reveals a dramatic shift in their allocation in recent decades; in particular, pension and mutual funds have registered major increases in their share of household financial assets at the expense of intermediaries such as banks and thrifts. The trend toward a growing reliance of households on pension and mutual funds has increased at an accelerating pace; from 1982 to 1994, pension and mutual funds alone accounted for approximately 67 percent of the net growth of households' total financial assets (Edwards 1996, 16-27).

Reflecting their growing importance in managing the savings of U.S. households, pension and mutual funds' shares of corporate equities have increased dramatically. Pension funds held 24 percent of U.S. corporate stock in 1997, with private pensions accounting for 13.8 percent and public pensions for 10.2 percent, compared with 0.3 percent in 1945. Over the same period, mutual funds increased their share of U.S. corporate stock from 1.5 percent to 16.2 percent. In contrast to the growing importance of institutional investors, the share of corporate stocks held directly by individuals has fallen from 93.0 percent in 1945 to 42.7 percent in 1997 (U.S. Board of Governors, various years). Institutional share ownership is even higher in the largest U.S.

corporations than in the population of corporate enterprises as a whole; in 1987, the institutional share of the equity of the top 1000 U.S. corporations was 46.6 percent, and, by 1995, it had increased to 57.2 percent (Brancato 1997, 21).

The importance of institutional investments, especially pension funds and mutual funds, as a repository of financial wealth in the United States is related to the process of population aging under way in that country. That the phenomenon has had such a dramatic effect on financial institutions reflects not so much the demographic trend, however, as the particular form that social provisions for retirement have taken in that country. One important factor is the smaller significance of the government pay-as-you-go pension scheme as a source of pension income in the United States relative to a country like Germany; social security accounts for about 40 percent of the retirement income of U.S. pensioners compared with nearly 70 percent for German pensioners (Turner and Watanabe 1995, 136). In the decades after World War II, an extensive system of private pensions was developed to fill the breach at least for the more fortunate Americans.

During the 1950s and 1960s, there were legal restrictions on the extent to which pension funds could include corporate equities in their investment portfolios. As investors in stocks and bonds, mutual funds had advantages over other institutional investors such as life insurance companies and pension funds in generating higher returns on household savings because they were not subject to the same stringent regulations concerning the types of investments that they could make. Moreover, even without the mutual funds as competitors, the inflationary conditions of the 1970s meant that, under current regulations, pension funds and insurance companies could no longer offer households positive real rates of return. The regulatory response was the Employee Retirement Income Security Act (1974), which, when amended in 1978, permitted pension funds and insurance companies to invest substantial proportions of their portfolios in corporate equities and other risky securities such as so-called junk bonds and venture funds rather than just in high-grade corporate and government securities as had previously been the case.

The stage was now set for institutional investors to become central participants in the hostile-takeover movement of the 1980s. An important instrument of the takeover movement was the junk bond, corporate or government bonds that the bond-rating agencies considered to be below investment grade. Financial deregulation brought, first, pension funds and insurance companies and, then, savings and loan institutions into the junk bond market. With the liquidity that these investors provided, it became possible to use junk bonds to launch hostile takeovers of even the largest corporations. The result was the emergence of a powerful market for corporate control.

When many savings and loans went bust and junk bond markets were thrown into disarray by insider trading scandals and the jailing of Michael Milken, the market maker, institutional investors increasingly turned to corporate equities as a source of higher returns on their portfolios. They sought levers other than the market for corporate control to influence corporate resource allocation. In particular, from the mid-1980s, a number of major institutional investors, led by the California State Public Employees Retirement System (CalPERS), a defined-benefit pension fund for California's public employees, began to take a more aggressive stance toward incumbent corporate managers in the proxy process.

What the foregoing account emphasizes is that institutional investors have significance in the U.S. system of corporate governance because they have ridden a wave of structural change in the U.S. economy that has created a large and growing minority of Americans who, with longer life spans, earlier retirements, and accumulated financial assets, find it in their interests to favor arguments for high returns on corporate equities.[2] Unlike the days when holding stock in any one company was fragmented among hundreds of thousands of household investors, the collective power of institutional investing now gives wealth-holding households greater opportunities to reap high returns. With their ever increasing holdings of corporate stocks, institutional investors can now put pressure on U.S. corporations to create shareholder value.

Yet it is important to recognize that, notwithstanding these changes, institutional investors are a long way from controlling corporate resource allocation even in the United States. Why? First, the ambitions of most activist institutional investors for transforming the U.S. system of corporate governance are far from radical. Activist institutional investors in the United States have tended to take a narrow view of the essence of good corporate governance. CalPERS, for example, focuses primarily on the board of directors and its relationship with corporate management. Moreover, for all the attention that the likes of CalPERS have garnered, they are in a minority when it comes to actively voting the shares that they hold and jawboning management and boards of directors about reforming their corporate governance practices. Most institutional investors display little interest in exercising themselves about governance issues. They focus their energies on churning their portfolios of shares and thus seem unlikely to have strong incentives to make the commitment required to push for fundamental changes in corporate resource allocation. Finally, the powerful opposition of corporate managers also acts as a constraint on investor activism in the United States. These executives continue to be quite successful at using the protection that the legal system affords them to avoid shareholder interference in their decision-making processes.

Senior managers still retain considerable power in the U.S. corporate economy. What has profoundly changed in recent years, however, are their incentives. The growing pressure for financial liquidity in the U.S.

economy has provided them with the opportunity to enrich themselves under the mantra of creating value for shareholders. So successful have senior corporate executives been in this endeavor that, to a greater extent than has ever been the case since the rise of the corporate economy, they have separated their fate from that of the rest of the working population. On average, the pay packages of chief executive officers of large U.S. public corporations increased from 44 times the average factory worker's wages in 1965, already a substantial multiple, to 419 times in 1998 (Executive Pay 1999, 72). It is with the active cooperation of top corporate managers, therefore, that shareholder value had by the 1990s become a firmly entrenched principle of U.S. corporate governance.

Germany

As recently as the late 1980s, confidence in the ability of the "Rhenish system of capitalism" to deliver economic performance without sacrificing social cohesion was running at an all-time high. From the early 1990s, however, as Germany wrestled with the challenges and costs of reunification and then plunged into its worst recession since World War II, talk of the strengths of German capitalism was replaced by anxious discussion of the viability of *Industriestandort Deutschland* (Germany as an industrial location). Employers warned that German companies would be forced to relocate production abroad if drastic reforms of corporate structures and, indeed, the foundations of the social market economy were not undertaken to ensure closer attention to the bottom line. Senior German managers seemed to be increasingly influenced by what was happening overseas, especially in the U.S. corporate economy. Indeed, companies such as Daimler-Benz and Deutsche Bank, formerly seen as synonymous with the distinctive German postwar system of managerial capitalism, emerged at the forefront of a shareholder value movement in Germany in the mid- to late 1990s.

Yet there are also many signs of business as usual in the German corporate sector. Within German companies, even those that are most strident in proclaiming their conversion to shareholder value, corporate resource allocation processes are only beginning to be overhauled to accord with its logic. Among serious proponents of shareholder value, moreover, there is a certain skepticism that German managers know what they mean and mean what they say when they speak of the merits of shareholder value for enhancing corporate performance. Many advocates of the current German corporate economic model, moreover, do not believe that corporate resource allocation in German enterprises will be fundamentally transformed to better serve financial interests.

It is certainly true that the institutional foundations of the postwar system of corporate governance in Germany have until recently proven to be more enduring than those in the United States. Nevertheless, various pressures have built up on the German system of corporate governance that raise questions about its sustainability in its current form. Many of these pressures are the result of structural changes in the German financial sector that are generating support in Germany for higher returns on corporate equities in particular and financial assets in general. As in the United States, these changes are rooted in the rising level of savings generated by the country's postwar economic success and an evolution of the way these savings are allocated. They have, however, assumed an institutional form in Germany that is substantially different from their form in the United States.

Recent changes in the allocation of German household financial assets are considerable in historical perspective, with a marked shift out of bank deposits into higher-yielding savings instruments since the early 1970s. Competing for savings has provided German financial enterprises with strong incentives to pursue higher yields on financial assets.

Germany has one of the most extensive banking networks in the world, and all three sectors of the banking industry—the savings banks, the cooperative banks, and the private banks (including the big banks)—have been active participants in "the battle over the piggy bank" that has been under way in Germany in recent decades (Oberbeck and Baethge 1989, 287). Arguably, it is the large private banks—Deutsche Bank, Dresdner, and Commerzbank (the alleged "patient capitalists" of the German economy)—that have particularly strong incentives to push for higher returns on financial assets. They have less to lose than the savings and cooperative banks (with a combined total of 80 percent of savings deposits) through the disintermediation that has already resulted and will continue to result from the widespread introduction of market-based savings instruments. Moreover, with their access to high-income Germans through their retail networks, and their experience in securities markets at home and abroad, they are well positioned to exploit the profit potential of this business. Reflecting these incentives, they have been particularly active in the introduction of new savings instruments and in attempts to promote an equity culture in Germany.

The major insurance companies, like Allianz and Munich Re, have also become formidable competitors for the savings of German people. They have been eyeing the business opportunities in asset management that are growing as competition for yields heats up in Germany.

The incentives of these financial enterprises to stimulate demands for higher financial returns in Germany have been reinforced by similar trends toward heightened competition in all segments of their business. A major overhaul of the regulatory framework of the German financial markets that has been under way since the mid-1980s has facilitated and fostered greater competition (Deeg 1996; Story 1997). Margins have thus become very tight in all sectors of German banking, and financial enterprises have been looking to new business opportunities to compensate. Asset management is one such opportunity. For the major

German banks, investment banking is another. The level of competition in German finance is likely to increase still further as the big banks and other German financial enterprises battle with foreign competitors for business and profits. If the European Commission succeeds in its attempts to sever the ties between the savings and cooperative banks and the public sector, competition will become even more intense (Monti to Challenge 1999, 1).

Given the business conditions that the big banks face, to assume that they can be characterized as "patient capitalists" seems particularly misguided in the final years of the twentieth century. Indeed, it has arguably long been a misnomer. The big banks have never been shy about advancing their profit interests and have done well from their postwar acquiescence in a system that provided German enterprise with financial commitment largely because of restrictions on competition, both among savings instruments and in the securities markets (O'Sullivan 2000, chap. 7). As Germans have grown wealthier and competition for their savings has intensified, however, the banks have increasingly seen their interests as being better served by promoting financial liquidity rather than financial commitment (Deutsche Bundesbank 1999b).

One important symptom of change, with direct implications for the German system of corporate governance, is the evolution of German financial enterprises' attitudes toward their industrial holdings. The big banks have been quietly reducing these holdings for some time; the number of companies in which banks held at least 10 percent of the shares (directly or indirectly) fell from 129 in 1976 to 86 in 1986, and the number in which they controlled a blocking minority of more than 25 percent fell from 86 to 45 (Deeg 1991, 201). In the 1990s, the reduction of big banks' industrial holdings gained apace. The major commercial banks, especially Deutsche Bank, have made no secret of the fact that they would like to receive higher returns from these holdings either by managing them more actively or by selling them. Until recently, the German tax system put a brake on the latter option; a major capital gains tax liability would have accrued on most of these holdings because they had been held by the banks for so long. As the banks have come under increasing financial pressures in their own businesses, however, that barrier has no longer proven prohibitive; in the last two years, they have sold off significant tranches of their participating interests (O'Sullivan 2000, 325). In December 1999, the German government promised to make the process of unwinding the cross-shareholding structure in Germany even easier when it proposed an important change in tax law that will, if approved, eliminate the tax liability incurred by the major banks and other large companies that sell off their participations in other companies.

This change in taxation is likely to be approved, although, even if successful, it will not take effect until 2002. Given the competitive conditions facing the leading financial enterprises in Germany, it seems entirely plausible that the banks and insurance companies will unwind most of their shareholdings, at least to the extent that they are unrelated to their core business interests. One can but speculate about the effect that such a change might have on German corporate governance. German banks, despite all the attention that their industrial shareholdings garner, held only 10.3 percent of the shares of German companies at the end of 1998 (down from 11.2 percent at the end of 1996). Yet one should not forget that mutual funds in the United States held only 10.2 percent of U.S. corporate stock in 1996. It is therefore likely that effects on the German corporate economy would be significant if the banks transferred ownership of the shares that they hold or if they managed them in a more aggressive manner. The likely effect of such changes also depends on what happens to the remaining 90 percent of German shares and in particular on the level of support that a stronger shareholder-value orientation finds among other shareholders. In the past, cross-shareholdings between nonfinancial enterprises in the German economy have acted as an important buffer against interference from outsiders, but the importance of these holdings has declined rapidly in recent years and, with the proposed tax changes, is likely to diminish even further; at the end of 1998, nonfinancial enterprises held 30.5 percent of all German shares, down from 37.6 percent at the end of 1996. The shares released from the cross-shareholding network seem to have been bought up by foreign investors (whose holdings of German shares increased from 11.7 percent to 15.6 percent during the same period) and investment funds, which increased their ownership of German shares from 9.1 percent to 12.9 percent (Deutsche Bundesbank 1999a).

The foregoing account underlines the fact that there are clear signs of change in the incentives and behavior of at least one group of actors who have the potential to transform a critical element of the postwar German system of corporate governance. Furthermore, change is not confined to the banks. Major German corporations are singing to the tune of shareholder value to a degree considered unimaginable as recently as the early 1990s, and they display a growing propensity to adopt innovations, from executive stock options to stock buybacks, that until recently were regarded as anathema in German business circles. The recent success of the *Neuer Markt* has substantially increased the number of listed companies in Germany, and it is "widely expected that the going public trend will continue since thousands of mid-size companies suffer from a deteriorating equity position and face a succession crisis from company founder to non-familial management" (Deeg 1996, 12). The appetite of German households for equities has also been increasing in recent years; the proportion of Germans owning shares increased from 5.4 percent in the early 1990s to 7.6 percent in 1995 and then again to 8.8 percent in 1997 (*Deutsche Bank Bulletin* 1995, 9; Germany's Capitalist Piglets 1997, 85). The financial assets of institutional investors have also increased substantially, from

36.5 percent of gross domestic product (GDP) in 1990 to 57.5 percent in 1997 (OECD 1998).

It is important, however, not to overstate the degree to which change has penetrated to the heart of the German system of governance. It is still the case today that most companies in Germany, including some of its most successful enterprises, have nothing at all to do with the stock market. Furthermore, notwithstanding changes in the structure of German savings in recent decades, equity holdings as a percentage of private financial assets remain low in international comparison (*Deutsche Bank Bulletin* 1995, 9). The German financial system has generated nothing approaching the vast liquid funds under management by U.S. financial institutions, whose assets increased from 123.8 percent of GDP in 1990 to 202.8 percent in 1997. The difference in absolute terms is even more striking; in 1997, for example, institutional investors in the United States held financial assets of approximately U.S.$15,868 billion compared with U.S.$1202 billion for their German counterparts (OECD 1998, 20).

Pension funds account for a substantial proportion of the difference, and if there is one area in which substantial change could induce a systemic shift in corporate governance in Germany, it is the pension system. The financial assets of German pension funds were, at 2.9 percent in 1997, negligible compared with their American counterparts, which had comparable holdings of 72.5 percent of GDP. There has been a significant increase since 1960 in personal provision for pensions in Germany, with most of it channeled through insurance companies. If we add the holdings of insurance companies, we arrive at a somewhat different picture (34.8 percent of GDP in Germany versus 115.6 percent in the United States), but the relatively vast scale of U.S. funds under management by institutional investors for pension purposes is still not in question (OECD 1998).

The most important reason for the differences between Germany and the United States in accumulated pension funds under management is the relative importance of the state pension system in Germany. As a pay-as-you-go system, the German government pension system generates no reservoir of surplus funds to be allocated. Instead, almost 75 percent of the financing for the system comes from employee and employer contributions on the basis of earnings up to a ceiling of 1.8 times the average gross earnings of all insured individuals; the remainder is paid by the federal government out of general revenues (World Bank 1994, 361).

Since 1960, there has been a steady increase in the contribution rate required to finance the pay-as-you-go pension system; it has risen from 14 percent in 1960 to 20.3 percent in 1997 (Deutsche Bundesbank 1997, 42). A further increase in the contribution rate to 21 percent in 1998 was forestalled only by the emergency measure agreed in April 1997 to raise the value-added tax by one point, to 16 percent. The levy is expected to rise still further in the decades to come as growing life expectancy and a decline in fertility contribute to a double aging process in Germany. The OECD has forecast that, by 2040, pension costs in Germany will amount to an enormous 18 percent of GDP (Roseveare et al. 1996).

Demographic trends are not, however, the only source of increased pressure on the financing of the German pension system. They are compounded by labor market pressures. All major OECD countries have experienced a strong decline in labor supply by the elderly, but the German participation rate for older people is now among the lowest of the major OECD countries. Some scholars have attributed the striking German trend to the structure of the state pension system, which provides generous incentives to retire and, until recently, pension benefits that did not decrease with age in a manner that was actuarially fair (Börsch-Supan 1991). The low average retirement age also reflects the use of early retirement as a means of contracting enterprise workforces; in 1994, for example, only 29 percent of new pension benefits awarded were paid to those retiring at normal retirement age (Queisser 1996, 18; see also Abraham and Houseman 1993). The extensive use of early retirement increases the pressures on the pension system beyond what the growing old-age dependency ratio alone would imply.

How Germany deals with the problem of supporting more and more people in old age will have critical implications for the sustainability of financial commitment to productive investment in the German economy. The growing concerns that have been expressed in Germany about the funding of pensions suggest that if the pressures for higher yields in Germany, especially from corporations, are to get a major push in the near future, it will come from changes in the pension system. To date, the initiatives undertaken by the government to improve the funding situation in the state pension scheme have focused on making adjustments within the framework of the pay-as-you-go pension system, but the financial pressures on the system have increased, and the proposed solutions are becoming more radical.

It is by no means assured that there will be a major shift to the funding of pensions through the equity markets. The political opposition in Germany to such a move would likely be enormous. The issue is not, however, solely dependent on domestic politics. What happens to pension provision in Germany will also depend on policy initiatives by the European Union. In its attempts to promote the mobility of capital and labor across European borders, the European Commission has for some time identified retirement provision as one of the key obstacles to achieving its objectives. In May 1999, the commission issued a blueprint for pension reform, "Towards a Single Market for Supplementary Pensions," which called for the liberalization of the European Union's pension fund market and reported that substantial progress had been made in gaining consensus between member states about the regulatory changes

that such a development would require (European Commission 1999). Major companies, especially in the financial sector, have been exerting pressure on the European Commission to develop a directive along these lines, but they have also been threatening to take the issue to the European Court of Justice if the commission does not comply with their demands. However it comes about, a move toward funding seems likely in the current political climate in Europe, notwithstanding serious concerns about the effects on pension security of such a move (see, for example, Boldrin et al. 1999).

The preceding account underlines the fact that Germany has not witnessed as dramatic a transformation in its system of corporate governance as the United States. The critical institutional supports for its postwar system of governance remain largely intact. However, there have been important developments in the financial sphere that call into question the future viability of the German postwar system because of changes in the abilities and incentives of key actors in the postwar system, especially the major financial enterprises, that they have induced. Systemic change is unlikely to occur, however, without greater structural change in the financial sector. The most likely impetus for such change, beyond the proposed tax reform, would be an overhaul of the pension system. To the extent that there is a major push toward individualization of pension provision with the greater resort to financial markets, and equity markets in particular, that such a strategy would almost inevitably entail, one important effect would undoubtedly be stronger pressures on corporations to generate higher yields for their shareholders.

To the extent that these pressures develop, the productive challenges that German enterprises face may prove complementary in bringing about a transformation of the German system of governance. Business elites are pointing to strong international competition from other parts of the world, especially Asia but also Eastern Europe, as a rationale for unwinding key elements of the postwar German model. As corporate enterprises struggle to deal with these challenges, the relationship between senior German managers and the rest of the corporate organization is an important one to watch. To the extent that the managers become increasingly segmented from the people whom they manage, share prices will undoubtedly become more and more important as an incentive either for their personal gains through stock options or for their empire building through mergers and acquisitions. As compared with their U.S. counterparts, however, the ability of top managers in Germany to go off in their own direction is restrained by the role ascribed to workers in the German system of corporate governance. If German managers try to follow their American counterparts down the path to shareholder value, they will have to contend with a politically powerful labor movement that has a voice in determining for whom and how corporations should be run.

UNDERSTANDING THE RECENT EVOLUTION OF CORPORATE GOVERNANCE

In the foregoing discussion, I emphasized certain similarities in the sources of recent pressures for change in both the U.S. and German systems of corporate governance. Of particular importance is the postwar accumulation of financial assets by certain groups in the population as well as the rise in intergenerational dependence that has resulted from population aging and, especially in Germany, the growth of early retirement. These two countries are not alone in experiencing these pressures. Similar tensions are apparent in other economies in which some or all of the following features are apparent: substantial accumulations of financial assets, broad-based expectations of a period of paid retirement at the end of people's working lives, and a rise in intergenerational dependence due to population aging and early retirement. In France, Japan, and Italy, for example, various combinations of these factors have created momentum for reform of corporate governance systems.

As the comparison of the United States and Germany also reveals, however, the nature of these pressures varies considerably across countries, as does their impact, as a result of national institutional diversity, especially in financial and pension systems. Without an analysis of the development of these, and other, national institutions, the pressures on corporate governance systems and the responses to them cannot be understood. An analysis of the productive pressures confronting national systems of corporate governance has not been undertaken here but would provide support for a similar conclusion. Different countries display distinct productive strengths and frailties that are closely related to their institutional formations. These patterns have had an important effect on the timing and seriousness of the vulnerability of their leading corporate enterprises to competitive challenges and, relatedly, the susceptibility of their extant systems of corporate governance to challenges for reform from within the domestic economy (O'Sullivan 2000, chaps. 5 and 8).

As important as, and arguably less understood than, the dynamics of corporate governance at the national level is the interaction between the evolution of national systems of corporate governance and the international economy. Given the weight of U.S. institutional investors in international securities markets, it is of particular importance that we understand the relationship between the internal realignment of the U.S. system of corporate governance and international developments. There is certainly a perception in the popular press, and among many academics, that U.S. investors (and their British counterparts) now exercise considerable influence over corporate resource allocation in continental Europe and Japan, as well as in many developing countries. Yet we know little about the mechanisms through which control over foreign corporations is exercised by Anglo-American institutional investors and

therefore about the true extent of that control.

The standard view is that if foreign executives resist pressures to deliver higher returns to shareholders, institutional investors will not invest in their shares and foreign corporations will find themselves short of capital. Common though that assumption is, it is mistaken. The markets for corporate stocks are predominantly secondary markets. That shares are exchanged on them has no necessary implications for the financing of productive investment. Moreover, it is not clear why major corporations in the leading advanced industrial economies need to raise cash to finance their investments. Retained earnings—undistributed profits and capital consumption allowances—have always provided, and continue to provide, the financial resources that are the foundations of investments in productive capabilities that make innovation and economic development possible (Lazonick and O'Sullivan 1997a, 1997b).

Why then do corporate executives care about their stock price to the degree that they are willing to succumb to the demands of foreign or domestic institutional investors? One answer is that the spread of stock options as a means of compensation for senior corporate managers gives them a personal interest in the stock price. Arguably even more important are foreign executives' battles for global dominance. Merger activity has been rising in advanced industrial economies for some time; it reached unprecedented levels in the 1990s. Cross-border merger activity in particular has exploded. Since shares are increasingly the currency of exchange, the lure of having a highly valued stock that can serve as a merger currency or a deterrent against undesirable bidders provides foreign executives with strong incentives to dance to the tune of shareholder value or to at least appear to do so.

From this point of view, foreign corporate executives are seen as to some extent complicit in driving forward the shareholder value movement because they have chosen particular paths to personal wealth and business success. The degree to which executives are willing to embrace these types of behavior differs across countries. An understanding of the social organization of corporate economies as productive entities is an important source of insight in analyzing the incentives and abilities of top managers to buy into pressures from the financial sphere to transform the extant system of corporate governance.

CONCLUSION

There are serious limits to the globalization thesis for understanding the types of development in corporate governance discussed here. The globalization argument with respect to corporate governance generally relies on the contention that greater capital mobility will lead to a more efficient allocation of capital in the world economy. In a world in which capital is mobile, German, French, Japanese, and other enterprises will have to ensure that investing in their corporate stock offers a competitive rate of return to foreign and domestic investors. If not, capital will move elsewhere. Given that U.S. and British corporations provide high returns to shareholders, the implication of being competitive on international equity markets is that other countries must go further down the path toward a corporate governance system that, as in the United States and Britain, promotes the interests of shareholders as the number-one priority, or risk undermining their productive capabilities because of a shortage of investment capital.

Yet what is the relationship between international capital flows and real investment in the economies to which they go? Most of what is described as portfolio investment involves exchanges of securities on secondary markets that have no direct implication for the productive economy at all. Moreover, the distinction between foreign direct investment, which many economists believe to be more desirable from the point of view of the real economy, and portfolio capital flows has become very blurred in recent years as the importance of cross-border asset swapping has grown; cross-border mergers and acquisitions accounted for 50.9 percent of foreign direct investment in 1997 and 63.8 percent in 1998 (United Nations Conference on Trade and Development 1999).

As in the case of portfolio investment, merger and acquisition (M&A) activity has no necessary implications for productive investment. In the aftermath of an acquisition, the acquiring company may make substantial investments in the acquired company, but levels of M&A activity tell us nothing about the extent to which this is happening, and they are certainly not a measure of such real investment. Moreover, the record of performance for M&A activity within countries is sufficiently negative that there are no grounds for assuming, a priori, that such investment, even if it occurs, will generate improved economic performance.

The supposed merits of international capital mobility have been subject to more contestation recently (see, for example, Bhagwati 1998), but what concerns most critics is the volatility of international capital markets that portfolio flows are alleged to induce. The more fundamental question of whether these flows play the role assigned to them in economic theory as suppliers of capital for investment continues to attract insufficient scholarly attention. Furthermore, what is still not widely recognized is that what Bhagwati (1998) calls the "capital myth" at the international level is merely an extrapolation of the problems encountered by mainstream economic theory in explaining the relationship between financial institutions and economic development within nations.

Nowhere are the deficiencies of the conventional view more striking than in the case of the stock market. The common assumption is that the stock market is an important institution for channeling finance from savers to investors. It is this assumption that underpins the shareholder theory of corporate governance that is such an important component of the globalization argument with respect to corporate governance; to the extent that countries develop well-functioning stock markets, and that the interests of corporate managers are aligned with shareholders' interests, overall economic efficiency will allegedly be enhanced.

In fact, the relationship between active stock markets and economic performance is based on conjecture rather than empirical proof. In none of the leading industrial economies of the twentieth century has the provision of capital through the stock market been a central element in the process of economic development. For all the talk of the merits of free-flowing capital for economic growth therefore, there is little evidence that the stock market performs its assumed function as a crucial conduit of resources from savers to investors. Nor are there strong theoretical grounds for the widespread assumption that the stock market should play such a role. There is, in fact, no theory within mainstream economics that supports the idea that stock market efficiency leads to economic efficiency. In an article provocatively entitled "Stock Market Efficiency and Economic Efficiency: Is There a Connection?" Dow and Gorton (1997) underline this point:

There is a large body of research on welfare economics, and an equally large one on efficient markets theory. However, there has been relatively little work linking these two literatures. By and large welfare economists have not studied corporate control or asset pricing, while efficient-markets researchers have taken for granted that informational efficiency implies economic efficiency. (1090)

Given the dependence by most corporate enterprises on retained earnings rather than equity issues, the stock market is not the primary mechanism through which capital is allocated to investment in the corporate economy. Moreover, even when the stock market does allocate capital, as it does to some degree through the initial public offering market, it is not at all clear that it does so in an efficient manner. The initial public offering market has been shown by a number of academic studies to be particularly prone to bubbles and fads (see the review in Heisler 1994, 88-89) and, as such, is a far cry from the efficient capital market of economic orthodoxy.

The weak conceptual and empirical underpinnings of the globalization argument, at least if we interpret it as an economic argument, make it unsuitable as the basis on which to interpret recent developments in corporate governance systems. There have been important intellectual challenges to the globalization thesis, especially those emanating from international political economy and the "varieties of capitalism" literature. However, with a few exceptions, these challenges have not focused directly on the issue of corporate governance. Given the importance of corporate resource allocation to economic and social outcomes, it is crucial that we develop a more sophisticated analysis of national and international developments that determines who makes investment decisions in corporations, what types of investments they make, and how returns from investments are distributed.

Notes

1. In describing the evolution of corporate governance systems in the United States and Germany, I emphasize developments in the financial sector of both of these economies that have implications for the viability of their systems of corporate governance. Pressures from the productive sphere have also been important in influencing corporate governance in both of these countries, especially the United States. I have discussed these pressures elsewhere (O'Sullivan 2000), but I treat them in a cursory fashion herein due to space constraints.

2. In 1995, 40.3 percent of U.S. households had direct or indirect stock holdings, compared with 31.6 percent as recently as 1989. These holdings accounted for, on average, 41.5 percent of the financial assets of all U.S. households in 1995, up from 28.6 percent in 1989 (U.S. Department of Commerce 1998, 532).

3. The contribution of internal funds to net sources of finance for nonfinancial enterprises during the period 1970-89 has recently been estimated as 80.6 percent for Germany, 69.3 percent for Japan, 97.3 percent for the United Kingdom, and 91.3 percent for the United States (Corbett and Jenkinson 1996).

References

Abraham, Katherine and Susan Houseman. 1993. *Job Security in America: Lessons from Germany*. Washington, DC: Brookings Institution.

Bhagwati, Jagdish. 1998. The Capital Myth: The Difference Between Trade in Widgets and Dollars. *Foreign Affairs* May-June: 7-12.

Boldrin, M., J. Dolado, J. Jimeno, and F. Peracchi. 1999. The Future of Pensions in Europe. *Economic Policy* 14(29): 289-320.

Börsch-Supan, Alex. 1991. Aging Populations: Problems and Policy Options in the U.S. and Germany. *Economic Policy* 12: 103-39.

Brancato, Carolyn. 1997. *Institutional Investors and Corporate Governance: Best Practices for Increasing Corporate Value.* Chicago: Irwin Professional.

Corbett, Jenny and Tim Jenkinson. 1996. The Financing of Industry, 1970-1989: An International Comparison. *Journal of the Japanese and International Economies* 10(1): 71-96.

Deeg, Richard. 1991. Banks and the State in Germany: The Critical Role of Subnational Institutions in Economic Governance. Ph.D. diss., Massachusetts Institute of Technology.

———. 1996. German Banks and Industrial Finance in the 1990s. Discussion paper FS I 96-323, Wissenschaftszentrum Berlin.

Deutsche Bank Bulletin. 1995, 9 Jan.

Deutsche Bundesbank. 1997. *Monthly Report,* Sept.

———. 1999a. *Gesamtwirtschaftliche Finanazierungsrechnung.* Frankfurt: Deutsche Bundesbank.

———. 1999b. *Monthly Report,* July.

Dow, James and Gary Gorton. 1997. Stock Market Efficiency and Economic Efficiency: Is There a Connection? *Journal of Finance* 52(3): 1087-129.

Edwards, Franklin. 1996. *The New Finance: Regulation and Financial Stability.* Washington, DC: AEI Press.

European Commission. 1999. *Towards a Single Market for Supplementary Pensions.* Brussels: European Commission. Available at http://europa.eu.int/comm/dg15/en/finances/pensions/cpensen.pdf.

Executive Pay. 1999. *BusinessWeek,* 19 Apr., 72-118.

Germany's Capitalist Piglets. 1997. *Economist,* 6 Dec., 88.

Heisler, Jeffrey. 1994. Recent Research in Behavioral Finance. *Financial Markets, Institutions & Instruments* 3(5): 76-105.

Lazonick, William and Mary O'Sullivan. 1997a. Finance and Industrial Development: Japan and Germany. *Financial History Review* 4(2): 113-34.

———. 1997b. Finance and Industrial Development: The United States and the United Kingdom. *Financial History Review* 4(1): 7-29.

Monti to Challenge Berlin. 1999. *Financial Times,* 22 Oct.

Oberbeck, Herbert and Martin Baethge. 1989. Computer and Pinstripes: Financial Institutions. In *Industry and Politics in West Germany,* ed. P. Katzenstein. Ithaca, NY: Cornell University Press.

OECD (Organization for Economic Cooperation and Development). 1998. Institutional Investors. In *Statistical Yearbook.* Paris: OECD.

———. 1999. *OECD Principles of Corporate Governance.* Paris: OECD.

O'Sullivan, M. 2000. *Contests for Corporate Control: Corporate Governance and Economic Performance in the United States and Germany.* Oxford: Oxford University Press.

Queisser, Monika. 1996. *Pensions in Germany.* Washington, DC: World Bank.

Roseveare, D., W. Leibfritz, D. Fore, and E. Wurzel. 1996. Aging Populations, Pension Systems, and Government Budgets: Simulation for 20 OECD Countries. OECD Working Paper, no. 168, Organization for Economic Cooperation and Development, Paris.

Story, Jonathan. 1997. Finanzplatz Deutschland: National or European Response to Internationalisation? *German Politics* 5(3): 371-94.

Turner, John and Noriyasu Watanabe. 1995. *Private Pension Policies in Industrialised Countries: A Comparative Analysis.* Kalamazoo, MI: Upjohn Institute.

United Nations Conference on Trade and Development. 1999. *World Investment Report 1998: Trends and Determinants.* New York: United Nations.

U.S. Board of Governors of the Federal Reserve. Various years. *Flow of Funds Accounts: Flows and Outstandings.* Washington, DC: Board of Governors.

U.S. Department of Commerce. 1998. *Statistical Abstract of the United States.* Washington, DC: Government Printing Office.

World Bank. 1994. *Averting the Old Age Crisis: Policies to Protect the Old and Promote Growth.* New York: Oxford University Press.

Sustainable Economic Development in Rural America

By ADAM S. WEINBERG

ABSTRACT: While globalization threatens many of the historical drivers of rural American economies, it also opens up new opportunities for economic development. In particular, globalization increases the ability of rural communities to establish sustainable forms of economic development. "Sustainable development" refers to practices that simultaneously create economic vitality, environmental stewardship, and social equity. Rural communities have increasingly embraced the concept of sustainable development as a mantra for expressing their desired pattern of development. In this article, the author draws on his experiences at Colgate University with a project called the Hamlets of Madison County to develop a theoretical model that outlines the conditions and factors that shape the ability of rural communities to develop sustainable economies.

Adam S. Weinberg is assistant professor of sociology at Colgate University. He has published widely on sustainable development, including Urban Recycling and the Search for Sustainable Community Development *(2000), coauthored with David Pellow and Allan Schnaiberg. He served as a member of the Metropolitan and Rural Strategies Task Force, part of President Clinton's Council on Sustainable Development. He has also worked with a range of communities, nonprofit organizations, and government agencies on sustainable development projects.*

THIS article is an argument on behalf of and an illustration of sustainable economic development as the means by which rural areas can successfully participate in the global economy (Audirac 1997; President's Council 1999). "Sustainable economic development" refers to practices that simultaneously create economic vitality, environmental stewardship, and social equity (Audirac 1997). Although the concept of sustainable development is subject to varying definitions, in general the use of the phrase suggests forms of economic vitality that enhance the quality of life for current and future community members (Weinberg, Pellow, and Schnaiberg forthcoming; President's Council 1999). At its core, sustainable community development is a political project that articulates strategies to empower rural communities to locate assets and tap into the global economy in ways that enhance their ability to control their own future.

Critical to the success of this approach is the presence of what in the literature is referred to as "high-road" firms. These are producers that employ the best workers and latest technology to yield products with a high value (Harrison 1997; Thurow 1996; Kanter 1995). Production is carried out in smaller facilities where workers and managers can concentrate on mastering a small range of tasks (Harrison 1997; Rubin 1996). Thus products are made in components across diverse geographic regions, creating global networks of production. In a major study of global production processes, the late New School for Social Research

economist Bennett Harrison (1997) stated, "The business system is increasingly taking the form of lean and mean core firms, connected by contract and handshake to networks of other large and small organizations, including firms, governments and communities" (220).

High-road production would allow rural communities to compete for good jobs and people in sectors that are attractive to them. This would be true in two ways. First, high-road firms emphasize quality control and product innovations. They therefore need back-line workers who can continually adapt to changing computer-aided technologies and who can solve problems on the shop floor. They need frontline workers who are educated, articulate, and computer literate to provide customer service functions. Both frontline and back-line operations can be located anyplace where labor is good and the infrastructure is available.

Second, high-road production relies on a growing professionalized service sector that identifies, analyzes, and solves information-related problems around product design, production, distribution, marketing, and finance. Firms go to extraordinary lengths to recruit and retain such professionals. The latter in turn use their bargaining power and wealth to seek an enhanced quality of life. Increasingly, this quality is achieved by relocating from traditional urban areas to rural communities (Dent 1998).

A number of studies have documented the anxiety that rural communities have concerning development. In part, this apprehension comes from prior patterns of dysfunctional development, including natural resource extraction, industrial waste facilities, low-road industry, tourism, and prisons. These activities often brought economic growth but also social and ecological disruption. The apprehension also arises from a desire of rural residents for economic growth but without significant social change. Thus a major study done by the Aspen Institute concluded that rural residents "have no desire to turn their communities into small cities. They want to preserve the culture, values and way of life that make rural places so special" (Salant and Marx 1995, 20).

High-road firms help to alleviate these anxieties because they tend to be locked into positive labor structures. Their market niches necessitate that machinery and labor continuously change to meet consumer demand and competitive pressures. To do this, they typically adopt flexible organizational structures and high-performance work practices that foster greater worker responsibility for quality control and problem solving. These structures and practices include work teams, flexible job assignments, and information sharing between labor and management (Appelbaum and Batt 1994; Jones and Kato 1995). High-performance work practices rely on skilled workers. To attract such employees, firms tend to offer above-average wages. They also tend to invest continuously in worker training (Kanter 1995), which tends to reinforce that high-wage structure. Further, the same need to recruit and retain high-quality labor results in firms' creating profit-sharing and employee stock ownership plans and other mechanisms that tie the workers' fate to corporate profits.

High-road firms also tend to be active partners in bringing about positive forms of development. First, high-road firms view environmental pollution as a production problem, in which pollution is seen as an inefficient use of raw materials (Harrison 1997). In his review of high-road strategic planning, economist Grant Ledgerwood (1997) states, "Key global enterprises are establishing and forcing a competitive advantage for themselves through environmental protection" (30). Likewise, high-road firms are willing to invest in the community because an elevated quality of life raises job retention rates for the professional sector. Kanter (1995) states, "Professionals are recruited on a national and international basis; companies need to make sure that their home city has maximum amenities and minimum problems in order to compete for talent in a global labor market" (179).

CREATING
HIGH-ROAD INDUSTRIES

While globalization opens opportunities for rural communities to develop high-road industries, it does not ensure that it will occur. There are three elements essential for success: human capital, physical infrastructure, and adequate financing.

The importance of human capital has been emphasized by Harvard economist Michael Porter, who argued that a community's comparative advantage is greatly enhanced by the presence of highest-quality workers (Porter 1990). His finding has been reiterated by others, most notably Robert Reich (1992) and Lester Thurow (1996). In a recent study, sociologist Rosabeth Kanter (1995) concluded,

To succeed in the global economy, places must nurture the core capability that gives them international distinction, but they must also invest in other skills to support their core strength. They must seek interactions among strategies: for example, offering both education for professionals who will pioneer in new technologies and new concepts and training for production workers in world class operations that can use those technologies. (361)

The availability of human capital is only a necessary, not a sufficient, condition for successful development. A second essential factor is infrastructure. New technologies reduce the communication and transportation problems that have isolated rural locales, but communities need infrastructure to implement the technologies. Increasingly this means access to high-speed data transmission, digital communication equipment, international airports, and overnight transportation services. Firms also require more traditional forms of infrastructure. Products are still constructed within the confines of physical spaces. Firms need buildings, roads, housing stock, and other amenities. Harrison (1997) states,

I also define "productive" local economic development policy (as contrasted with a tax- and wage-cutting race to the bottom,

in which localities compete with one another by reducing their standard of living) as the building of stronger attractors for catching multilocational or networked capital. This is done by providing high-quality infrastructure—roads, bridges, waste disposal, telecommunications, transportation—and highly skilled labor. (33; see also Clark 1989)

Without appropriate infrastructure, a community is isolated whether it is only two miles from a city or in the middle of barren desert.

Untapped or unmobilized talent in many rural communities represents a key resource in the effort by rural communities to stimulate high-road development. In this, finance plays a critical role in encouraging otherwise dormant local entrepreneurial energies. Shulman (1998), for example, finds that communities are often unaware that they have preexisting firms that could be used in this effort. Many of these small businesses are underdeveloped because they have been undercapitalized by existing financial institutions. They have also been underserved by state agencies that tend to provide technical assistance to large firms.

Recent studies suggest that many small operations, commonly called microenterprises, have potential payoffs for rural community development. But the emergence of such firms requires seed money. Fortunately, these units are inexpensive to start, thus reducing the constraint that financing represents. Most microenterprises need under $20,000 for start-up costs. This contrasts favorably with Shuman's estimate that when businesses are recruited, the cost per job is $50,000

(Shuman 1998). Second, micro-entrepreneurs are "anchored to the community" through personal ties. When compared to non-locally owned firms, Shuman (1998) found that locally owned firms tend to pay well, contribute to the community, and eschew relocating as they grow. With therefore only modest financial support, microenterprise development can also help diversify the local economy and put it on a development path satisfactory to its residents.

A CASE STUDY: THE
HAMLETS OF MADISON COUNTY

Together, human capital, infrastructure, and financing provide the economic capacity needed to develop high-road industries. While these links are relatively straightforward, what is less clear is how a community goes about mobilizing itself to achieve sustainable economic development. To gain insight into this, I will discuss the experience at Colgate University to foster local economic capacity enhancement. In the fall of 1996, Peter Cann, the executive director of the Madison County (New York) Industrial Development Agency (IDA), developed a project called the "Hamlets of Madison County." The project was designed to reinvigorate the rural hamlets of central New York. These are small communities with populations of roughly 500-1800. Initially, I agreed to help Cann run community meetings in the hamlets with the objective of encouraging people to think more proactively about community development.

From the fall of 1997 through the winter of 1998, 31 Colgate students and I participated in 7 community meetings, averaging 55 people at each. We also participated in 15 smaller meetings, averaging 13 people. These meetings were difficult. We met intense resistance. A local mayor reflected the pervasive skepticism: "People have been here before. These things never really pan out, and we get left with the apathy." According to another person, "Change is always bad. It's always helpin' the person who tells you it's going to help you. Never does. Always helps them, and you get more taxes." In addition to these doubts, the environment was made difficult because the communities were rife with internal factions. Typical of the hamlets, in one community of 500 people, there were three quarreling groups revolving around a church, a volunteer fire department, and a women's club. None of the members of one would sit in the same room with members of the others.

To build attendance, we met individually with each social faction. This was an extremely labor-intensive process that often failed. Initially, we offered arguments about economic development and political organization. When this did not work, we used more explicit incentives. We announced that the U.S. Department of Agriculture (USDA) and the IDA had funds to implement projects. Although this did not minimize skepticism, it did create the perception that the project was real. A local organizer stated, "All of a sudden, people thought maybe there was something here. Nobody wants to be left out either." Finally, we brought students to the meetings, because community factions were less willing to fight in front of them. According to one person, "We were not going to embarrass ourselves in front of the students. We [didn't] want to seem small minded in front of them by bickering" (Weinberg 1999, 809).

In attending the meetings, we were able to see that there were a variety of untapped assets in the community that could be leveraged into enhanced developmental capacity. Furthermore, the resources needed to turn these assets into capacity were readily available. The difficulty was that we lacked the organizational infrastructure to mobilize the resources. These resources were grouped in four clusters: microentrepreneurs, midsize firms, infrastructure, and human capital.

First, we mapped 83 small microentrepreneurs (Weinberg and Vaughn forthcoming). Approximately 25 of them were developing innovative businesses that were selling products outside the area. Included was a contractor who purchased a computer numerically controlled (CNC) machine for subassembly furniture production; a weaver who raised sheep and used the wool to make high-end sweaters; a woodworker who made display cases for retail stores; and a machinist who produced a part for public transportation systems and who was attempting to use his profits to purchase suppliers adjacent to him. The problem was that these businesses were invisible; few people knew that they existed. Yet they paid good wages:

$10-$15 an hour, twice the average area manufacturing wage. In interviews, all of the businesses reported a desire to expand, if they could locate small loans and technical assistance.

As we did further research, we located a gap between the banks and microentrepreneurs. In theory, the Small Business Administration (SBA) had loan guarantee programs, making microenterprise loans attractive for the banks. In practice, the loans were too small to produce revenue for the banks, resulting in their lack of interest in the program. Furthermore, most of the microentrepreneurs could not qualify even for these SBA programs because they lacked conventional forms of equity and a documented business history. What we realized was that if we could obtain an initial first loan for them, it appeared that the banks would be able to make subsequent loans, because the microentrepreneurs would then have established a credit history and would presumably seek a larger loan later. We also learned that there was money readily available for technical assistance to increase human capital to run a small business. A number of federal agencies and foundations had funding programs, including the U.S. Department of Housing and Urban Development, the USDA, the U.S. Department of Commerce, the Aspen Institute, and ACCION International. Our difficulty was that although support was at least potentially available, we lacked the capability to tap these sources. We did not have anybody with the time or expertise to write competitive grants.

The second resource was midsize firms. We located four such firms with expansion goals of 20-50 percent. They also paid between $10-$15 an hour to their labor forces. They offered stable, skill-enhancing work with full benefits. The paradox here was that their expansion efforts seemed to be hampered by a scarcity of labor, although our community meetings were packed with people who claimed they were unemployed or underemployed. Here was another gap in our resources. While we had a potentially good workforce, too many people lacked basic employment soft skills: dependability, initiative, and interpersonal skills. The firms blamed the schools for not being rigorous enough with students. The schools claimed that local jobs were poor, thereby diminishing the aspirations of students. Both the schools and the firms were willing to be creative, but there was no mechanism for them to meet and develop programs.

The third resource cluster involved infrastructure. We found two empty buildings and a proposed airport business park that could house small firms, if needed improvements were made to them. While these buildings were sitting empty, local entrepreneurs were complaining that there was no vacant space for development. Again, there were funds available from the Department of Housing and Urban Development and the USDA for infrastructure development, but, as with funding sources generally, we were hampered because none of us possessed the expertise to write professional grant applications.

The final resource was human capital. We found hidden talent. As our meetings generated media coverage, we received unsolicited phone calls from local people with skills in community development, business recruitment, professional support skills (graphic design, Web page development, marketing), and grant writing. It turned out that there were a lot of people who lived in the community but commuted elsewhere for interesting work opportunities. They wanted to help but did not know how to do so.

Starting in the spring of 1998, Cann and I began to create informal and also formal groups that would mobilize the resources to turn the four assets into capacity, thereby encouraging high-road development. The two of us initiated a series of conversations between the four midsize firms and the school superintendents in their area. Initially, these meetings were frustrating. After each one, I felt certain that no one would come back to the next one. One person summarized, "We are all busy people who run organizations. These meetings are just talk. It's not clear about an outcome." But the participants in these discussions did return, and they did so for two reasons. First, both sides were under intense pressure to deal with a specific and vexing problem. Firms needed labor. Schools had to find some way to get the mid-quartile of high school students to be more engaged with the dynamics of the labor market. In addition, we were the only group with the potential to deal with the issues that arose. Cann and I both appeared to have the resources to create a program for them, if we all could agree on one.

Over the course of eight months, Cann and I worked aggressively with the group. Progress was slow. We brought in experts on school-business partnerships. We also gathered data on successful programs. Gradually, we began to identify specific ways in which we could share resources. This process has crystallized in a pilot school-to-work program for 35 high school students. One of the high-road companies went even further. It collaborated with the local branch of the State University of New York (SUNY) to pilot a two-year on-site manufacturing degree program. The classes will be taught at the company's site by SUNY faculty for the company's workers.

Our second effort was to bring the banks and microentrepreneurs together. We asked a senior vice president at each of the banks in the county to start visiting the microentrepreneurs. This yielded some mild success. The banks made two loans to small firms, permitting those companies to hire staff. Additionally, three of the businesses were encouraged to look elsewhere and were successful in finding financing sources. For example, one microentrepreneur located a CNC machine maker over the Internet who financed the purchase of a CNC machine. He also found a Web site for small firms to acquire subassembly contracts. Within three weeks of purchasing the machine, he had three large orders. Three other contractors joined with him. They legally incorporated, and built a small shop. Within four months, they hired two people and were expanding the shop.

It became clear to Cann and me that present was a large group of microentrepreneurs who could grow if they had access to technical assistance and capital. As a group, however, they were not organized. They were isolated businesses, struggling to get off the ground. Because they were unable to organize themselves, we began to think more broadly about developing an organization that could champion their efforts.

We were joined in this endeavor by the Town of Hamilton Long Range Planning Committee (LRPC). The LRPC had begun its efforts in 1993 but had mostly floundered. Committee members had little idea how to create a plan. In 1997, they had hired a consultant. As the LRPC and the consultant began to formulate a draft, it became clear that they shared with Cann and me an interest in starting a microenterprise development program. They also saw potential in the airport, if we could develop the infrastructure.

The consultant convinced the LRPC to focus less on the plan and more on the process of creating the plan as a mechanism to get people mobilized. If we could organize enough support, we could mobilize the funds to hire the consultant to write federal grants for projects. With this in mind, we convinced the committee to hold a town meeting in June 1998 to solicit input for the initial draft of the plan. In the face of skepticism within the LRPC that we could get more than 25 people to the meeting, the consultant and I put our experience as organizers to work. We mapped social groups and found appropriate community leaders to call members of each group (often multiple groups) to secure commitments to attend. On 18 June, over 125 people were present at the meeting.

The success of the meeting led to a series of smaller community meetings. It was during these meetings that Colgate first provided institutional support for the LRPC effort. Over the course of the fall, the groups worked diligently under the guidance of the consultant. It became apparent that if we could stay organized, there was lots of potential for acquiring outside funding for economic development projects. This point of synergy created an incentive for representatives of the various entities to start to understand each other and to come to trust each other enough to work together. In February, these efforts were formally institutionalized in the Partnership for Community Development (PCD).

At this writing (July 1999), the PCD is extremely fragile. Meetings often turn tense as competing agendas emerge. One of the largest problems has been tension over the impact of growth on the local community. Many community residents fear that local economic growth will destroy the small-town character of the community through rapid population growth or that it will contaminate the local environment with industrial pollution. The focus on high-road development has allowed us to manage this tension, as the PCD has championed projects that either develop local businesses that will not lead to sizable population growth or attract nonpolluting firms involved in subassembly, cybermarketing, or new emerging professionalized service sectors.

Thus our largest problems remain organizational. We hired the consultant to write grants and facilitate the organization of the PCD. However, most of her time goes to facilitation. There seems to be a constant stream of issues that require her to devote too much attention to local politics. She spends a good deal of her time making phone calls, returning hostile e-mail messages, and facilitating small meetings to manage political disputes. Each of the disputes arises from mistrust, which allows minor issues to become community controversies.

Still, we have started to generate some increased economic capacity. We have started the long process of raising funds to provide technical assistance and financing to entrepreneurs and to improve local infrastructure for a business park at the airport. A number of grant applications have been submitted to state and federal programs. This activity has generated other outcomes. The grants have created excitement from Colgate alumni, who have stepped forward and offered to fund a number of the projects. Likewise, a number of community residents are providing pro bono services in project development and administration, significantly reducing our costs.

A THEORY OF RURAL SUSTAINABLE ECONOMIC DEVELOPMENT

How do I account for our struggles and emerging gains? The key factor for us was local mobilization. We had untapped assets that could be used to increase capacity. However, we lacked the organization to mobilize them.

The importance of local mobilization has been underscored by recent social science research. Initially, this research emerged as a number of scholars noted the correlation between strategic planning programs and community development gains, especially in the Midwestern states. In 1995, a team of leading rural social scientists concluded an extensive review of these communities and concluded that strategic planning works because it makes "major progress towards building grassroots efforts and developing a sense of long-term commitment for local economic development" (Walzer and Deller 1996, iii). In a follow-up review of the published literature, Gruidl (1996) noted that "success does not depend on the plan itself, but on the process of creating it" (134). The process generates local mobilization.

Sociologists Jan Flora, Jeff Sharp, and Corneila Flora (1997) have traced the link between local mobilization and economic development to more specific factors. In a study of 1,099 rural communities, they found that mobilization matters because (1) it depersonalizes controversy, thereby allowing communities to engage in the conflict necessary to solve problems without fractionalizing; (2) it solicits participation from a diversity of individuals and institutions, thereby helping to mobilize the available resources within a community; and (3) it assists in the formation of community networks, linking groups internally to one another and linking the community to regional and national networks. In this way, it increases the potential resource base. Flora, Sharp, and Flora attempted to capture these dynamics with the concept of entrepreneurial social infrastructure (ESI). According to them, "Certain styles of interaction and manners of collectively approaching problems represent an additional 'bundle' of factors contributing to a locality's ability to respond to challenges in a rapidly changing context" (624).

In our case, ESI allowed schools and firms to stop blaming each other and to recognize that, by sharing resources, they could develop a mutually beneficial school-to-work program. It allowed for a comprehensive set of interactions between local entrepreneurs, banks, and the PCD. These conversations led the banks and entrepreneurs to recognize points of synergy, and they allowed the PCD to locate the gaps that needed to be overcome in order to develop a microenterprise program. Our deficiencies in ESI continue to slow us down, forcing the PCD to spend too much time engaging in organizational management and not writing grant applications. Most recently, the community has become split over a park and a library improvement project. The projects do not compete, but people are fearful that they might. We had to spend the better part of a week facilitating a series of formal and informal meetings to resolve the conflict.

If the link between mobilization and economic capacity is ESI, still unanswered is the question of how ESI is achieved: how do communities get organized? Incentives obviously matter. People must see that mobilization will have a payoff—either financially or otherwise. Capacities also matter. If adequate resources are not available, no level of good intentions will be sufficient. But aside from sufficient incentives and capacities, mobilization also is dependent upon elements of social chance. The British sociologist Sibeon (1999) defines social chance as the "contingent and indeterminate phenomena that are unplanned and which do not extend widely across time and/or social space" (84). These are the fortuitous events that are both critical and exogenous. The larger literature on community mobilization is rife with random events that spark mobilization: two people happen to meet; a disaster occurs. These are the events that cannot be created or planned for but play an important role in human behavior. Thus the Hamlets project emerged because the IDA solicited the help of a professor at the exact time that the latter (I) was looking for a project. The LRPC succeeded because it hired a consultant who had just moved into the community and who was also a strong community organizer.

Social chance is more than blind luck, because it can be enhanced. As ESI increases, so does the possibility of social chance. ESI increases internal networks, thereby increasing the chance that the right people will meet. ESI increases external networks. For example, we are likely to get a new business because somebody mentioned our project at a party in Syracuse that was attended by someone who knew an organization that was looking for empty space in a rural community. The fact is, however, that it was the rise of ESI that was responsible for people's talking to others outside the community about the empty building and the community's development efforts.

Thus we can postulate a theory of rural economic development as follows. A well-organized community is one that is able to define what it wants to accomplish and is able to do so to the extent that it is well organized. Incentives can play a powerful role as they encourage communities to engage in the kinds of activity that lead to ESI or specific programs to build capacity. Incentives involve more than the available money that can be leveraged. They also encourage people to believe that things can be done. They help them to have hope and thereby to engage in local mobilization activities. Capacity, ESI, and social chance all are enabling elements. The role of social chance is important. Hold communities constant with regard to ESI and capacity, and social chance—such as the presence of an active individual—can make all the difference. With these factors in place, rural communities can create the context for the development of high-road industries and sustainable community development. Figure 1 diagrams the theory.

CONCLUSION

Madison County has not yet succeeded in achieving the high road of economic growth outlined in this article. It therefore has not yet

FIGURE 1
A THEORY OF RURAL SUSTAINABLE ECONOMIC DEVELOPMENT

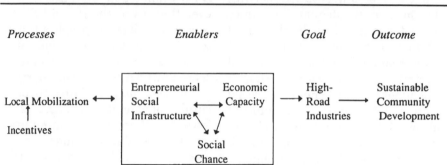

integrated itself as a producer in the global economy. Whether it will do so in the future is contingent on its continuing efforts at nurturing and mobilizing its resources. But a start has been made, and enough has been achieved to suggest that the effort is not foredoomed. Sufficient organization and resources are available to suggest that production for the global market is not out of the question. One day it may be possible to point to this county in central New York as an example of how a rural area can restructure itself to become an active agent of globalization.

References

Appelbaum, Eileen and Rosemary Batt. 1994. *The New American Workplace.* Ithaca, NY: ILR Press.

Audirac, Ivonne. 1997. *Rural Sustainable Development in America.* New York: John Wiley.

Clark, Gordon. 1989. *Unions and Communities Under Siege.* New York: Cambridge University Press.

Dent, Harry. 1998. *The Roaring 2000s.* New York: Simon & Schuster.

Flora, J., J. Sharp, and C. Flora. 1997. Entrepreneurial Social Infrastructure and Locally Initiated Economic Development in the Nonmetropolitan United States. *Sociological Quarterly* 38: 623-45.

Gruidl, John. 1996. Participant Evaluation of Strategic Planning Processes. In *Community Strategic Visioning Programs,* ed. Norman Walzer. Westport, CT: Praeger.

Harrison, Bennett. 1997. *Lean and Mean.* New York: Guilford Press.

Jones, Derek and Takao Kato. 1995. The Productivity Effects of Employee Stock-Ownership Plans and Bonuses. *American Economic Review* 85(34): 391-414.

Kanter, Rosabeth. 1995. *World Class.* New York: Simon & Schuster.

Ledgerwood, Grant. 1997. Environmental Stewardship of the Planet. In *Greening the Boardroom,* ed. Grant Ledgerwood. Sheffield, England: Greenleaf.

Porter, Michael. 1990. *The Comparative Advantage of Nations.* New York: Free Press.

President's Council on Sustainable Development. 1999. *Towards a Sustain-*

able America. Washington, DC: President's Council on Sustainable Development.

Reich, Robert. 1992. *The Work of Nations*. New York: Vintage Books.

Rubin, Beth A. 1996. *Shifts in the Social Contract*. Thousand Oaks, CA: Pine Forge Press.

Salant, Priscilla and Julie Marx. 1995. *Small Towns, Big*. Washington, DC: Aspen Institute.

Shuman, M. 1998. *Going Local*. New York: Free Press.

Sibeon, Roger. 1999. Governance and the Postnational Policy Process. In *Global Futures: Migration, Environment and Globalization*, ed. Avitar Brah, Mary Hickman, and Mairtin Mac an Ghaill. New York: St. Martin's Press.

Thurow, Lester. 1996. *The Future of Capitalism*. New York: Penguin Books.

Walzer, Norman and Steven Deller. 1996. Rural Issues and Trends. In *Community Strategic Visioning Programs*, ed. Norman Walzer. Westport, CT: Praeger.

Weinberg, Adam. 1999. The University and the Hamlets. *American Behavioral Scientist* 42(5): 800-813.

Weinberg, Adam, David Pellow, and Allan Schnaiberg. Forthcoming. *Urban Recycling and the Search for Sustainable Community Development*. Princeton, NJ: Princeton University Press.

Weinberg, Adam and Heather Vaughn. Forthcoming. The Home Based Businesses of Madison County: Creating Categories and Assessing Local Mechanisms for Local Self-Development. *Journal of the Community Development Society*.

Book Department

INTERNATIONAL RELATIONS AND POLITICS 186
AFRICA, ASIA, AND LATIN AMERICA 192
EUROPE 194
UNITED STATES 196
SOCIOLOGY 207
ECONOMICS. 214

INTERNATIONAL RELATIONS AND POLITICS

BARNETT, MICHAEL N. 1998. *Dialogues in Arab Politics: Negotiations in Regional Order*. Pp. xiii, 376. New York: Columbia University Press. $40.00. Paperbound, $17.50.

The first work of serious scholarship by an international relations scholar using the Middle East as a laboratory was *The Origins of Alliances* (1987) by Stephen Walt. The work under review takes primary aim at that neorealist analysis and proposes that a constructivist approach can better explain the region's interstate relations.

Michael Barnett's basic argument is that a reconceptualization of Arab politics that examines the actions of states and leaders within a normative context—in this case, that of Arab nationalism—better explains why Arab states competed the way they did and how that competition changed over time. In this detailed examination of 70 years of high politics, Barnett delineates five distinct periods, which he contends are characterized by changes in "conversations" between Arab leaders about the appropriate bases of the regional order.

The importance of Arab nationalism to the region's interstate politics will come as no surprise to those who have studied the Arab world over the years, although Barnett's book is the first attempt systematically to come to terms with its salience. In that respect, the work is a contribution. Unfortunately, on other fronts it is quite problematic.

In the first place, in his desire to discredit neorealism (which he conflates with realism), Barnett has set up a straw man. It is certainly true that traditional approaches have had trouble accounting for interstate behavior in areas outside the East-West theater, but that does not justify Barnett's dismissal of many of the clear bases of power in the region nor his regular assertions that "symbolic politics" was of primary importance. His first major misstep comes on page 1 where he writes, "Arab states have shunned any noticeable effort to enhance their security by amassing weapons." To the contrary, for most of the post–World War II period, this has been a highly militarized region. To downplay the reasons for this militarization and its role in shaping politics lays a very faulty basis for subsequent analysis.

To effectively challenge neorealism, Barnett apparently felt a need to explain everything based on norms; yet he (quite rightly) retreats on numerous occasions, admitting that other factors—military, political, economic—are at work as well. This leaves the reader wondering just how central the norms are to effective explanation and how the causal chain supposedly works.

There are numerous other problems as well. Barnett decided to limit his discussion to a handful of core countries because, he argues, they were "at the forefront of and defined the debate about regional order." But this begs the question of just how salient the norms of Arab nationalism in fact were to Arab states in general, as opposed to this core group that he examines. He also ignores numerous historical cases where it appears norms were of little import, and he fails seriously to entertain the possibility that there were norms other than Arab nationalism at work. Most glaring here is the absence of any discussion of Islamism, an increasingly potent force in the region after 1967, based on his erroneous claim that Islamists have been interested only in state-society rather than interstate relations. He also ignores the role of superpower competition in affecting the evolution of interstate relations, and he seems strangely naïve about Israel's role in the region: "That Israel represents a threat to the Arab nation is derived from Arab identity."

Finally, for a work that stresses—at least in theory—the importance of understanding the social and the cultural, this discussion remains largely at the level of superstructure or leadership. With the exception of the first historical period, in which he details the relationship between the emergence of Arab nationalism and the anticolonial movement, no attempt is made to link changes in the content of these "conversations" to ground-level developments. This is particularly odd given that there are a number of theoretically informed works by scholars with regional expertise who make strong cases for the impact of domestic politics and economics on Arab state foreign policy.

Constructivist approaches certainly have a contribution to make to the study of international relations. But to make it, they must more analytically appreciate the material realities of the states whose behavior they seek to explain.

LAURIE A. BRAND

University of Southern California
Los Angeles

BERGER, THOMAS U. 1998. *Cultures of Antimilitarism: National Security in Germany and Japan*. Pp. xiii, 256. Baltimore, MD: Johns Hopkins University Press. $38.00.

How to explain the ingrained aversion to military power in contemporary Germany and Japan, each a paragon of aggressive militarism in its own right earlier in the twentieth century? In *Cultures of Antimilitarism*, Thomas Berger looks for answers in culture, specifically the belief systems formed in the crucible of crushing military defeat in World War II and the stark lessons drawn subsequently by elites and masses from their troubled pasts. Discounting alternative explanations based on history, geopolitics, and postwar multilateralism, Berger develops a model of foreign policy formation that highlights the causal role of the "political-military cultures" that formed in each country during the first two decades after the war. Once consolidated, they influenced German and Japanese defense and security policy in profound ways, serving as a reservoir of goals and norms for political actors, shaping elite and mass perceptions of both the domestic and international political environments, and influencing the capacity of political actors to mobilize national resources for military ends.

In chapters that lay out a comparative chronology of postwar foreign policy in each country, Berger shows that political-military cultures did not spring full-blown from the head of Jove but emerged fitfully and conflictually out of debates among established political groupings or "subcultures" that were "bound by common ideological interpretations of history and definitions of reality." Once established through pluralist contestation, each political-military culture was subject to change, albeit on the margins (hence the strong policy continuities in each country), as shifting domestic and international realities intruded.

Berger carefully traces manifest differences between German and Japanese approaches to military power to variations in their wartime experiences and the lessons gleaned therefrom, and then links differences in their political-military cultures to variations in behavior and outcomes along several key dimensions of policy, such as alliance politics, military doctrine and force structures, and civil-military relations. Berger employs counterfactual analysis repeatedly to good effect, demonstrating plausibility that in situations that called for a response based on military power, Germany or Japan chose to act in a manner consistent with its political-military culture, usually because governing elites feared an antimilitarist public backlash.

The shortcomings of this volume are common to scholarship that relies on culture as an explanatory variable. For one, culture, however much it incorporates a dynamic element (as does Berger's), is best at accounting for continuity, not change. As such, cultural explanations can easily be overtaken by events. Bonn's recent decision to permit German bomber pilots to take part in North Atlantic Treaty Organization air strikes on Serbia is difficult to reconcile with Berger's characterization of its political-military culture as "permanent." It may be permanent in the sense that the cabinet decision elicited an uneasy reaction from the public and opened up a deep divide within the Red-Green coalition, but it is impermanent insofar as the cabinet sanctioned the use of military force.

This volume also confirms that it is extremely difficult to catch ideas in action—that is, to disentangle and then isolate the effects of belief systems from those of material interests and institutional structures. In some ways, Berger complicates his task by casting the country narratives in terms of the clash of contending subcultures—struggles over foreign policy appear to be driven as much by political-electoral interest as they are by antimilitarist beliefs. But perhaps that is precisely the point—culture matters, not to the exclusion of all else but along with other factors or, in some cases, as a chief influence. *Cultures of Antimilitarism* shows that there is something truly distinctive about the approach to military power in contemporary Germany and Japan, something that resides in the realm of belief.

JEFFREY J. ANDERSON

Brown University
Providence
Rhode Island

COOK, TIMOTHY E. 1998. *Governing with the News: The News Media as a Political Institution.* Pp. xi, 289. Chicago: University of Chicago Press. $48.00. Paperbound, $17.95.

Scholars who have acceded to a trend in modern dictionaries by treating the word "media" as grammatically singular will find support for their concession in *Governing with the News.* In this book, Timothy Cook argues that news media constitute a political institution. He has crafted a succinct (192 pages of text) theoretical essay that draws on studies and insights from social science, communication, and journalism. Communication specialists may ponder how much Cook adds to long-standing understandings of interrelations between politicians and reporters. Social scientists may contest the author's many interesting derivations from "American political development" and "the new institutionalism." The nonspecialist, however, should delight in Cook's perceptive view of journalists and journalism. To oversimplify, this book argues that reporters, editors, and publishers are, on the whole and as a whole, political and often even governmental.

To advance that thesis, Cook reviews the history of reciprocal relations between those officials and institutions that have long been recognized to be political or governmental and those journalists and editors who have held themselves apart from politics and government. Cook's learned reexamination reiterates that politicians and reporters have always been at least somewhat interdependent and sometimes outright symbionts.

Subsidies, sponsorship, and solicitude have intertwined governors and journalists throughout the history of the Republic. Even if they do not refuse blandishments, news media may assert their independence by cultivating professionalism. Indeed, plausibly professional independence often makes the press more useful politically.

Media professionalism has grown throughout recent history, so canons and formats are expected or demanded of newspeople. The greater the professionalization of news gathering, the greater the standardization of form and content in news reporting. As news becomes more formalized and formulaic, routines and practices become taken for granted, natural, and normal. Cook argues that, as the profession standardizes routines and practices, the news business tends to converge on a unified set of expectations and roles. In sum, the recent history of the news media suggests to Cook that, to some nontrivial extent, they constitute a unity.

Whether the news business is an aggregation of recipients of patronage, a pack of freebooters, a multiplicity of competing journalistic paradigms, or a coalescing singularity, it must set itself apart from politics and government in theory because it cannot get away from politics and government in fact. Rather, it ends up in the middle of what it covers. While it is hardly news that journalistic observers are also participants, Cook explores the nature of their institutional, as opposed to individual, participation in politics and government.

Viewed as an institution, the news is a prerequisite for even a semblance of democracy. To reach constituents, those in office must employ intermediaries who can deliver the constituents in multitudes that are predictably large and homogeneous enough to maximize the performance of carefully selected symbols and artfully crafted messages. Because governmental and political entities must secure coverage, they must control coverage. As governors and politicians start to practice journalism, members of the news profession must anticipate how governors and politicians will attempt to use them. Inevitably, journalists do politics, if not government. Theoretically, independent institutions come to participate in each other's routines and practices.

If Cook is correct, the news media constitute an institution apart from but in the middle of government and politics. This thesis will provoke a profitable debate. Even readers who cannot go all the way with Cook's thesis will enhance their appreciation of the media as they follow his provocative arguments.

WILLIAM HALTOM

University of Puget Sound
Tacoma
Washington

FRIMAN, H. RICHARD. 1996. *Narcodiplomacy: Exporting the United States War on Drugs.* Pp. xiii, 170. Ithaca, NY: Cornell University Press. $29.95.

Conventional wisdom among those who study the Latin American cocaine trade is that source countries such as Peru, Bolivia, and Colombia have a weak state apparatus and, therefore, cannot accomplish the goals of U.S. anti-drug policy. Put another way, these countries expend so much energy and so many resources trying to govern that they cannot really accede to U.S. demands. Some scholars assert that the fact that the cocaine trade has not been eliminated in such countries has been the result of not willfulness but incapacity. To others, U.S. policy demands threaten to destabilize these countries. It is an important issue for both scholars and policymakers. Both are going to have to rethink the issue of state capacity after reading this book. The issue is not as straightforward as we thought.

Richard Friman examines U.S. narcodiplomacy in Germany and Japan in the twentieth century. The scope of the study meant that he was able to examine Japan and Germany when they were independent actors, through the occupation, and, finally, as independent nations once again. Germany and Japan were major producers, exporters, and traffickers, had their domestic drug laws rewritten by the United States during the occupation, and then emerged as two of the most powerful nations in the world, fully capable of being major financial centers of the drug trade. Because both have played these various roles in narcodiplomacy, studying them tells us a lot about state capacity and the ability to withstand external pressures.

The drug trade in these countries was not just in cocaine, although Germany was a major producer before World War II. The countries responded to their own particular perceptions of the problem and needs. Japan did not want the Chinese experience with opium, so it adopted and enforced strict drug laws. However, its military was willing to foster the drug trade in order to undermine China as it sought to conquer that country in the

1920s and 1930s. Pre-1945 Germany—whether the Weimar Republic or the Nazi regime—selectively resisted international control attempts. Since 1945, Japan has not been much worried about domestic drugs except for some concern about amphetamines; it has not been much of a player in the international arena. Germany, faced with a growing heroin problem, created in part by usage among American military forces and also by the importation of cocaine via Spain, has passed tougher domestic drug laws. This fit the U.S. agenda. However, Germany also declared drug usage a disease and sought therapeutic approaches rather than just the U.S.-preferred punishment route.

Friman draws upon British and American diplomatic files, German documents, and the most important studies in the field. Ideally, one would have liked to see the use of Japanese original sources, of course, but he makes a case without them. His research allows him to draw important conclusions.

He organizes the work into six chapters. After an introductory chapter, he devotes a chapter each to Germany and Japan before World War II and a chapter to each country in the period since that war, followed by a concluding chapter. Such an organization allows him to sketch the policies of Japan and Germany without bogging the reader down in too much detail.

In terms of the study of drug diplomacy, Friman asserts that domestic and international drug policies are not simply a matter of state capacity. Even when strong, Japan and Germany addressed their own agendas. At times, they have acceded to some of the wishes of the United States in order to pacify the latter but, weak or strong, they have sought their own destinies.

DONALD J. MABRY

Mississippi State University
Mississippi State

MUELLER, DENNIS C. 1996. *Constitutional Democracy*. Pp. xii, 370. New York: Oxford University Press. $65.00.

Dennis Miller, a professor of economics, applies economic theories in general—externalities, prisoners' dilemmas, and public goods—and the public choice theory in particular to his analysis of national governmental institutions and development of normative recommendations for a constitutional democracy.

After briefly listing "governmental failures" in the United States, Mueller attributes them to geographic representation, centralization, and separation of powers. He is convinced that Article I, section 8, of the U.S. Constitution "limits the Congress to eighteen rather narrowly defined powers" and concludes that the growth in the power of the national government is due to reinterpretation of these power grants by the U.S. Supreme Court.

The scope of the book is extraordinarily wide and stresses the connections between the constitutional structure of governments and policy outcomes by comparing the U.S. system with other national systems. To develop normative precepts for members of a constitutional convention, Mueller explores democracy in other nations, purposes of government, the nature of a constitution, federalism, direct and representative democracy, voting systems, parliamentary democracy, referenda, bicameralism, citizens' rights, redistribution of resources, the executive branch, the judiciary, citizenship, and a constitutional convention.

Mueller is an advocate of the principle of subsidiarity that holds that governmental functions should be performed by the government closest to the people capable of performing the functions. Furthermore, he recommends direct democracy in the form of neighborhood and town assemblies of voters and the use of referenda.

Proportional representation (PR) is viewed as an electoral system that overcomes the major problems of geographic representation. Mueller is convinced that the problem of governmental instability in certain parliamentary nations, often attributed to PR, "stems from the practice of combining" PR "with the requirement [that] the parliament also form the executive," and the cure, he feels, is separation of executive and legislative powers.

This book is overly ambitious in addressing important topics. In consequence, space limitations result in inadequate coverage of many topics, minor factual errors, and overgeneralizations, including the following.

Mueller writes, "In Germany, the number of seats a party can occupy is determined by the number of votes each party receives across the entire nation" (105). He fails to indicate that one-half of the Bundestag members are elected by single-member districts. Similarly, he writes, "Germany has a bicameral parliament" (199). The Bundesverfassungsgericht (constitutional court) has opined that the Bundesrat is not the upper house of parliament.

Mueller also writes, with respect to voting rights, "To date, it has been only black minorities who have been protected by the courts" (145). The Voting Rights Act Amendments of 1975 extended the act's coverage to four "language" minorities.

The book's epilogue concludes, "Crime in the United States has several causes. The alienation of minorities, drugs, and easy access to guns are prominent among them" (342). The term "minorities" apparently is a code word for blacks and possibly Hispanics. Mueller believes that "a system of proportional representation would increase minority representation . . . and remove this source of alienation" (342). Although the single-transferable vote system of PR has provided proportional representation for blacks, Hispanics, Asian Americans, and other groups on New York City community school boards, the percentage of eligible voters casting ballots has declined since the system was installed in 1971, and only 7 percent voted in the last election, suggesting alienation has not been eliminated.

Mueller recognizes that it is improbable that his suggestions will be accepted by the United States and West European nations, but he believes East European and developing nations may be more receptive.

JOSEPH F. ZIMMERMAN

State University of New York
Albany

AFRICA, ASIA, AND
LATIN AMERICA

EHRET, CHRISTOPHER. 1998. *An African Classical Age: Eastern and Southern Africa in World History, 1000* B.C. to A.D. 400. Pp. xvii, 354. Charlottesville, VA: University Press of Virginia; Oxford, UK: James Currey. $45.00.

Recovering the early eastern and southern African past, given the scarcity of written records or even conscious historical memory, is a difficult and highly specialized endeavor. Christopher Ehret has been an important part of this endeavor since he began publishing work based on his dissertation more than thirty years ago. *An African Classical Age* showcases the technical skills, extensive and creative research, mature reflection, and wide-ranging insights that Ehret has developed over these years.

Ehret's basic approach in this book is to place in the background the comparative, historical-linguistic evidence central to his reconstruction and interpretation. The most important of this evidence—relating to the processes of dialect divergence, sound change, word borrowing, and semantic shifts—is summarized in some 46 tables located throughout the text and 33 pages of appendices. The text narrative is thus freed for broad, imaginative interpretations of social, cultural, and economic developments and interactions over nearly 1,500 years concerning most of the significant ethnolinguistic groups then on the historical stage. These included Khoisan gatherer-hunters as well as the predominantly farming and/or herding Central Sudanian-, Eastern Sahelian-, Southern Cushitic-, and Bantu-speaking communities.

Bantu-speaking groups receive the greatest attention. It was, after all, during the last millennium B.C. and first millennium A.D. that Bantu-speaking communities established themselves across much of the region, often absorbing or pushing out previous settlers of different cultural and language backgrounds in the process. This is by now a relatively well-known story, which typically includes the establishment of ironworking among the Bantu as the driving force behind their expansion. Ehret augments and challenges the standard view. First, he moves away from identifying "Bantu expansion" as *the* defining dynamic of the era, treating it instead as part of broader, more inclusive developments involving peoples from other ethnolinguistic groups. For example, he emphasizes the complex and shifting nature of social, cultural, and economic borrowings back and forth, over time, between Bantu-speaking communities and others, with neither side consistently in the contributing or receiving role. He also argues that the fundamental factors explaining Bantu expansion were not those associated with the development of ironworking technology but the gradual adoption by Bantu speakers of grain cultivation technology from non-Bantu peoples. This allowed Bantu groups, Ehret argues, eventually to spread from earlier settlements in wet, low-lying forests (especially suited to the cultivation of root crops) into a variety of higher, dryer, and more open grassland environments "where grain cultivation often was essential to farmers' survival."

The book also investigates a range of other topics, including architecture, ceramics, other artistic developments (personal adornment, sculpture, rock painting, and music), settlement geography, demographic trends, residential patterns, domestic furnishings, kinship, age organizations and other social customs, and authority (including early forms of chiefship). Importantly, in all of these areas, Ehret investigates change as well as continuity over time. Moreover, particularly in the three crucial realms of agropastoral innovation, changes in tool technology (especially ironworking), and early long-distance commerce, Ehret explicitly situates eastern and southern Africa squarely within the context of related changes in world history during the period.

This is not easy or light reading. Still, despite the remote time period and the highly technical nature of most of the evidence, Ehret's interpretive narrative is relatively free of jargon, usually clear, and almost always sensible. The result is a remarkably rich, evocative social and cultural history, offering many new and deeper insights into the lives of people living in eastern and southern Africa from 1000 B.C. to A.D. 400. *An African Classical Age* will itself become a classic and shape future scholarship in early African history for many years to come.

RONALD R. ATKINSON

University of South Carolina
Columbia

FABIAN, JOHANNES. 1998. *Moments of Freedom: Anthropology and Popular Culture.* Pp. xv, 172. Charlottesville: University Press of Virginia. Paperbound, $17.50.

Moments of Freedom is fashioned from four lectures that Fabian gave as the 1996 Page-Barbour lectures at the University of Virginia. Fabian has characterized the lectures as a "reflexive project," which it most certainly is; maybe the term "confessional" might be more accurate. He also writes in the first person, a convention now often utilized in ethnographic research. Using the first person gives Fabian's book a dramatic quality, as he traces his experiences over 30 years in a region once called Katanga and now Shaba, in a country once called the Belgian Congo and more recently Zaire.

Fabian deals with four topics: popular culture in anthropology; genres and their relation to power and popular culture; time and movement in popular culture; and "terrains of contestation" in African popular culture. In the middle of his book, he recalls his first visit to Kinshasa, once called Leopoldville, which he was visiting for a few days before he went on to Katanga-Shaba.

I was in bed in a room at a mission . . . trying to get some sleep. Around the square where the mission buildings lay, loudspeakers from what seemed at least four bars or dance halls blasted Zairean music in the night air. . . . Here was African life that assaulted me physically, made its presence painfully felt. I was about to go out of my mind, as the saying goes, when a tropical downpour swept all noise from the square. (85, 86)

He thought of African music as noise because music was not of interest to him; he had his research paradigm (or might we say that he had theoretical blinders on?) that told him to focus on the study of a religious movement. Everything else was irrelevant. Later, of course, he was to discover the importance of popular culture, and his book can be seen as an argument for the importance of the study of popular culture by anthropologists.

Fabian's essays retrace the steps that led him to recognize the importance of "inquiries into popular language, theater, painting, and to a lesser extent other expressions such as music and material culture." Topics such as these, representing "vast portions of contemporary African life," he suggests, have traditionally been ignored by anthropologists and ethnologists.

So far so good. The main problem I have with *Moments of Freedom* is that Fabian becomes so concerned with talking about popular culture and why it is important that he forgets to analyze any of it. For example, he reproduces four paintings in the book but does not say much about them. On the cover of the book, we see one of these paintings. In it, a mermaid, wearing a wristwatch, is lying on some grass, and a thin snake is coiled around her tail. In the background, we see water and trees.

This painting is also reproduced in the book, and in the caption underneath it, Fabian tells us that the mermaid is a "key" symbol in Zairean popular culture. What does that mean? Why does he not analyze this painting and the other paintings in the book in more detail to show us how popular culture reflects and affects the beliefs and values of the people in Shaba whom he was studying? He also might have dealt in depth with music and other popular culture texts from Shaba. Moving from theory to interpreting popular culture texts would have greatly enriched this fascinating book.

ARTHUR ASA BERGER

San Francisco State University
California

EUROPE

PELINKA, ANTON. 1999. *Politics of the Lesser Evil: Leadership, Democracy and Jaruzelski's Poland*. Pp. 259. New Brunswick, NJ: Transaction. $44.95.

Wojciech Jaruzelski, the only general-dictator of the Communist bloc, was the head of both the Polish state and the Polish Communist Party during most of the 1980s. He was anything but a charismatic leader and was generally regarded by his countrymen as a collaborator. Nevertheless, Anton Pelinka, Austria's leading political scientist at the University of Innsbruck and director of the Institute of Conflict Research in Vienna, cites Jaruzelski as an excellent example of a political leader who was wise enough to recognize the lesser evil among difficult choices.

Pelinka's larger purpose is to make comparisons between decision making by political leaders in democracies and dictatorships. His thesis is that the range of real choices for democratic leaders is reduced to practically nothing by the perceived necessity to accommodate public opinion. By contrast, choices confronting a dictator like Jaruzelski during the 1980s were actually considerably greater despite the external restraints imposed on him by the Soviet threat to intervene militarily during the Solidarity crisis in 1981.

The first and last chapters of *Politics of the Lesser Evil* deal first with Jaruzelski's decision to suppress the Polish trade union Solidarity and then his efforts in 1989 to arrange for the Soviet bloc's first truly free election. Pelinka argues that public opinion in a democratic Poland would have forced the general to make a heroic but disastrous military resistance to Soviet troops in 1981 with the same results as those that affected Hungary in 1956 and Czechoslovakia in 1968. Because he was not a democratic leader, Jaruzelski made the wise if unpopular decision not to resist. On the other hand, he did not adopt a Stalinist policy of executing or imprisoning for long periods of time the leaders of Solidarity, nor did he exile or humiliate them. In 1989, he reversed his earlier position by being the first Warsaw Pact leader to persuade a national Communist Party to accept democratic elections. In so doing, he unselfishly put himself out of a job.

In making these decisions, the Polish dictator was twice forced to make difficult choices. In 1981, he opted to temporarily intensify the Cold War rather than to risk a nuclear confrontation between East and West. Although technically a collaborator, he was not responsible for his dependence on Moscow, nor did he have the latitude within which to maneuver enjoyed by the leaders of Vichy France. In 1989, although he did not march against the trends of the time, he also did not simply follow in the footsteps that had been laid down by Gorbachev's reforms.

The 23 chapters between the first and last ones, although occasionally referring to Jaruzelski, concentrate on leadership styles in democracies and dictatorships like Hitler's Germany, Stalin's Russia, and Mao's China. Real moral leadership, Pelinka insists, can be exercised only by people who do not hold public office, such as Martin Luther King, Jr., and Mahatma Gandhi. Once they are in power, public opinion forces leaders to avoid making difficult decisions altogether or to mislead the public. Pelinka cites World War I as the classic case of democratization of war—a crusade against the powers of darkness that made a reasonable compromise and an early end of the war impossible.

Politics of the Lesser Evil is not for beginners. Individuals and situations are frequently cited with little or no background information. However, political scientists and historians who do have the necessary foreknowledge will find Pelinka's book fascinating and stimulating. Based on numerous secondary works and a lifetime of reflection, *Politics of the Lesser Evil* demonstrates the sometimes depressingly limited choices facing dictatorial and especially democratic leaders.

BRUCE F. PAULEY

University of Central Florida
Orlando

REYNOLDS, ELAINE A. 1998. *Before the Bobbies: The Night Watch and Police Reform in Metropolitan London, 1720-1830.* Pp. x, 235. Stanford, CA: Stanford University Press. $49.50.

Before the Bobbies provides a vital supplement to our knowledge of the evolution of modern policing, demonstrating that creation of the Metropolitan Police was not a revolutionary event but the culmination of an evolutionary process. In the words of one of Reynolds's sources, "England . . . [was not] an unchanging 'ancien régime,' awaiting the reforms of the nineteenth century," and professional policing did not spring full-armored from the heads of Peel, Rowan, and Mayne.

Reynolds's focus is not the central government of Whitehall but local parish vestries and committees: though fiscal considerations and a resistance to centralization slowed the process, professional policing was developed at the local rather than national level, addressing problems of crime well before the industrialization process brought the specter of riots to London's streets. Her sources are official records: minutes of parish vestries and committees, local government correspondence, and court and parliamentary records.

The development of policing parallels developments in government, and the chapter "Westminster, 1720-39" traces the struggles of various governing bodies to establish a local power to regulate their territories through court-leets, beadles, headboroughs, constables, and especially the night watch. Fluctuations in robbery rates, the introduction of the gin trade, and discipline problems are covered. "An Expanding Watch, 1748-76" traces the expansion of that authority; the evolution of shared watches; the need for paving, lighting, and guarding turnpikes; the structure and influence of mobs and riots; a growing property crime rate; and tensions between large and small property owners.

"Collaboration, 1750-74" documents Parliament's increasing role in the establishment and maintenance of the watches, and crime control measures. The early attempts of Henry and John Fielding and others to regulate and improve the watch are treated here. "New Means to Old Ends" covers the impact of the American Revolution and the Gordon Riots, which spurred the reforming interests toward central control of local justice institutions. The quality, conduct, deployment, and supervision of watch personnel receive special focus, as do contemporaneous developments in social thought on justice issues in the face of rising property crime.

Within the historical context of the French Revolution and the Napoleonic era, "The War Years, 1793-1815" examines the philosophical shifts within English governance, balancing liberty and order: threats of invasion intertwined with political struggles with domestic radicals. The 1792 Middlesex Justices Act and the appearance of Loyal Associations and the Volunteer societies presage the Wilberforce Proclamation Society and Patrick Colquhoun's role in promoting the idea of a "general police."

Deteriorating social conditions in London, the celebrated Ratcliffe Highway murders, and the appearance of immigration problems all proved insufficient to overcome ingrained fears of a centralized police force. "Night Watch to Police, 1811-28" then covers the political conditions that overcame those fears: demobilization, the Corn Law protests, labor unrest, a general unwillingness of the general public to aid the government voluntarily, the Peterloo massacre and other scandals. Robert Peel's early, incremental reforms as home secretary are outlined. The final chapters, "Why 1829?" and "Charlies to Bobbies," provide details on the conditions that permitted the founding and the success of the London Metropolitan Police force.

The book is well written, cogent, and extensively documented. One of the unexpected treats of reading it is the discovery that seventeenth-century London dealt with many of the issues—crime displacement, invasion and change in neighborhoods, deteriorating social conditions, municipal "low bid" policies, and the media's fascination with crime—that bedevil our modern metropolises.

MICHAEL E. BUERGER

Northeastern University
Boston
Massachusetts

UNITED STATES

BYBEE, KEITH J. 1998. *Mistaken Identity: The Supreme Court and the Politics of Minority Representation*. Pp. x, 194. Princeton, NJ: Princeton University Press. $55.00.

The Supreme Court's ruling in *Shaw v. Reno* ushered in a period of sharply divided Supreme Court rulings over majority-minority districting under the

Voting Rights Act (VRA). The narrow majority in the post-*Shaw* rulings, usually 5 to 4, and the absence of common ground between majority and minority guarantees that the already conflictual process of redistricting after the 2000 census will be clouded by questions of how far jurisdictions can go to ensure the election of minority officeholders. In *Mistaken Identity*, Keith Bybee traces the roots of this impasse and suggests that, if a solution is to be found, Congress must take the lead.

Bybee's analysis is built on a series of meticulous readings of scholarly and judicial interpretations of the VRA. Linking Bybee's readings is the question of how the notion of the people (the political community that the Constitution and the VRA seek to protect) is understood by analysts and judges. Over time, Bybee contends, the Supreme Court has divided on this question into advocates of individualist solutions (who would limit or eliminate VRA protections) and group-based solutions (who see majority-minority districting as necessary). He finds no potential for a compromise between these two camps.

Bybee's solution is to return to the intellectual foundation of the first VRA case to reach the Supreme Court, *South Carolina* v. *Katzenbach*. Writing for an eight-justice majority, Chief Justice Warren held the act to be constitutional based on the Fifteenth Amendment and, more important for Bybee, on the process that Congress engaged in to deliberate the law. This deliberation included multiple hearings and an extensive legislative history that documented voting discrimination so as to justify a remedy as unprecedented as the VRA. In the final, quite brief section of *Mistaken Identity*, Bybee asserts that a return to such a process of legislative deliberation can restructure the voting rights debate away from the individualist and group underpinnings of

political identity that paralyze the Court today.

Unfortunately, Bybee does not apply the same critical eye to his own proposal that he does to the numerous judicial opinions and scholarly understandings of the VRA that he analyses. As a result, the discussion of legislative deliberation reads almost as an afterthought, taking up just half of the final chapter.

Can Congress find common ground where the courts have not? Clearly, Congress was able to deliberate in 1965 and pass a bill whose impact was revolutionary. Perhaps, however, 1965 was unique. An activist president used his legislative skills to force the bill through the Senate, and sectional cleavages supplanted party. Even so, Congress passed a bill with narrow geographical impact that would expire after five years.

Admittedly, the VRA has been extended and expanded four times since 1965, but as these were modifications of an existing practice and their political costs could be more easily calculated, they were far less contentious than the original debate. A new deliberation would be closer to the original debate—without presidential leadership—than any of the subsequent congressional actions. Finally, in 1965, Congress could not look to the courts to address voting rights concerns. Today, members of Congress can blame the courts for any failures in this area.

In sum, Bybee offers a rich reading of the judicial history of the VRA. Scholars of the act will benefit from his clear and close reading. His efforts to design a remedy for the conflict that he documents, however, is less well developed and unconvincing in its current form.

LOUIS DeSIPIO

University of Illinois
at Urbana-Champaign
Urbana

DERICKSON, ALAN. 1998. *Black Lung: Anatomy of a Public Health Disaster.* Pp. xiv, 237. Ithaca, NY: Cornell University Press. $22.95.

The history of coal mining has been largely the same regardless of the region or even the country considered. The work has been physically demanding, and it has entailed high levels of risk from injuries due to accidents or due to diseases that arose out of the unhealthy environment. The focus of Alan Derickson's volume is on the travails that American coal miners endured in the past century that resulted from their occupational exposure to dust. As a result, the sad story that emerges is one that leaves the author with obvious anger at those whom he finds responsible. There is considerable blame that can be widely shared by the miners' employers, their unions, the health professions, and the government. In his view, the miners were able to overcome these combined forces and earn themselves a measure of justice only in the late 1960s.

Basically, there are two principal problems that Derickson identifies. First, there is the issue of prevention, which, sadly, has long been underemphasized not simply by employers and state governments but also by the miners and their representatives. Undoubtedly, those who had concerns about the conditions in the mines were stymied by others who denied that any health risks from coal dust even existed. The motives of those who denied the hazards of coal dust exposure cannot be known. Yet Derickson makes clear his position that the mine owners and operators would use any resource to suppress information that suggested that the work was hazardous. Nonetheless, the miners were not unaware of the risks.

The second problem that Derickson identifies is the lack of any compensation for those miners who developed occupational disease. Derickson does argue at some length that coal miners with respiratory disease did not have silicosis but, instead, were sickened by coal dust itself. The purpose of this point is never made clear, however. Workers with silicosis also had extreme difficulty in obtaining compensation for their condition. Further, if a coal miner was found to be suffering from silica-caused respiratory disease, he had no less an entitlement to compensation than one with coal-dust-induced illness.

Derickson seems to be unaware that collecting workers' compensation benefits for almost any occupational disease has not been a simple matter, particularly prior to the 1980s. For many possible reasons, states have seemed to err on the side of restrictiveness with respect to such claims. Curiously, workers' problems were not easier in Ohio or West Virginia, both important coal mining states where private insurers have not been permitted to sell workers' compensation insurance. One might have expected that worker-supportive political administrations would have surfaced, at least periodically, in those jurisdictions, thereby enabling more workers to succeed in their claims.

Ultimately, the miners took matters into their own hands, aided and abetted by a small number of radical physicians. In some cases, the motivation of these doctors for leading or participating in the cause of gaining compensation for the miners is not known. One of the activist doctors regularly told crowds of miners, "You've all got black lung" and "You're all gonna die." The miners were also stirred into action by a dedicated group of young outsiders who were in the area serving in Volunteers in Service to America (VISTA). They brought with them a willingness to organize and agitate along with a sense of power that the civil rights and antiwar movements conferred on many young persons in the late 1960s. The result was some initial legislative success in West Virginia that became the forerunner of the federal black lung provisions of the 1969 Coal Mine Health and Safety Act. The federal legislation was enacted in response to the national trauma following the mine disaster in Farmington, West Virginia, that killed 78 miners in 1968.

There are a variety of shortcomings in this book that I believe have undermined what could have been a significant contribution to the understanding of occupational illness. The anger that motivates Derickson is as palpable as it is understandable, but it also creates a highly ideological piece of work. The entire framework for this book is one of class struggle: noble workers largely helpless against those motivated by greed; the powerful and the powerless; the victims and the victimizers. As such, the volume lacks any measure of objectivity that could have made it more persuasive. The 45 pages of notes that follow the narrative are not a measure of the depth of inquiry here. Derickson is bent on persuasion and makes little effort to mask this. He has constructed a brief and has done it well, if not entirely persuasively. The book is likely to persuade only those who are convinced already of the reality of the struggle of the working masses.

I also would have preferred Derickson to have brought his history to a later date than he did. His book ends with the enactment of the 1969 law that created the black lung benefits program. The implication is that the struggle for the miners has succeeded by dint of their entitlement to compensation for respiratory disease. Yet almost three decades have passed, and one might ask whether this legislation has met its goals and if it has served the needs of miners and their families. Did the statute succeed in identifying and compensating victims of occupational disease, or was this a pension program that placed relatively small amounts of money per household in the hands of large numbers of miners and their families? Because the miners and their survivors of earlier years were not compensated for coal-dust-induced disease, did this justify a program that compensated many who never had such illness? Did the large (in the aggregate) program cost, seemingly unanticipated in 1969, serve to discourage any future federal legislation from providing compensation for victims of occupational diseases who were not coal miners? Curiously, this history concludes with its focus entirely on compensation, although it seems apparent that this public health disaster has been significantly minimized by the prevention provisions of the Coal Mine Health and Safety Act. That part of the story warrants telling also. Perhaps Derickson plans to undertake such a study in the future.

PETER S. BARTH

University of Connecticut
Storrs

EISINGER, PETER K. 1998. *Towards an End to Hunger in America*. Pp. xi, 177. Washington, DC: Brookings Institution Press. $39.95. Paperbound, $16.95.

Peter Eisinger uses secondary data sources to give readers a compelling social and political history of the variety of food assistance programs in the United States. He begins by citing figures from the 1995 Current Population Survey that suggest that more than 4 million households in the United States can be considered "food insecure with hunger." The central question of the book is, "Why is it that so many Americans are hungry?" To answer this question, Eisinger examines America's policy response to hunger. He concentrates on the response side of the equation but does not examine the factors that lead individual households to demand food assistance.

I found Eisinger's political history of a variety of hunger programs and his characterization of U.S. government food assistance—an untargeted program (food stamps) supplemented by a variety of targeted programs—very useful. He writes that "food stamps sit at the pivot point between American society's compassion for hungry people and its disdain for public welfare." What he does not consider is that the existence of "targeted" programs (for example, targeted to children, pregnant women, reservation Native Americans) is evidence of the government's lack of faith that the food stamp program actually alleviates food insecurity and hunger among all household members.

Eisinger discusses how domestic hunger became part of the national agenda in the 1960s and the precarious nature of the committee structure in the House of Representatives and Senate to address hunger issues. He devotes a chapter to anti-hunger advocacy groups and another chapter to "charitable food assistance." The literature review in this latter chapter seems haphazard.

Eisinger does little questioning of the structure of food assistance in the United States, especially of private food assistance. He takes people standing in lines at food pantries as a given and does not present the reader with an alternative structure of food assistance that would reduce the shame that food pantry clients feel, increase the consistency of services and goods received, and respond to hunger in an equitable manner.

His answer to why hunger exists in the United States is that Americans lack the political will to eradicate hunger. He places all blame for the existence of hunger on the response of Americans. He writes,

Americans harbor unshakable doubts about the scope and severity of hunger, and the result is a failure of political will. It is not that Americans have done nothing: it is simply that they have not done enough. Thus we have designed an arsenal of programs because hunger in a rich land is deeply troubling, but at the same time many believe that those who get free food are freeloaders, that people who do not work ought not rely on those who do to pay for their food, that failing to get enough to eat in a food-rich society is the fault of the hungry, that many immigrants have come to the United States to feed in the welfare trough, and that the best help is given in the form of charity by volunteers. So food assistance policy is grudging: we erect administrative hurdles to participation in public programs, we eschew outreach, we bar whole categories of people from the eligibility rolls to suit the political temper of the times, and we limit funding in a way that almost guarantees insufficiency. (125-26)

While his criticisms of the supply of food assistance are valid, he does not consider the conditions that create a demand for food assistance. Eisinger cites the statistic that 84 percent of persons below 100 percent of poverty report that they get enough to eat. He does not contrast the factors that result in food insecurity in comparably poor households. Unraveling the ultimate source of food insecurity (be it insufficient income; poor budgeting, cooking, and/or shopping skills; or a lack of time to cook and shop) and access to affordable grocery stores will enable America to attack the problem of food insecurity using a framework that is politically and morally acceptable and promises to eradicate hunger in this land of plenty.

BETH OSBORNE DAPONTE

University of Pittsburgh
Pennsylvania

ERENBERG, LEWIS A. 1998. *Swingin'
the Dream: Big Band Jazz and the Rebirth of American Culture.* Pp. xxi,
320. Chicago: University of Chicago
Press. $28.00.

Lewis A. Erenberg's *Swingin' the
Dream* is the latest addition to a burgeoning jazz studies literature that relates
jazz's internal aesthetics and sociology to
broader trends in American race relations, gender dynamics, leisure habits,
and political culture. In his ambitious
central claim, Erenberg argues that the
big band swing movement from 1935 to
1948 heralded a tolerant, pluralist, democratic ideal that challenged the
white-supremacist foundations of U.S.
national culture. Even as America's
neighborhoods, schools, courts, armed
forces, and sports leagues remained
racially segregated, a mass youth culture
of jitterbuggers and record hounds joined
forces with left-leaning critics and entrepreneurs to confer deep social significance on the sounds and images of the
racially integrated Benny Goodman
band and the African American bands of
Duke Ellington, Count Basie, Jimmy
Lunceford, and others.

While passionately invoking this
"vision of democratic community rooted
in ethnic and racial pluralism" (202),
Erenberg also richly documents how
radio and record company executives,
booking agents, and hotel operators
favored white performers over black
ones, often justifying their decisions on
the grounds that they could not afford to
alienate their southern clients. Indeed,
after reading about Jim Crow's hounding
Billie Holiday out of an engagement with
Artie Shaw's band, or about New York
City policemen's unleashing violence on
musicians and fans who had built an
interracial culture in the 52nd Street
("Swing Street") clubs, or even about
Glenn Miller's crafting a wartime

celebrity image out of a whitened version
of swing that left blacks out, one wonders
whether Erenberg has been justified in
embracing swing as the basis of a democratic cultural rebirth. Erenberg, in fact,
faces up to the failure of swing's "ecstatic
promise" in the last pages of the book,
arguing that the bebop movement of the
late 1940s was not merely a formal artistic development but also a protest
against the "failed expectations embodied in swing."

If, finally, this book registers swing's
limitations as a transformative social
force, its great power—and its pleasure—
lies in the ecstasies and hopes engendered in the music of Holiday, Shaw,
Goodman, Ellington, and Basie.
Erenberg's sober duties as a historian do
not get the better of his passion: the book
throbs with his love for this music and his
admiration for the people who made it,
enjoyed it, and lobbied on its behalf. This
energy owes in no small part, I suspect, to
Erenberg's having solicited testimony
from the swing audience—the
jitterbuggers and record hounds themselves—through newspaper queries and
follow-up correspondence.

One wishes, in fact, to hear more
about and from these correspondents.
Too rarely do their voices drive the narrative. The very sound of such testimony—imbued as it no doubt is with sen-
timent, nostalgia, and even the
inconsistencies and inaccuracies of personal memory—is itself an important
dimension of swing culture. In an age
when it is commonplace for our national
leaders to call for a national dialogue on
race, it would be especially interesting to
hear how vintage white and black swing
enthusiasts remember this core experience from their youth. Having given us a
richly textured account of swing's glories
and disappointments in its own time,
perhaps Erenberg can now turn to a

fuller reckoning of how swing has lived on in American cultural memory.

JOHN GENNARI

University of Virginia
Charlottesville

ETZIONI, AMITAI. 1999. *The Limits of Privacy*. Pp. vii, 280. New York: Basic Books. $25.00.

In *The Limits of Privacy*, Amitai Etzioni confronts what he argues is an unhealthy preoccupation with privacy. While fully acknowledging the importance of privacy to a free society, he also maintains that too much emphasis on privacy can be dysfunctional if not kept in balance with other societal concerns: "immoderate champions of privacy have not merely engaged in rhetorical excesses but those excesses have had significant and detrimental effects." In contrast to what he calls the "alarmist" position, Etzioni advocates a communitarian approach to privacy that "systematically provides for a balance between rights and the common good." He also maintains that a contemporary conceptualization of privacy must recognize that the greatest threat to privacy comes not from "Big Brother" but from "Big Bucks" (the private sector).

Etzioni does not shy away from difficult issues. He tackles five controversial procedures in the area of privacy: HIV testing of infants; Megan's Laws, which require registration of sex offenders; government mandates that encryption devices include deciphering technology; the use of identification technology; and the dissemination of medical records.

For each topic, Etzioni presents an impressive amount of research to explain the problem. Next, he canvasses privacy advocates' arguments against the various practices. As to this step of the analysis, I must admit initial skepticism over how fairly a critic would voice the opposing viewpoint, but Etzioni's articulation of the strong privacy position for each topic was fair and objective. Finally, Etzioni applies his communitarian balancing approach to determine what intrusions upon privacy are justified to meet the societal problem being addressed. His conclusions are sometimes surprising; for example, his solution for sex offenders who still pose a high risk is not to use registration laws (Megan's Laws), but to keep the high-risk offenders in a "guarded village" where they would stay until no longer a risk. It also initially may come as a surprise that in a book arguing that privacy rights have become too privileged, Etzioni advocates controls over the use of medical records that actually would strengthen privacy protections (in fact, this position is consistent with his overall argument that each procedure must be individually examined and that the greatest threat to privacy is from the private sector, not the government).

Etzioni concludes that currently we do not have a conception of privacy that adequately encompasses all necessary policy factors. From his view, the legal right to privacy has evolved to the point where it is "privileged" over "the common good." He also makes the intriguing argument that allowing for more public scrutiny may, in the end, actually reduce the need for government control. His solution is to model privacy analysis after the Fourth Amendment's command that searches be "reasonable" based upon balancing the individual's privacy interests against society's need for the search. For Etzioni, the Fourth Amendment gives express legal voice to the communitarian balancing of individual privacy needs and society's good.

Privacy issues invoke such strong reactions that the book undoubtedly will not convince everyone. Certain sectors of society, for example, are privacy alarmists because they are legitimately concerned that personal information (such as HIV test results) will be misused no matter what formal assurances are made. Similarly, those familiar with the Supreme Court's recent interpretations of the Fourth Amendment are likely to raise a skeptical eyebrow that a reasonableness balancing test is the panacea for resolving complex privacy issues. Such caveats, however, do not diminish the book's importance in taking on current thinking about privacy and providing thoughtful analysis that forces readers, whether they agree or disagree, to rethink their own views.

SCOTT SUNDBY

Washington and Lee University
Lexington
Virginia

GLAZIER, JACK. 1998. *Dispersing the Ghetto: The Relocation of Jewish Immigrants Across America*. Pp. x, 245. Ithaca, NY: Cornell University Press. $39.95.

Several million Jewish immigrants from Eastern Europe came to the United States between 1880 and 1924 and most settled in New York City. Living conditions were bad, unemployment was high, radical and socialist ideas were common among the immigrants, urban values and living conditions were under attack by nativist Americans, and "immigrants were closely identified with the social problems and moral derangements of urban life." Upper-class German American Jews felt an obligation to help their Jewish coreligionists, but they also wanted the new immigrants to Americanize as rapidly as possible in order to minimize the dangers of anti-Semitism and threats to German American Jewish prestige and acceptance in U.S. society.

In February 1901, the Industrial Removal Office (IRO) was founded as part of the nascent Jewish Agricultural and Industrial Aid Society. Although part of the aid society, the IRO was concerned only with small-town occupations and played no part in the small effort to settle Jews on farms. The IRO's immediate goal was to distribute refugees to other towns and cities, where they might more easily find employment. The IRO did not recruit immigrants; the immigrants had to come to the IRO for help. But, once giving help, the IRO expected the immigrants to become industrious and self-supporting. The immigrants were to determine the extent of their own cultural practices and observances, but the German American Jews expected that dispersal to small towns with small Jewish communities to help with jobs and socialization would speed up the process of Americanization.

From 1901 to 1917, the IRO, working with local Jewish communities, expedited the resettlement of 78,995 people to more than a thousand towns and cities. About 5000 immigrants were resettled from Boston and Philadelphia, but almost all the remainder were resettled from New York City. These resettled Jews probably encouraged others to follow them, so that the total number resettled was larger. The numbers were small compared to the size of the Eastern European migration, but the resettlement undertaking was an important part of U.S. Jewish history that has not been told previously in detail. Glazier shows, for example, that Ohio received the largest number of immigrants, followed by Illinois, Missouri, and Michigan. Over half of the immigrants went to these four states or the adjoining states of Indiana, Minnesota, Wisconsin, and Iowa. One of the strengths of Glazier's book is the extensive amount of data presented in appendices as well as throughout the book.

Glazier discusses in detail how, why, and the extent to which German American Jews in the United States helped resettle the immigrants and the major extent to which the recent immigrants joined in the resettlement debate concerning themselves. He demonstrates how the immigrants were not passive but actively involved in the debate and activities. Glazier also gives a detailed and insightful discussion of how the IRO's efforts related to the larger national debates over immigration, economics, eugenics, and prejudice. A 38-page chapter discusses Indianapolis and Terre Haute, Indiana, showing in detail the consequences of resettlement for local areas. In the concluding chapter, Glazier compares immigration issues in the United States today with issues of the IRO era. Whether or not the reader agrees with his views, the comparison is enlightening.

Dispersing the Ghetto is a well-researched, well-written, and informative study of a small but important aspect of American Jewish life. It is highly recommended for students of immigration and Judaica.

ABRAHAM D. LAVENDER

Florida International University
Miami

MAYERS, DAVID. 1998. *Wars and Peace: The Future Americans Envisioned, 1861-1991.* Pp. viii, 184. New York: St. Martin's Press. $45.00.

David Mayers explores the role of ideas in shaping American foreign policy by analyzing wartime views about the future peace from the Civil War through the end of the Cold War. His quest is shaped by a concern over the failure of American leaders to offer a coherent set of principles to guide the nation in the chaotic post–Cold War years of the 1990s.

Mayers demonstrates a sound grasp of the fundamentals of American diplomacy and its relationship to the changing world scene during the five wars he discusses. Although his primary focus is on the presidents and their associates who offered the official justification for our wars, he does not neglect the voices of dissent. Thus he gives as much weight to those who spoke in protest, from Mark Twain and his opposition to imperialism in 1898 to Paul Robeson and his critique of containment during the Cold War, as he does to Woodrow Wilson's call to make the world safe for democracy or George Bush's proclamation of a New World Order.

The one thing he finds in common in all these conflicts is our failure to realize our wartime visions. Reconstruction proved to be a far cry from Lincoln's plea for a peace of reconciliation to bind up the nation's wounds; our desire to free Cuba ended up with that island's becoming an American protectorate, as well as with the acquisition of the distant Philippines; Wilson's call for peace without victory resulted in the vindictive Treaty of Versailles and another world war just 20 years later; FDR's appeal for a world based on the freedom from fear led instead to the Cold War, with its threat of nuclear annihilation for all mankind; even the Cold War, which ended in an apparent American triumph with the disintegration of the Soviet Union, was soon followed by the Persian Gulf war, massive ethnic violence in Africa, and brutal civil war in Bosnia. Mayers thus effectively shows the underlying truth in the classic American folk saying, "The United States always wins the war and loses the peace."

The explanation for this unhappy state of affairs is more difficult to determine. In part, Mayer suggests, the very diversity of American life precludes a simple solution to complex international situations. The idealism that lies at the heart of the American experience provides a useful and important corrective to attempts to use our great economic and military power to impose our will on the rest of the world. "U.S. history," Mayers reminds us, "is a story of experience chastised by conscience." It is this moral concern, expressed by such dissenters as Norman Thomas, Henry Wallace, and Jane Addams, that has tempered our latent imperialism and led to what Mayers calls "democratic universalism."

The ambiguous outcome of American wars, according to Mayers, is also due to what he terms "the classical wisdom" in international relations: "Each solution leads to fresh problems." In fighting to right a wrong, whether slavery in the South, Germany's attempt at European hegemony, or Soviet totalitarianism, we end up with new challenges that are equally difficult to resolve. This sense of futility—fighting and winning wars again and again, only to face new and awesome challenges—fuels the continuing temptation to embrace isolationism. It is thus not surprising that the phrase "perpetual war for perpetual peace," coined by Charles A. Beard and popularized by Harry Elmer Barnes, still has considerable appeal to a nation that has experienced such difficulty in enjoying the fruits of victory.

ROBERT A. DIVINE

University of Texas
Austin

MELISH, JOANNE POPE. 1998. *Disowning Slavery: Gradual Emancipation and "Race" in New England, 1780-1860*. Pp. xvii, 296. Ithaca, NY: Cornell University Press. $35.00.

Fifteen years in the making, this is an unusually mature and finished first book. It is also a major contribution to the study of the construction of American national identity. Every province in colonial America protected slavery by law, and, as Joanne Pope Melish reminds us, the New England colonies were no exception. Following earlier scholars such as Lorenzo Greene and Edgar McManus, she emphasizes "the unexceptional and commonplace" character of slavery in New England from 1638 on and its importance in the region's economic expansion and diversification. She does not suggest that the region's economy was based on slavery, as was the case with the British colonies below Pennsylvania. But she does make a powerful argument for the central economic role of slaves in New England households and communities, especially close to the seacoast and in agricultural southern New England. In 1774, one in four Connecticut households owned slaves. Unlike the laws in colonies with larger proportions of slaves, New England law permitted slaves to hold property and to testify in court against white people, but this did not mean that slavery was benign. Rather, it functioned as a "crucial system of social control" for managing a "different" category of people by defining them as a "class of permanently 'debased' strangers."

The core of the volume is its discussion of the relationship between emancipation, race, and identity between 1780 and 1860. The declining economic importance of slavery made it relatively easy for New Englanders to respond to the Atlantic antislavery movement by emancipating their slaves. But, for whites, the promise of abolition was black removal. If, for blacks, abolitionism and republicanism were ideologies of inclusion, for whites they were instruments of exclusion. Antislavery or pro-slavery, whites shared a set of assumptions about black incapacity and dependence that they employed to construct a discourse of race associating whiteness with self-control and citizenship and blackness with savagery and servility. As a result, Melish writes, "the new entitlement of blacks to freedom was everywhere circumscribed by the persistence of whites' imagined entitlement to control," and "people of color never became [true] citizens." If emancipation enabled blacks to acquire "a property right," the deepening racism of whites effectively precluded them from "a citizenship right."

The volume's most important contribution is to uncover and analyze the process by which white New Englanders after 1820 succeeded in constructing "a triumphant narrative of a historically free, white New England in which a few people of color were unaccountably marooned" and the extensive indigenous experience with slavery "was either suppressed entirely or revised to emphasize its extreme brevity and mildness and its triumphant early abolition." In this narrative, New England assumed a "central role . . . as birthplace of the nation and steadfast, loyal defender of the union." Throughout the free states, whites eager to disassociate the American Republic from slavery could use this narrative as the foundation for a still grander "historical interpretation of America—the *true* America, the free America outside the South—as a white republic" that had always abhorred slavery. Abetted by the complicity of subsequent generations of historians who have preferred to see the institution of slavery as outside the mainstream of American life, this comforting myth of a deviant slave South and a normative free North held sway until the recent past. By explaining its origins and providing a rich analysis of the dynamics of race relations in pre–Civil War New England, Melish has made a promising entry onto the stage of American historical writing.

JACK P. GREENE

Johns Hopkins University
Baltimore
Maryland

ROSSINOW, DOUG. 1998. *The Politics of Authenticity: Liberalism, Christianity, and the New Left in America.* Pp. x, 500. New York: Columbia University Press. $32.50.

While radical protest movements of the 1960s often viewed themselves as profoundly new, lacking significant historical origins or precedents, they were sure of making history themselves. Almost immediately after flagship organizations like Students for a Democratic Society (SDS) broke up, protest veterans began writing the history of sixties activism, and by our own time, literature in the field has even passed through a couple of stages: first, a flurry of studies trying to define the tenor of a "New Left" possessing a unique sensibility or ideology; then, from around 1980, a number of particular "movement (or sub-movement) histories" such as Clayborne Carson's *In Struggle* on the Student Nonviolent Coordinating Committee, Sara Evans's *Personal Politics* on early women's liberation, and Amy Swerdlow's *Women Strike for Peace.* Doug Rossinow's *Politics of Authenticity* synthesizes the two strands: while offering a particular "movement history" concerning student protest at the University of Texas–Austin, the book also stakes out a big claim about *the* differentiating trait (or differentia) of the New Left: this movement pursued existential "authenticity" (personal truth and integrity beyond the mortifying conventions of social life) via political action intended to expand and enrich democracy. Meticulously researched and documented, and exceptionally well informed on the burgeoning scholarly literature, this book will rank alongside the consummate movement histories cited previously, though its aim of disclosing the differentia of the New Left remains problematic.

To escape a New York–centric bias in other accounts of the Left, there are few better places to examine than Austin.

Significant figures such as SDS and women's liberation pioneer Sandra (Casey) Hayden and "new working class" theorist Greg Calvert were Austin activists. By the mid-1960s, Austin had the second-largest SDS chapter in the country. Other causes célèbres such as the dissident GIs named the "Fort Hood Three" and the abortion-rights cases leading to *Roe* v. *Wade* began nearby. And all this developed in the conservative, evangelical milieu of the postwar sunbelt. Here Christianity on campus served as a filter through which Texas's embattled populist liberalism, along with existentialist doctrines of alienation and its desired opposite, authenticity, reached idealistic young whites. Holding to a latter-day social gospel linked with an ideal of self-realization, this student constituency was politicized, and soon radicalized, by the rising civil rights movement. Then it was ready to engage with SDS, antiwar activism, the counterculture, and feminism.

This rich narrative is first-rate, but the book's larger claims raise questions. Why is the "New Left" a useful category at all, and why should authenticity be considered its essential trait (while "community," for instance, appears here as merely a "talismanic" phrase of the time)? Committed as he is to recognizing the movement's uniqueness, how much of the New Left should Rossinow credit as original and how much will he cede to the influence of other, older traditions? He does not wish to avoid the decades-long development, or impact, of Texas liberalism, the social gospel, and existential theology; yet, relying on the self-image of the New Left, he insists there was a decisive breach with the "old" Left, and he disregards or derides almost everything an older leftwing tradition offered the younger generation. Even the anti-imperialism of antiwar radicals, despite the prominence of that theme in twentieth-century Marxism, was really a New Left invention, Rossinow claims. By the end of the book, it becomes clearer why Rossinow is adamant on such points. Given its search for authenticity aimed at transforming personal life and local surroundings, the New Left by the early 1970s, he writes, had become "quietly unhitched from demands for broad social change" and revealed its basic "tropism toward liberalism." By insisting on the "new," Rossinow obscures much of what was "left" about the New Left.

HOWARD BRICK

Washington University
St. Louis
Missouri

SOCIOLOGY

DEUTSCH, FRANCINE M. 1999. *Halving It All: How Equally Shared Parenting Works.* Pp. 327. Cambridge, MA: Harvard University Press. $24.95.

During the last two decades, the persistence of inequality in contemporary relationships has been widely documented. In short, over 60 percent of married women with husbands present, including those with children under age six, are now in the paid labor force. Less than 40 percent of married men now serve as the main breadwinner for their families, but wives continue to do approximately two-thirds of both child care and housework, as well as a disproportionate amount of the work of relationships, including emotion work. Literally hundreds of studies have tried to understand why such inequality persists. These studies usually seek to identify the extent to which factors such as ideology, spouses' relative earnings, and time in paid labor differentiate between husbands who share the work of the home, children, and relationships and husbands who do not.

Most of these studies show that neither earnings, nor job prestige, nor time in paid labor are associated with the same outcomes for women as for men, and, in the end, the best predictor of who does what in the context of the family is simply gender.

Francine Deutsch, in *Halving It All*, takes a somewhat different tack. Believing that gendered parenting is the key to inequality, Deutsch personally interviewed 150 dual-earner couples divided into four groups based on how child care was divided. Three of the groups were upper middle class—the equal sharers who divided the work of child care 50-50, as well as two other groups among whom the work was divided 60-40 and 75-25. The fourth group was a sample of blue-collar workers who worked split shifts so that they could care for their young children without outside help. Deutsch is part of a growing group of feminist social scientists who work from a theory that defines gender as a system of stratification based on categorization that is created and re-created daily. Consistent with this theoretical perspective, Deutsch finds that relationship equality is created by the accumulations of large and small decisions and acts that make up couples' everyday lives as parents. Couples become equal or unequal in working out the details: who makes the children's breakfasts, washes out their diaper pails, kisses their hurts, or takes off work when the children are sick. According to Deutsch, couples who share parenting are more likely to become equal as a solution to the overwhelming labor demands of a two-job household than to fulfill an ideological agenda. Although she found that equally sharing husbands and wives had the most similar incomes of the four groups, Deutsch would argue that the similarity in earnings was more likely the consequence than the cause of equal sharing at home. Many of the wives in the unequal sharing groups earned as much as or more than their husbands at the time that their children were born. It was the decision for the wives to cut back on career commitments in order to assume primary responsibility for child care that brought about the earnings discrepancy with their husbands.

The achievement of equality, according to Deutsch, requires strong women and fair men. The strength and assertiveness of the equally sharing mothers is matched by the sense of fairness evident in the behavior of the equally sharing fathers. Men continue to feel their self-worth is tied to paid work. A woman's self-worth is usually more tied to motherhood than her husband's is to fatherhood. Thus women are torn between ambition and their love for their children. Men are torn between fairness and their need to achieve. Women fight with their husbands to get them to do more work, but they also fight within themselves. Equal sharing requires women to buck maternalism. They have to make their own needs for achievement, success, and autonomy more central than their mothers did and grapple with the issue of whether they are doing right by their children.

This is a book based on strong scholarship written for the lay reader. It comprises 11 chapters followed by careful documentation of the methodology and exhaustive notes. Its focus is the presentation of extensive excerpts from the couples supporting Deutsch's assertion that equality or inequality is created and re-created through the details of daily decisions. It outlines the strategies men use to resist change and, in a particularly interesting chapter, details the double standard of praise and criticism focusing on the insidious nature of praise. Thirty-six percent of the equally sharing women in Deutsch's sample received compliments about their husbands (mostly from other women). By contrast, only 2 percent of the husbands received compliments about their wives, and women were never praised for making money.

Deutsch's position is clear. She believes that the benefits of equal sharing far outweigh the costs and would like to see a future in which our children do not feel the pressure to choose between parenting and working, nurturing and achieving, loving and succeeding. Her book aims to support the realization of that goal by presenting the examples of others to show that, despite the negative findings of the last 20 years, equal parenting is possible.

JANICE M. STEIL

Adelphi University
Garden City
New York

FLEISHER, MARK S. 1998. *Dead End Kids: Gang Girls and the Boys They Know*. Pp. 336. Madison: University of Wisconsin Press. $24.95.

Dead End Kids takes us deeply and intimately into the daily world of violent and drug-selling adolescent gangs in Kansas City, Missouri. Fleisher, a highly skilled ethnographer and cultural anthropologist, hung out with the Fremont Hustlers and Northeast Gangstas from 1995 to 1997, trading rides, meals, cigarettes, legal advice, and companionship for the privileges of entering the gangs' inner circles and probing freely concerning their social relationships, drug use, and criminal activities.

Fleisher vividly re-creates his contacts with the gangs, replicating conversations and events in stunning detail (a drawback of this detail is the phonetic spelling of gang members' speech, which gets a bit tiresome as the book progresses). Fleisher is an expert at capturing firsthand the precarious and catastrophic nature of gang members' lives. Disputing the stereotype of the street gang as a closely knit band—risking their lives for honor or territory—he provides powerful evidence that members' selfish economic interests usually supersede the needs of the gang. Members' relationships are often tenuous, loyalties are easily transferred from one gang to another, and memberships can be ephemeral. In Fleisher's words, a youth gang is a "shifting network of social ties driven by economic need and a quest for material goods."

The book focuses on Cara and Wendy and their entangled webs of companions. All their lives are a continuing series of crises: money problems, shoddy housing conditions, teenage pregnancies, drug addictions, and interpersonal violence. The intergenerational quality of kids' problems is repeatedly documented in Fleisher's descriptions of Hustler kids' mothers who became pregnant in adolescence and who are selling or using drugs themselves and of Hustler kids' children who are wantonly neglected or abused. This never ending cycle will invariably turn Hustler kids' children into mirror images of their parents and grandparents.

Dead End Kids demonstrates that ethnographic studies of hidden populations are highly demanding and often dangerous. Fleisher spent much of his time communicating with drug sellers and users and with armed and volatile adolescents. He even ran afoul of the police, who became suspicious of his long-standing interest in the gangs. Ethnographic research also poses challenging moral and legal dilemmas regarding the decision to report illegal activities (such as child abuse and neglect). Such studies are so compelling that investigators are often drawn intensely and personally into their subjects' lives.

Fleisher's paternalism toward the kids and the painful emotional reactions that he sometimes experiences after his interactions with them hint that he is struggling to maintain his scientific distance and objectivity. This struggle is especially apparent in his relationship with his principal informant, Cara. He becomes her friend, confidant, and surrogate father. Fleisher's high expectations that Cara attend school and turn her life around, however, are eventually dashed by the powerful lure of the gang culture.

The final chapter of *Dead End Kids* explains the ethnographic method. Along with the book's chapter notes, the last chapter places the work within the larger body of social science research on gangs and argues for changes in the root causes of gang activity. Fleisher advocates that, instead of finding more ways to arrest and lock up disadvantaged teenagers, we attempt to ameliorate the pernicious conditions that propel poor kids into crime and drug use. These conditions include poverty, unemployment, school failure, social alienation, child sexual and physical abuse, and punitive crime control strategies that completely ignore the social, psychological, and material needs of at-risk kids.

ARTHUR J. LURIGIO

Loyola University of Chicago
Illinois

KILPATRICK, ALAN. 1998. *The Night Has a Naked Soul: Witchcraft and Sorcery Among the Western Cherokee.* Pp. xviii, 160. Syracuse, NY: Syracuse University Press. Paperbound, $19.95.

Fanciful titles aside, this book is a valuable addition to ethnographic studies of witchcraft and sorcery and expands our knowledge in significant ways. First, it demonstrates the continuing vitality of these beliefs among Native Americans. Widely recognized by ethnographers, this phenomenon continues to be encountered throughout North and South America. Second, this book provides a deepened understanding of witchcraft and sorcery beliefs among one of the largest North American tribal groupings, the Cherokee. As such, it continues the research of the elder Kilpatricks, whose son, the author of this book, has further enriched the Cherokee ethnographic record.

This book combines rich ethnographic accounts of Cherokee witchcraft and sorcery with stimulating theoretical insights. As a whole, it documents a compelling need for reexamination of classical problems such as function and dysfunction, psychoanalytic interpretation, status competition, status ambiguity, the problem of good and evil, the taxonomics of witchcraft and sorcery, the limitations of cross-cultural comparisons, and problems of acculturation. Perhaps most significantly, it provides a valuable study of Western Cherokee witchcraft and sorcery that will stimulate useful comparisons with Kluckhohn's classic *Navajo Witchcraft*. When considered with my own *Witchcraft and Sorcery of the American Native Peoples* and *Navajo Witchcraft*, this Cherokee study also provides a basis for hemispheric and broader comparisons concerning this universal phenomenon.

Realizing that it is unfair to criticize an author for what he has not done, I shall conclude by inviting him to undertake further comparative analysis. The continued vitality of witchcraft and sorcery in the world's cultures demands more systematic investigation. Alan Kilpatrick has provided us an excellent stimulus to this renewed research on a topic of abiding anthropological interest.

DEWARD E. WALKER, JR.

University of Colorado
Boulder

MITCHELL, LAWRENCE E. 1998. *Stacked Deck: A Story of Selfishness in America.* Pp. xiv, 249. Philadelphia: Temple University Press. No price.

Stacked Deck is an interdisciplinary attempt to make sense out of American selfishness. Drawing upon materials from law, philosophy, and the social sciences, Lawrence Mitchell makes a compelling assessment of American society that points to a lack of real fairness.

Why does a George W. Bush, the current governor of Texas, perform in what at best appears to have been average fashion in the prep school he attended and then proceed to attend the best universities for undergraduate and graduate work? Could it be class advantage? While not addressing this specific example, Mitchell does construct hypothetical cases that illustrate such a possibility. People born at positions in our stratification system considerably lower than that of George W. Bush would not be contemplating attendance at Yale and Harvard if their high school performance was average or less. Mitchell compares such cases and indicates that for many of us in America, where we start in the stratification system is very influential in determining where we will wind up in the race of life.

Nevertheless, as *Stacked Deck* indicates, what has developed in America is the myth of individualism, which exaggerates the role of the individual in achieving success and tends to overlook the role of initial, advantaged position in aiding one on the path to success. At the same time, we are led to a lack of sympathy for those who do not succeed. We blame them for failing. Those who do not make it are to blame for their situation. Moreover, and very important for Mitchell's arguments, we do not see many of those who do not succeed as vulnerable. Vulnerability is not seen. It is masked and denied even though it is universal to all. Furthermore, the myth of individualism downplays the structural limitations that make sure that the vulnerable stay that way.

The foregoing circumstances are ingrained in the laws of America according to Mitchell. He shows how they get perpetuated in private and public law and, in turn, how this makes people, even at their most vulnerable, take care of themselves. Autonomy is championed in the law rather than vulnerability, according to Mitchell. What undergirds this? Answer: our philosophical approaches to fairness. Here, Mitchell examines three brands of liberal theory: social democracy, resource equality, and wealth maximization. He finds them all lacking from the standpoint of explaining fairness and then proceeds to explore what he calls the heart of the matter: vulnerability. We are brought along a path of many thoughtful challenges and insights that eventually leads to the need to refashion liberal theory so that it keeps the value placed upon autonomy while also including the reality of vulnerability.

Beyond modifying liberal theory, similar changes are called for in our laws, institutions, and overall society. Indeed, Mitchell calls for redistribution to correct for what he refers to as the radical inequality of our society. Ideally, this would give everyone a real chance to choose good options as they advance in the race of life. As Mitchell indicates, we can decide to move in this direction as a society. From his standpoint, however, we will have to rethink what vulnerability is all about. He argues that this will lead to a fairer society and one where community may be realized to a greater extent.

I found many of the book's hypothetical cases and thought experiments quite convincing with respect to Mitchell's specific points. What is left for him and others to pursue is the fundamental task of changing key American societal institutions toward the conception of fairness that he presents. As we approach the millennium, we are left with a seemingly eternal American dilemma: how to move beyond making a fetish of individualism and see the strength of fostering community. One hopes that this book helps us to make some progress in this direction.

JOHN R. DALPHIN

Merrimack College
North Andover
Massachusetts

SOWELL, THOMAS. 1998. *Conquests and Cultures: An International History.* Pp. xvi, 493. New York: Basic Books. $35.00. Paperbound, $16.00.

Thomas Sowell's *Conquests and Cultures* is the third and final volume of a trilogy that also includes *Race and Culture* (1994) and *Migrations and Cultures* (1996). Like its predecessors, it is a work with a thesis. It argues that the socioeconomic position of racial, ethnic, and national groups is determined more by each group's cultural values than by the attitudes of the surrounding society. Sowell aims to refute two "prevailing doctrines": first, the guilt thesis that "society" is responsible for the unfavorable socioeconomic position of certain groups; second, the diversity argument that cultural differences are valuable regardless of content and should therefore be respected and preserved.

Sowell defines "culture" in a broad sense as "the working machinery of everyday life"—the aggregate choices made by millions of individuals over a period of centuries. Culture is their "human capital." Trained economist that he is, Sowell regards the benefits of economic development as self-evident. He evaluates each of the cultures under consideration by the practical standard of "how well it works," and he claims to base his judgments on the actual facts of history.

Conquests and Cultures discusses four very large aggregations: the British (from Roman times to the present), the Africans, the Slavs, and the Western Hemisphere Indians, with extra attention to certain subgroups. The British represent the advanced Western society of the conquerors. Africans and Indians are examples of conquered peoples. The Slavs, though less severely oppressed than the latter two, lived for centuries in large multinational empires relatively distant from major trade arteries. Four such inclusive categories naturally require Sowell to paint with a very broad brush, ignoring important differences within each group. The advantage of this approach—a very significant one—is to reveal certain striking similarities that occur across very disparate cultures. The juxtaposition demonstrates that many forms of human behavior—exploitation and cruelty, among others—are virtually universal and hardly unique to a few demonized nations.

Sowell is well aware of the negative aspects of European global dominance, though he does not dwell on them. Rather, he cites the rise of the West to military, economic, and technological preeminence as proof of the effectiveness of Western cultural attitudes. He argues that precisely those liberal values that developed initially in British society—the rule of law, rejection of royal absolutism, and respect for individual rights—have proved far more successful than their alternatives, in both practical and moral terms.

Critics might argue that valid international history on the scale of Sowell's trilogy is ipso facto impossible—an objection I would dispute. Unquestionably, the enormous expansion of knowledge in modern times means that no single individual can claim expertise in more than a limited field. The specialist will regard with horror the occasional factual errors that inevitably crop up in an undertaking as ambitious as the one considered here. (I noted a few in *Conquests and Cultures*). More to the point, Sowell's choice of sources is sometimes inadequate—another limitation difficult for the generalist to avoid.

Nonetheless, *Conquests and Cultures* is an impressive achievement. Sowell has identified some of the major forces determining the course of human events. He writes history not as an exercise in antiquarianism but as a contribution to the discussion of contemporary issues. His prose is consistently straightforward and readable, making the work easily accessible to the general reader. Sowell's views are strongly held, sometimes provocative, but unquestionably relevant. Whether or not the reader agrees with his conclusions, the net effect is decidedly stimulating.

JEAN W. SEDLAR

University of Pittsburgh
Johnstown
Pennsylvania

STOCKER, MARGARETA. 1998. *Judith, Sexual Warrior: Women and Power in Western Culture*. Pp. ix, 278. New Haven, CT: Yale University Press. $30.00.

Mythology has given us our most prodigious heroes—Hercules, Oedipus, Aeneas—and their stories speak to a superhuman greatness and pathos. Legend, with its residual sense of an actual historical past, provides us with men of lesser though still marvelous stature: the Chevalier Roland, Arthur of Britain, Paul Bunyan. Heroines of a comparable character are less common and often ambiguous: Hippolyta, Ariadne, Joan of Arc. As women approach heroic status, they seem to become like men and hence to betray the fixed hierarchy of patriarchy. As Stocker's extensive study shows,

the apocryphal Judith is perhaps the most sensational of them.

Literature and the arts have pictured her in various guises, all derived from her account in Scripture, which tells of her beheading Holofernes the Assyrian, her rapist and the enemy of her people, the Israelites. Her story conflates two distinct though related zones of endeavor, the domestic and the political. Woman as subject to man within the household also exemplifies the collective and structurally feminine political subject, the men and women who obey a local authority, virtually always masculine. By destroying a rapist and a tyrant, Judith actualizes the possibility that authority, whether domestic or political, can be illicit. She becomes the figural incarnation of resistance theory. Her actions frame the limits of patriarchy, prone paradoxically to invalidate its fundamental assumption: that man (not woman) is naturally the rational head of human society and that masculinity is naturally correlative with a right to govern. Judith illustrates the enduring tension between her own kind of challenge to orthodoxy and the cultural matrices in which men and masculinity have been celebrated as guarantors of social order and decency. Her story in all its forms constitutes a powerful pretext upon which patriarchy has been questioned and even rejected.

From antiquity through the Renaissance, Judith exemplified chastity, the virtue of womankind, yet also instanced *fortitudo*, a cardinal virtue demonstrated in battle. In different contexts, her conquest over Holofernes is attributed to a reprehensible shrewishness or to a laudable patriotism. Both cases are ironic to a degree: they show her supporting the institution from which her oppression derives. She is featured in the *querelle des femmes*, in treatises on woman's rule, in defenses of tyrannicide. The post-romantic Judith is more complicated. She can justify actions for liberty, yet, as an exponent of Hebraism, she can also validate eugenicist views of race. She even has a Nazi version. Her postmodern representations are frequently indebted to Freudian views of sexual difference. Stocker finds her in fictions about women who take up arms (illustrating, as Stocker suggests, an assumed penis envy); she even locates her as the mythic archetype behind the remarkable account of Lorena Bobbitt, who cut off her rapist-husband's penis while he slept.

Stocker's study is a hugely ambitious work that succeeds in proving its thesis by virtue of the overwhelming evidence she brings to the reader's attention. The feminist issues Stocker raises are not new, but their coherent reference to a single legendary heroine does, I think, contribute importantly to feminist scholarship. Unfortunately, readers have not been well served by the publisher's decision to let the author document her sources in a cursory and incomplete way. This practice may be what editors think will popularize scholarly books. But there is no reason to sell short the critical interest of the so-called general reader by giving her inadequate references. Stocker's excellent study deserves a better representation.

CONSTANCE JORDAN

Claremont Graduate University
California

ECONOMICS

McNAMARA, PETER. 1998. *Political Economy and Statesmanship: Smith, Hamilton and the Foundation of the Commercial Republic.* Pp. xi, 191. DeKalb: Northern Illinois University Press. No price.

I was puzzled by the juxtaposition reflected in the title of this book, for I knew something about Smith and little about Hamilton but had given no thought to their possible connection. One of McNamara's purposes is to make "a contribution to the construction of a truly *political economy* that would supplement or, perhaps, replace mainstream neoclassical economics" (emphasis in the original). His attempt to accomplish this is through the engaging notion of combining the ideas of a scholar of economics with those of a politician-statesman to generate "a political economy" that is widely "recognized as being needed by both scholars and policymakers across the political spectrum." Much of this "need," it is argued, is generated by the absence of realism in neoclassical economics. This is a frequent and tiresome charge made by those who misunderstand the nature of theory or modeling whether the economics at issue is neoclassical or not. While I agree with McNamara's notion that political economy encompasses political and moral discourse, particularly when he speaks of developing "a" political economy, such a development is best viewed as a field or subdiscipline under the normative division within economics, something akin to welfare economics, and not as a correction to or replacement of neoclassical economics.

McNamara concludes that the "example of Hamilton's words and deeds" is more useful for a liberal statesman than the "economic model" of Smith's "science of political economy." Such statements cry out for an analysis of usefulness but are understandable in the sense that, if some morning I cannot start my car, it is probably more immediately useful to call my neighbor the mechanic than my colleague the professor of physics. But this position also derives from McNamara's conception of political economy. He seems to want to reserve this term for that area of study used to prepare individuals who wish to work in public service, whether as elected officials or public policy wonks.

While this may be a useful function of "a" political economy, it should not be considered as being coterminous with political economy as a field. This is especially the case if one purpose of any new political economy, as stated earlier, is to replace neoclassical economics. There is more to economics than a practical concern with public policy.

While there are many points of this book that many economists would take issue with (for example, the seeming equating of rational self-interest with selfishness, the argument that political economy should move from trying to be a social science to being a study of statesmanship, that Smith is greatly overrated, or that there has been little or no advance in economic theory for 200 years), there is much to engage one's interest in the sense of challenging one to clarify one's own thinking and vowing to exercise more care when talking economics with noneconomists. The book contains an uneven review and interpretation of Smith's contributions but some interesting comparisons with and adulation of Hamilton's economic policies. One example of the unevenness is the statement that "Smith makes statesmanship subordinate to political economy, practice to theory." I think few would interpret Smith's definition of political economy at the beginning of Book IV in this manner. A more accurate interpretation of Smith would be exactly the reverse, for he places political economy in the service of the statesman and legislator.

COLIN WRIGHT

Claremont McKenna College
California

MINK, GWENDOLYN. 1998. *Welfare's End.* Pp. xii, 180. Ithaca, NY: Cornell University Press. $21.00.

Mothering is work, argues political scientist Gwendolyn Mink in *Welfare's End*, and, as such, deserves recognition and financial compensation. But in the American context, such acknowledgment has rarely been forthcoming; instead, married, non-wage-earning mothers depend on their husbands, while single mothers are compelled to turn to the state for grudging support. With the passage of the Personal Responsibility and Work Opportunity Act of 1996 (PRA), the law that tolled "welfare's end," solo mothers now are being forced to work outside the home, thus losing the right to care for their children. In this concise but elegant analysis, Mink explains the precedents and implications of this drastic turn in legislation.

For Mink, American motherhood has always been perilous, lodged as it is in a nexus between social policy and social custom. Married women have often endured domestic violence in exchange for financial support, while single mothers, many of whom used "welfare" (Aid to Families with Dependent Children) to exit from abusive relationships, faced surveillance and stigmatization. For both groups, support has thus been erratic and conditional, with the result that they have been deprived of "the means for independence."

Married women tend to fare better, however, in a policy climate that privileges "earned" over "gratuitous" benefits and marital over nonmarital families. As Mink points out, the wives of men covered by social security (whether they are retired or deceased) enjoy nonstigmatized state support for themselves and their children (though the benefits are presented as being derived from their husbands' wage-earning status, not as direct recognition for their caring work). At the same time, a series of court decisions and state and federal laws have reinforced a preference for marital families by making paternity establishment mandatory only for welfare applicants, attempting to push poor solo mothers into marriage, and offering states incentives to reduce nonmarital births. Such measures, according to Mink, not only curb women's independence and expose them to potential domestic violence but also discriminate between married and unmarried women with regard to their right to bear (or not to bear) children.

This pattern is rooted in the Social Security Act of 1935, which from the outset created separate programs for wage earners (Old Age Insurance) and caregivers (Aid to Dependent Children). As Mink documents, Congress consistently extended entitlements to the families of "covered" wage earners (even including divorced spouses) while contesting, reducing, and eventually withdrawing benefits for nonmarried and poor caregivers, often using racialized stereotypes as a rationale.

Mink's solution to these blatant inequities is to treat women engaged in mothering and other forms of caregiving as workers and, by guaranteeing unconditional state support, allow them to become financially secure and independent. Like the feminist demand for "wages for housework" of the 1970s, this runs the risk of "essentializing" women by assigning them once again to full-time caring and not allowing for the possibility that, given the wherewithal, some might prefer to work outside the home. Indeed, Mink initially dismisses the idea of job programs for welfare recipients as the narrow-minded projection of "middle-class feminists." But, as she herself concedes, many poor mothers do express a desire to work outside the home and, when possible, prefer to combine wage earning with public assistance.

By the end of the book, Mink seems to have modified her position somewhat, as she calls for programs that would allow poor solo mothers "to voluntarily receive education, training, and assistance in job placement," and "labor market reforms to make outside work feasible" for women in this group. Such measures come across as more balanced and, even in the present political climate, perhaps within our reach.

SONYA MICHEL

University of Illinois
Urbana-Champaign

OTHER BOOKS

ABIZADEH, SOHRAB and ALLEN MILLS, eds. 1999. *The Return of Mitteleuropa: Socio-Economic Transition in Post-Communist Central Europe.* Pp. ix, 213. Commack, NY: Nova Science. No price.

ADELMAN, HOWARD and ASTRI SUHRKE, eds. 1999. *The Path of a Genocide: The Rwanda Crisis from Uganda to Zaire.* Pp. xxii, 414. New Brunswick, NJ: Transaction. $44.95.

ADITJONDRO, GEORGE J. 1999. *Is Oil Thicker Than Blood? A Study of Oil Companies' Interests and Western Complicity in Indonesia's Annexation of East Timor.* Pp. 119. Commack, NY: Nova Science. $59.00.

ALLEN, ANITA L. and MILTON C. REGAN, JR., eds. 1999. *Debating Democracy's Discontent: Essays on American Politics, Law, and Public Philosophy.* Pp. xvi, 391. New York: Oxford University Press. $80.00. Paperbound, $19.95.

AMOS, GARY and RICHARD GARDINER. 1998. *Never Before in History: America's Inspired Birth.* Pp. ix, 212. Dallas, TX: Haughton. No price.

ANDERSON, BRIAN C., ed. 1999. *On Cultivating Liberty: Reflections on Moral Ecology.* Pp. vii, 359. Lanham, MD: Rowman & Littlefield. $27.95.

ARNSON, CYNTHIA J., ed. 1999. *Comparative Peace Processes in Latin America.* Pp. xiii, 493. Stanford, CA: Stanford University Press. $49.50. Paperbound, $19.95.

BABKINA, A. M. 1999. *Nuclear Proliferation: An Annotated Bibliography.* Pp. 239. Commack, NY: Nova Science. No price.

BARTHOLOMEUSZ, TESSA J. and CHANDRA R. DE SILVA, eds. 1998. *Buddhist Fundamentalism and Minority Identities in Sri Lanka.* Pp. viii, 212. Albany: State University of New York Press. Paperbound, $23.95.

BERNSTIEN, ANN and MYRON WEINER, eds. 1999. *Migration and Refugee Policies: An Overview.* Pp. xx, 300. New York: Cassell & Continuum. $75.00.

BHARGAVA, RAJEEV, ed. 1998. *Secularism and Its Critics.* Pp. xii, 550. New York: Oxford University Press. $39.95.

BISCHOF, GUNTER, ANTON PELINKA, and FERDINAND KARLHOFER, eds. 1999. *The Vranitzky Era in Austria.* Vol. 7. Pp. 305. New Brunswick, NJ: Transaction. Paperbound, $35.00.

BOSTON, JONATHAN, PAUL DALZIEL, and SUSAN ST. JOHN, eds. 1999. *Redesigning the Welfare State in New Zealand: Problems, Policies, Prospects.* Pp. xi, 356. New York: Oxford University Press. Paperbound, $39.95.

BRANDS, H. W., ed. 1999. *The Foreign Policies of Lyndon Johnson: Beyond Vietnam.* Pp. vi, 194. College Station: Texas A&M University Press. $29.95.

BRETTSCHNEIDER, MARLA. 1996. *Cornerstones of Peace: Jewish Identity Politics and Democratic Theory.* Pp. xii, 201. New Brunswick, NJ: Rutgers University Press. $48.00. Paperbound, $16.95.

BRODY, J. KENNETH. 1999. *The Avoidable War: Lord Cecil and the Policy of Principle, 1933-1935.* Vol. 1. Pp. x, 389. New Brunswick, NJ: Transaction. Paperbound, no price.

BROWN, MACALISTER and JOSEPH J. ZASLOFF. 1998. *Cambodia Confounds the Peacemakers, 1979-1998.* Pp. xviii, 326. Ithaca, NY: Cornell University Press. No price.

BRUSTEIN, ROBERT. 1998. *Cultural Calisthenics: Writings on Race, Politics, and Theatre.* Pp. vii, 291. Chicago: Ivan R. Dee. $26.00.

BURNS, JEFFREY M. 1999. *Disturbing the Peace: A History of the Christian Family Movement, 1949-1974.* Pp. xiv, 296. Notre Dame, IN: University of Notre Dame Press. Paperbound, $25.00.

BUZO, ADRIAN. 1999. *The Guerilla Dynasty: Politics and Leadership in North Korea.* Pp. xi, 323. Boulder, CO: Westview Press. Paperbound, no price.

CAMERON, MAXWELL A., ROBERT J. LAWSON, and BRIAN W. TOMLIN, eds. 1998. *To Walk Without Fear: The Global Movement to Ban Landmines.* Pp. xvi, 491. New York: Oxford University Press. Paperbound, $24.95.

CASHMORE, ELLIS and CHRIS ROJEK, eds. 1999. *Dictionary of Cultural Theorists.* Pp. x, 497. New York: Oxford University Press. $75.00. Paperbound, $19.95.

COCKCROFT, JAMES D. 1999. *Mexico's Hope: An Encounter with Politics and History.* Pp. viii, 435. New York: Monthly Review Press. $48.00. Paperbound, $18.00.

COHEN, RICHARD E. 1999. *Rostenkowski: The Pursuit of Power and the End of the Old Politics.* Pp. 311. Chicago: Ivan R. Dee. $27.50.

COX, MICHAEL, ed. 1999. *Rethinking the Soviet Collapse: Sovietology, the Death of Communism and the New Russia.* Pp. ix, 294. New York: Cassell & Continuum. $75.00. Paperbound, $26.50.

DERSHOWITZ, ALAN M. 1998. *Sexual McCarthyism: Clinton, Starr, and the Emerging Constitutional Crisis.* Pp. x, 275. New York: Basic. $23.00.

DUFFY, EAMON. 1999. *Saints and Sinners: A History of the Popes.* Pp. ix, 326. New Haven, CT: Yale University Press. $37.50. Paperbound, $18.95.

EBAN, ABBA. 1999. *Diplomacy for the Next Century.* Pp. 191. New Haven, CT: Yale University Press. $27.50. Paperbound, $11.95.

EYSENCK, HANS J. 1999. *The Psychology of Politics.* Pp. xxvi, 317. New Brunswick, NJ: Transaction. Paperbound, $29.95.

GINSBURG, NANCY and ROY GINSBURG, eds. 1999. *Psychoanalysis and Culture at the Millennium.* Pp. xii, 394. New Haven, CT: Yale University Press. $40.00.

GOLD, MARTIN and ELIZABETH DOUVAN. 1997. *A New Outline of Social Psychology.* Pp. xiii, 287. Washington, DC: American Psychological Association. $39.95.

GOSSMAN, PATRICIA A. 1999. *Riots and Victims: Violence and the Construction of Communal Identity Among Bengali Muslims, 1905-1947.* Pp. xi, 186. Boulder, CO: Westview Press. $59.00.

GREENE, ROBERTA R. and MARIE WATKINS, eds. 1998. *Serving Diverse Constituencies: Applying the Ecological Perspective.* Pp. xii, 376. Hawthorne, NY: Aldine de Gruyter. $53.95. Paperbound, $27.95.

GUTIERREZ, JOSE ANGEL. 1999. *The Making of a Chicano Militant: Lessons from Cristal.* Pp. xiii, 334. Madison: University of Wisconsin Press. $50.00. Paperbound, $19.95.

HADDAD, WILLIAM W., GHADA H. TALHAMI, and JANICE J. TERRY, eds. 1999. *The June 1967 War After Three Decades.* Pp. v, 215. Washington, DC: Arab Studies Quarterly. Paperbound, $19.95.

HAGLUND, DAVID G., ed. 1999. *Pondering NATO's Nuclear Options: Gambits for a Post-Westphalian World.* Pp. 208. Ontario, Canada: Queen's Quarterly. Paperbound, no price.

HANSEN, THOMAS BLOM and CHRISTOPHE JAFFRELOT, eds. 1998. *The BJP and the Compulsions of Politics in India.* Pp. viii, 332. New York: Oxford University Press. $35.00.

HARRINGTON, JOHN P. and ELIZA-
BETH J. MITCHELL, eds. 1999. *Poli-
tics and Performance in Contemporary
Northern Ireland*. Pp. vi, 234.
Amherst: University of Massachu-
setts Press. Paperbound, no price.

HART-LANDSBERG, MARTIN. 1998.
*Korea: Division, Reunification, and
United States Foreign Policy*. Pp. 266.
New York: Monthly Review Press.
$48.00. Paperbound, $18.00.

HEROD, ANDREW, ed. 1998. *Organizing the Landscape: Geographical
Perspectives on Labor Unionism*.
Pp. xix, 372. Minneapolis: University
of Minnesota Press. $54.95. Paper-
bound, $21.95.

HEYWOOD, ANDREW. 1999. *Political
Theory*. 2d ed. Pp. xvi, 400. New York:
St. Martin's Press. $59.95. Paper-
bound, $22.95.

HOPKINS, NICHOLAS S. and
KIRSTEN WESTERGAARD, eds.
1999. *Directions of Change in Rural
Egypt*. Pp. viii, 398. New York: Columbia University Press. $27.50.

HURRELL, ANDREW and NGAIRE
WOODS, eds. 1999. *Inequality, Globalization, and World Politics*. Pp. ix,
353. New York: Oxford University
Press. $70.00. Paperbound, $24.95.

IKEDA, KEIKO. 1999. *A Room Full of
Mirrors: High School Reunions in
Middle America*. Pp. x, 205. Stanford,
CA: Stanford University Press.
$35.00.

JONES, BILL, ed. 1999. *Political Issues
in Britain Today*. 5th ed. Pp. xiii, 433.
New York: Manchester University
Press. $69.95. Paperbound, $18.95.

KALDOR, MARY and IVAN VEJVODA,
eds. 1999. *Democratization in Central
and Eastern Europe*. Pp. xiv, 194. New
York: Cassell & Continuum. $75.00.

KHALILZAD, ZALMAY M. and JOHN P.
WHITE, eds. 1999. *The Changing Role
of Information in Warfare*. Pp. xxiii,
452. Santa Monica, CA: Rand. Paperbound, $25.00.

KINLOCH, GRAHAM C. 1999. *The Com-
parative Understanding of Intergroup
Relations: A Worldwide Analysis*.
Pp. xii, 207. Boulder, CO: Westview
Press. $60.00.

LEIBOVITZ, CLEMENT and ALVIN
FINKEL. 1998. *In Our Time: The
Chamberlain-Hitler Collusion*. Pp.
319. New York: Monthly Review
Press. $48.00. Paperbound, $18.00.

LEONARD, THOMAS M. 1999. *Castro
and the Cuban Revolution*. Pp. xxv,
188. Westport, CT: Greenwood Press.
$39.95.

LESSER, IAN O., BRUCE HOFFMAN,
JOHN ARQUILLA, DAVID
RONFELDT, and MICHEL ZANINI.
1999. *Countering the New Terrorism*.
Pp. xxiii, 153. Santa Monica, CA:
Rand. Paperbound, $15.00.

LIEVEN, ANATOL. 1999. *Ukraine and
Russia: A Fraternal Rivalry*. Pp. xvi,
182. Washington, DC: United States
Institute of Peace. Paperbound,
$19.95.

LIGHT, PAUL C. 1999. *The President's
Agenda: Domestic Policy Choice from
Kennedy to Clinton*. 3d ed. Pp. xiii,
312. Baltimore, MD: Johns Hopkins
University Press. $49.95. Paper-
bound, $16.95.

MARSO, LORI JO. 1999. *(Un)Manly Citi-
zens: Jean-Jacques Rousseau's and
Germaine de Stael's Subversive
Women*. Pp. xiv, 172. Baltimore, MD:
Johns Hopkins University Press.
$38.00.

MATTOX, GALE A., GEOFFREY D. OL-
IVER, and JONATHAN B. TUCKER,
eds. 1999. *Germany in Transition: A
Unified Nation's Search for Identity*.
Pp. xv, 254. Boulder, CO: Westview
Press. $65.00.

McCRONE, DAVID. 1998. *The Sociology
of Nationalism*. Pp. ix, 207. New York:
Routledge. $75.00. Paperbound,
$24.99.

MENDEZ, JUAN E., GUILLERMO
O'DONNELL, and PAULO SERGIO

PINHEIRO, eds. 1999. *The (Un)Rule of Law and the Underprivileged in Latin America.* Pp. ix, 357. Notre Dame, IN: Notre Dame Press. $48.00. Paperbound, $28.00.

MIALL, HUGH, OLIVER RAMS-BOTHAM, and TOM WOODHOUSE. 1999. *Contemporary Conflict Resolution: The Prevention, Management and Transformation of Deadly Conflicts.* Pp. xviii, 270. Malden, MA: Blackwell. $59.95.

MISHEL, LAWRENCE, JARED BERNSTEIN, and JOHN SCHMITT. 1999. *The State of Working America, 1998-99.* Pp. xi, 445. Ithaca, NY: Cornell University Press. No price.

PACINI, ANDREA, ed. 1999. *Christian Communities in the Arab Middle East: The Challenge of the Future.* Pp. xiii, 365. New York: Oxford University Press. $80.00.

PATTON, DAVID F. 1999. *Cold War Politics in Postwar Germany.* Pp. iv, 220. New York: St. Martin's Press. $49.95.

PFIFFNER, JAMES P., ed. 1999. *The Managerial Presidency.* 2d ed. Pp. xv, 351. College Station: Texas A&M University Press. $29.95. Paperbound, $16.95.

POND, ELIZABETH. 1999. *The Rebirth of Europe.* Pp. xiii, 290. Washington, DC: Brookings Institution Press. $26.95.

PORETTE, MARGARET. 1999. *The Mirror of Simple Souls.* Pp. lxxxvii, 209. Notre Dame, IN: University of Notre Dame Press. Paperbound, $24.00.

PREVOST, GARY and HARRY E. VANDEN, eds. 1999. *The Undermining of the Sandinista Revolution.* Pp. xiv, 226. New York: St. Martin's Press. Paperbound, $22.95.

ROBERTS, JOSEPH K. 1999. *In the Shadow of Empire: Canada for Americans.* Pp. xi, 142. New York: Monthly Review Press. $43.00. Paperbound, $15.00.

RODRIK, DANI. 1999. *The New Global Economy and Developing Countries: Making Openness Work.* Pp. x, 168. Baltimore, MD: Johns Hopkins University Press. Paperbound, $13.95.

SAIZ, MARTIN and HANS GESER, eds. 1999. *Local Parties in Political and Organizational Perspective.* Pp. xi, 350. Boulder, CO: Westview Press. $70.00.

SANDHOLTZ, WAYNE and ALEC STONE SWEET. 1998. *European Integration and Supranational Governance.* Pp. viii, 389. New York: Oxford University Press. $85.00. Paperbound, $24.95.

SATHYAMURTHY, T. V., ed. 1998. *Region, Religion, Caste, Gender and Culture in Contemporary India.* Vol. 3. Pp. xvi, 606. New York: Oxford University Press. Paperbound, $19.95.

SCHMOOKLER, ANDREW BARD. 1999. *Debating the Good Society: A Quest to Bridge America's Moral Divide.* Pp. viii, 378. Cambridge: MIT Press. $29.95.

SCOTCHIE, JOSEPH, ed. 1999. *The Paleoconservatives: New Voices of the Old Right.* Pp. viii, 212. New Brunswick, NJ: Transaction. $29.95.

SKIDMORE, MAX J. 1999. *Social Security and Its Enemies: The Case for America's Most Efficient Insurance Program.* Pp. xiii, 192. Boulder, CO: Westview Press. Paperbound, $14.00.

SMYTH, PAUL and BETTINA CASS, eds. 1999. *Contesting the Australian Way: States, Markets, and Civil Society.* Pp. vii, 280. New York: Cambridge University Press. $64.95. Paperbound, $25.95.

SOARES, JOSEPH A. 1999. *The Decline of Privilege: The Modernization of Oxford University.* Pp. viii, 322. Stanford,

CA: Stanford University Press. $45.00.

SOLOMON, RICHARD H. 1999. *Chinese Negotiating Behavior: Pursuing Interests Through "Old Friends."* Pp. xvi, 204. Washington, DC: United States Institute of Peace Press. Paperbound, $14.95.

WANG SHAOGUANG and HU ANGANG. 1999. *The Political Economy of Uneven Development: The Case of China.* Pp. xii, 267. Armonk, NY: M. E. Sharpe. $65.95.

WATERMAN, RICHARD W., ROBERT WRIGHT, and GILBERT ST. CLAIR. 1999. *The Image-Is-Everything Presidency: Dilemmas in American Leadership.* Pp. xv, 183. Boulder, CO: Westview Press. $55.00. Paperbound, $15.95.

WOOD, ELLEN MEIKSINS. 1999. *The Origin of Capitalism.* Pp. vii, 138. New York: Monthly Review Press. $30.00. Paperbound, $13.00.

INDEX

Aid, international, 120, 123

Amsden, Alice H., 17

AMSDEN, ALICE H. and TAKASHI HIKINO, The Bark Is Worse than the Bite: New WTO Law and Late Industrialization, 104-14

Anti-dumping duties, 109-10

Apparel industry, international, 92-103

Apparel Industry Partnership (AIP), 95-97

Asia
financial crisis (1997) in, 23, 59-62, 125, 133
labor in, 88

Barber, Benjamin, 146-47

BARK IS WORSE THAN THE BITE: NEW WTO LAW AND LATE INDUSTRIAL-IZATION, THE, Alice H. Amsden and Takashi Hikino, 104-14

Brazil, development bank of, 107-8

Business loans, to microentrepreneurs, 178, 180, 182

Capital, speculative, movement of, 120-21, 122

Coclanis, Peter A., 17

COCLANIS, PETER A. and TILAK DOSHI, Globalization in Southeast Asia, 49-64

Cold War, and labor movements, 82

Collective bargaining, in the international apparel industry, 96, 97, 99-102

Commission on Global Governance, 121-22, 123-24

COPING WITH GLOBALIZATION: A SUG-GESTED POLICY PACKAGE FOR SMALL COUNTRIES, Frank B. Rampersad, 115-25

CORPORATE GOVERNANCE AND GLOB-ALIZATION, Mary O'Sullivan, 153-72

Culture
diversity of cultures, 127, 130
homogenization of cultures, 134-37, 142-45, 151
hybridization, 148-51
polarization of cultures, 145-48, 151

Debt relief, for poor countries, 120

Democracy, political, 42-44

Developing countries, small, and globaliza-tion, 115-25

Doshi, Tilak, 17

DOSHI, TILAK, see COCLANIS, PETER A., coauthor

Easterlin, Richard A., 17

EASTERLIN, RICHARD A., The Globaliza-tion of Human Development, 32-48

Economic development, sustainable, 173-85

Education
role in globalization, 8-11, 20, 21, 30
standard of living, 41
see also School-to-work transition

Entrepreneurial social infrastructure (ESI), 182-83

European Trade Union Confederation (ETUC), 84-86, 89

European Union (EU)
labor and, 84-86
pension funds and, 165

FERLEGER, LOUIS, see MANDLE, JAY R., coauthor

Fertility rate, 39-41

Foreign investment, 111, 112
foreign direct investment in Southeast Asia, 59

Free-trade agreements
international migration and, 67, 68
see also European Union (EU); North American Free Trade Agreement (NAFTA); North American Free Trade Area (NAFTA)

General Agreement on Tariffs and Trade (GATT), 12-13, 30, 56, 105, 108-9, 110, 118
immigration and, 68

General Agreement on Trade in Services (GATS), and immigration, 71, 72

Germany
banks, 160-63
corporate governance, 153-56, 159-72
pension funds, 163-66
shareholder value, 160, 163, 166

Global resource dividend (GRD), 131-34, 137

Globalization, definition of, 20-21, 50-52

GLOBALIZATION AND JUSTICE, Jon Mandle, 126-39

GLOBALIZATION IN SOUTHEAST ASIA, Peter A. Coclanis and Tilak Doshi, 49-64

GLOBALIZATION OF HUMAN DEVELOP-MENT, THE, Richard A. Easterlin, 32-48

GLOBALIZATION: THE PRODUCT OF A
    KNOWLEDGE-BASED ECONOMY,
    Lester C. Thurow, 19-31
GLOBALIZATION'S CULTURAL CONSE-
    QUENCES, Robert Holton, 140-52

Hannerz, Ulf, 148-49, 150
Hikino, Takashi, 17
HIKINO, TAKASHI, see AMSDEN, ALICE H.,
    coauthor
Holton, Robert, 17
HOLTON, ROBERT, Globalization's Cultural
    Consequences, 140-52
Human development, globalization of, 32-48
Huntington, Samuel, 146, 147, 148

Immigration
    culture, 147, 150
    free-trade agreements, 67, 68
    General Agreement on Trade in Services
        (GATS), 71, 72
    illegal immigration, 23
    immigration policy, 65-77
    International Monetary Fund (IMF), 67
    North American Free Trade Agreement
        (NAFTA), 68, 71, 72
    World Trade Organization (WTO), 68
Inequality, economic, and globalization, 24-27
Intellectual property rights, 28-29
International Labor Organization (ILO),
    100-102
International Monetary Fund (IMF)
    international migration and, 67
    small developing countries and, 116-23

Knowledge-based economy, 19-31, 105, 112
    nation-state and, 21-24, 30

Labor
    in Asia, 88
    European Union (EU) and, 84-86
    in Latin America, 87-88
    Mercosur and, 88
    North American Free Trade Agreement
        (NAFTA) and, 86-87
    in Southeast Asia, 88
    World Trade Organization (WTO) and, 89
Labor movements, 78-91
    Cold War, 82
    female labor force participation, 83
    political influence, 83-84
    student anti-sweatshop movement, 92-103
    see also Labor unions
Labor unions
    global economy and, 25
    see also Labor movements

LABOR VERSUS GLOBALIZATION, George
    Ross, 78-91
Latin America, and labor, 87-88
Life expectancy, 36-39, 44
Living wage, 96-99
Long Term Capital Management, 21-22, 26

Mandle, Jay R., 17
MANDLE, JAY R., The Student Anti-Sweat-
    shop Movement: Limits and Potential,
    92-103
MANDLE, JAY R. and LOUIS FERLEGER,
    Preface, 8-18
Mandle, Jon, 17
MANDLE, JON, Globalization and Justice,
    126-39
Marking and origin requirements, 109
Mercosur, and labor, 88
Morbidity, 37-39
Multilateral Trade Agreement, 118

Nation-state, sovereignty of, 21-24, 30, 62, 66,
    69-73, 76 n. 1, 84
North American Free Trade Agreement
    (NAFTA)
    immigration and, 68, 71, 72
    labor and, 86-87
North American Free Trade Area (NAFTA),
    109

O'Sullivan, Mary, 17
O'SULLIVAN, MARY, Corporate Governance
    and Globalization, 153-72

Poverty, relief of, 128-29, 131-34, 137
Protectionism, see Trade protection

Rampersad, Frank B., 17
RAMPERSAD, FRANK B., Coping with Glob-
    alization: A Suggested Policy Package
    for Small Countries, 115-25
Rawls, John, 127, 129, 130
REGULATING IMMIGRATION IN A
    GLOBAL AGE: A NEW POLICY
    LANDSCAPE, Saskia Sassen, 65-77
Religion, globalizing tendencies of, 147
Ross, George, 17
ROSS, GEORGE, Labor Versus Globalization,
    78-91

Sachs, Jeffrey, 116, 117, 119-20, 122, 123
Said, Edward, 145-46
Sassen, Saskia, 17
SASSEN, SASKIA, Regulating Immigration
    in a Global Age: A New Policy Land-
    scape, 65-77

School-to-work transition, 179-80, 182
Shareholder value, 156, 159, 160, 163, 166-70
Southeast Asia
    definition of, 52-53
    globalization in, 49-64
    labor in, 88
    see also Asia, financial crisis (1997) in
STUDENT ANTI-SWEATSHOP MOVE-
    MENT: LIMITS AND POTENTIAL,
    THE, Jay R. Mandle, 92-103
SUSTAINABLE ECONOMIC DEVELOP-
    MENT IN RURAL AMERICA, Adam S.
    Weinberg, 173-85

Tariffs, 108-9, 111, 124
Thurow, Lester C., 16-17
THUROW, LESTER C., Globalization: The
    Product of a Knowledge-Based Econ-
    omy, 19-31
Tobin tax, 121, 133-34, 137
Trade protection, 130
    small developing countries and, 118
    see also Anti-dumping duties; Marking and
    origin requirements; Tariffs; Voluntary
    export restraints (VERs)

United States
    corporate governance, 153-59, 166-72
    mutual funds, 157-59
    pension funds, 157-59
    rural economic development, 173-85
    shareholder value, 156, 159

Voluntary export restraints (VERs), 108

Weinberg, Adam S., 17
WEINBERG, ADAM S., Sustainable Eco-
    nomic Development in Rural America,
    173-85
Women
    labor force participation, 83, 136
    roles, 39, 44
World Bank, and small developing countries,
    116, 118-23
World Trade Organization (WTO), 12, 13, 15,
    66
    immigration and, 68
    labor and, 89
    new rules of, and late industrialization,
    104-14
    small developing countries and, 121